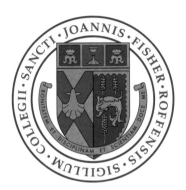

Lavery Library

St. John Fisher
College
Rochester, New York

ADVANCE PRAISE

"Schwandt and Marquardt capture the essence of the new organizational realities and what it takes to succeed. A timely book for a business world that is in a state of flux and chaos — a survival guide for organizations and individuals — both provocative and practical — a must read — destined to be a classic!"

— **Doug Bryant**
Director, Organization Development
AutoNation, Inc.

"The complex issues of organizational learning has never been presented so clearly and so well. I strongly recommend this book to any individual or organization looking for success in the workplace in the 21st century."

—**Anthony Hii**
Executive Director,
Institut Teknologi Pertama
Malaysia

"The long-awaited book to help organizations learn in the global workplace!"

—**Nikki Adams**
Director of Training
Seagate Technology International
Singapore

"Schwandt and Marquardt provide a timely resource for systematically analyzing and dynamic processes of organizational learning in the contemporary workplace. The Organizational Learning Systems Model should be applied within all organizations looking to survive and prosper in the 21st Century."

—**Martin B. Kormanik,**
Director of Human Resources and Diversity Program
O.D. Systems, Inc.

ORGANIZATIONAL LEARNING
From World-Class Theories
to Global Best Practices

David R. Schwandt
Michael J. Marquardt

foreword by

Betty S. Beene
President and CEO
United Way of America

S^t_L

St. Lucie Press
Boca Raton   London   New York   Washington, D.C.

Library of Congress Cataloging-in-Publication Data

Schwandt, David R.
  Organizational learning : from world-class theories to global best practices / David R. Schwandt and Michael J. Marquardt.
       p. cm.
    Includes bibliographical references and index.
    ISBN 0-57444-259-7 (alk. paper)
    1. Organizational learning. I. Marquardt, Michael J. II. Title.
HD58.82.S39 1999
658.3'124—dc21   99-28722
                                                                            CIP

© 2000 by CRC Press LLC
St. Lucie Press is an imprint of CRC Press LLC

No claim to original U.S. Government works
International Standard Book Number 0-57444-259-7
Library of Congress Card Number 99-28722
Printed in the United States of America   2 3 4 5 6 7 8 9 0
Printed on acid-free paper

Foreword

Fasten your seatbelts. The pace of change in the 21st century will be a blur. The world of work will continue to be transformed by the twin forces of technology and globalization. Organizations will become more virtual than physical. Workers will be more closely linked to customers across the country than to co-workers across the hall. Products and services will have ever-shorter shelf-lives.

As a result, only organizations that can adapt quickly and continuously will be able to survive and succeed in the new millenium. The corollary is also true. Organizations which cannot learn to adapt more quickly and constantly than the changes and chaos of the surrounding environment will become irrelevant, if not extinct.

This ability to adapt and innovate with increasing speed requires a new way of organizational thinking, acting, and, most importantly, learning. Only by organizationwide learning will companies have the speed, innovation, and quality essential to respond with competence to the ever-growing expectations of their customers. Simply put, organizational learning itself must become a core competency to compete.

Over the past 10 years, especially since the publication of Peter Senge's *The Fifth Discipline*, a number of books and articles in professional journals have appeared offering tools and techniques to enable the transformation to a learning organization. While the information whetted the organizational appetite for change mechanisms, they oversimplified a complex process. In my opinion, the essential underpinning of deep learning was lacking: a solid theoretical base and comprehensive systemic analysis necessary to guide organizations on their journey in organizational learning.

Following this simplified advice has resulted in missteps and failures in building learning organizations.

Organizational Learning: From World-Class Theories to Global Best Practices is different. It is a book that for the first time presents a comprehensive model for organizational learning that incorporates the best thinking of the field with the best practices in the world. The Organizational Learning Systems Model is one that has been tested and is working in many places, including the United Way of America. It has become our collective compass as we, like other institutions, confront a future in which the change is ever more rapid and unpredictable.

It has been said that learning is the only sustainable competitive advantage, individually or collectively. This book will enable organizations to become deliberate and effective in learning, unlearning, and relearning essential to progress. It provides no shortcuts; rather, a jumpstart to gaining and sustaining competitive advantage.

Betty Stanley Beene
President and Chief Executive Officer
United Way of America

Preface

It is almost trivializing to speak about the speed at which information and knowledge are transmitted around the globe. It has become a reality that both political and economic information quickly determine the behavior and actions of all organizations, whether they see themselves as global or as local. This avalanche of information also has a profound impact on the people in these organizations and the cultures that they generate. Companies around the world are beginning to recognize that by increasing the speed and quality of their learning they can succeed in a rapidly changing global marketplace. Simply stated, developing organization-wide learning and becoming a learning organization have become critical for adaptation and survival.

Unfortunately, organizational learning in the context of a fast-moving environment is much simpler to proclaim than it is to implement. Leaders of organizations have found the process of becoming a learning organization confusing and downright overwhelming. Much of the difficulty centers around the lack of understanding the connection between the envisioned "learning organization" and the everyday operations and actions of people in the organization.

Reengineering Not Enough

In recent years there have been numerous efforts by organizations to reengineer or reinvent themselves to achieve more efficient and effective global orientations. Whether we call these actions of organizations reengineering, downsizing, or even rightsizing, these changes result in large losses in employee commitment and very little long-term productivity gains.

In fact, many organizations find that they lose much of their organizational knowledge through these restructuring processes that ultimately reduce their competitiveness. In addition, these restructuring acts are accompanied by questions concerning the organization's ability to understand its environment and capacity to make adjustments that would have precluded radical restructuring over short periods of time.

On a less dramatic level of change these questions can also draw focus on the organization's failure to recognize that it continues to fall into repeated actions that result in errors. In many cases, what organizations saw as actions to increase their learning capacity became much more traditional acts directed at performance measures to secure short-term gains in profitability. However, these incidents have drawn attention to the importance of knowledge and learning and their dependence on both local and global organizational structures.

From Theory to Practice

This book provides a bridge for organizations to span the gap between vision and implementation, between hope and reality, from theory to practice. Through its action-based model and descriptions of successes and failures, we will address the question, "How do we, as an organization, have to change our actions and behaviors to increase our learning capacity as an organization?" More specifically, we will address questions concerning:

- Complex information interfaces between the organization and its environment
- Competing demands of knowledge creation goals relative to performance goals
- Critical breaks in systems integration abilities of organizations that affect the dissemination and diffusion of knowledge
- Intricate relationship of organizational and national cultures to the organization's ability to create new usable knowledge

Overview of Book

In Chapter 1 we describe how the seven paradigmatic shifts of the late 20th century force 21st century organizations to transform the way they operate and learn, thus demanding organizational learning for survival.

Chapter 2 examines five key questions important to an understanding and appreciation of organizational learning; namely, are there differences between (1) organizational vs. individual learning, (2) organizational learning and organizational change, (3) organizational learning and learning organization, (4) descriptive and dynamic models of organizational learning, and (5) world views associated with organizational learning?

The history and key theories of organizational learning are presented in Chapter 3, including the social action theory of Talcott Parsons which serves as the foundation for the Organizational Learning Systems Model.

In Chapter 4 an overview of the Organizational Learning Systems Model is presented. Chapters 5 through 8 then provide an in-depth description of each of the four subsystems of the model: Environmental Interface, Action/Reflection, Dissemination and Diffusion, and Memory and Meaning. Interspersed throughout these chapters are case studies of 20 companies around the world that are leaders in these subsystems of organizational learning — companies such as General Electric, Shell, CIGNA, Andersen, McKinsey, International Association of Machinists and Aerospace Workers, Federal Express, Canadian Imperial Bank of Commerce, Semco, National Semiconductor, Spring Branch Schools in Houston, and Pricewaterhouse-Coopers.

The final chapter, Chapter 9, provides the reader with specific steps and challenges for implementing organizational learning, how to address these challenges, and the success of Rover and Whirlpool in implementing organizational learning.

Getting Started in Your Organization

Organizational learning is no longer an option as we enter the 21st century. We either learn as an organization or we die. It is hoped that this book will provide you with the guidance and energy you and your organization will need to implement world class organizational learning theories and put the Organizational Learning Systems Model into practice in your company. We wish you much success on your journey!

David R. Schwandt
Ashburn, Virginia

Michael J. Marquardt
Reston, Virginia

The Authors

Dr. David Schwandt is Professor and Director of the Center for the Study of Learning at George Washington University. Prior to joining the university, Dave served as the Director of Organizational and Human Development for the U.S. General Accounting Office for 11 years. He has presented at various national and international conferences and workshops and has published more than 60 articles and chapters in scholarly works, including "Learning as an Organization: A Journey Into Chaos" in the book, *Learning Organizations* and "Using Organizational Learning in an Action Research Intervention to Maintain Technical Knowledge and Skills," selected as top paper of the 1996 Academy of HRD National Conference.

Dr. Schwandt utilizes a multidisciplinary approach (drawing from the fields of sociology, management, anthropology, the hard sciences, and psychology) in analyzing organizational structures and processes. His current research centers around sensemaking and cognition in organizational settings. He received his Ph.D. from Wayne State University in 1978. He has served in a variety of leadership roles in the Academy of HRD, the Academy of Management, the American Sociological Society, National Training Laboratory, Organizational Development Network, and the Systems Dynamic Society.

Dr. Michael Marquardt is Associate Professor of Human Resource Development and Program Director of Overseas Programs at George Washington University. He also serves as President of Global Learning Associates, a premier consulting firm assisting corporations around the world to become successful global learning organizations.

He has held a number of senior management, training, and marketing positions with organizations such as Grolier, World Center for Development and Training, National Coffee Service Association, Overseas Education Fund, TradeTec, and the U.S. Office of Personnel Management. Dr. Marquardt has trained over 25,000 managers in 85 countries since beginning his international experience in Spain in 1969. Consulting assignments have included Marriott, DuPont, Pentax, Motorola, Nortel, COMSAT, Rover, the United Nations Development Program, Xerox, San Miguel, Nuclear Regulatory Commission, Arthur Andersen, National Semiconductor, Warner-Lambert, TRW, Citicorp, Price Waterhouse, and Singapore Airlines as well as the governments of Indonesia, Laos, Ethiopia, Zambia, Egypt, Kuwait, Saudi Arabia, Turkey, Russia, Jamaica, Honduras, and Swaziland.

Dr. Marquardt is the author of over 50 professional articles and 11 books in the field of leadership, learning, and organizational change including *Building the Learning Organization* (selected as Book of the Year by the Academy of HRD), *The Global Advantage, Action Learning in Action, Global Human Resource Development*, and *Technology-Based Learning*. He has been a keynote speaker at international conferences in Australia, Japan, England, the Philippines, Malaysia, South Africa, Sweden, Singapore, and India as well as throughout North America.

Dr. Marquardt's achievements and leadership have been recognized through numerous awards including the International Practitioner of the Year Award from the American Society for Training and Development. He presently serves as a Senior Advisor for the United Nations Staff College in the areas of policy, technology, and learning systems. He is a Fellow of the National Academy of Human Resource Development and a cofounder of the Asian Learning Organization Network.

Table of Contents

1   Critical Need for Organizational Learning in a World of Rapid Change

Learning is the new form of labor.

Shoshana Zuboff
In the Age of the Smart Machine:
The Future of Work and Power, 1988

Transformations of the 21st Century

As we approach the 21st century, we are entering a new era in the evolution of organizational life and structure. The immense changes in the economic environment caused by globalization and technology have forced organizations from around the world to make significant transformations in order to adapt, survive, and to succeed in the new world of the next millennium.

The change we are talking about is not just the external elements of the organization — its products, activities, or structures — but rather its intrinsic way of operating — its values, mindset, even its primary purpose. Harrison Owen (1991, p. 1) states this message well in *Riding the Tiger: Doing*

1

Business in a Transforming World, when he writes, "There was a time when the prime business of business was to make a profit and a product. There is now a prior, prime business, which is to become an effective learning organization. Not that profit and product are no longer important, but without continual learning, profits and products will no longer be possible. Hence the strange thought that: the business of business is learning — and all else will follow."

The popular literature for managers is now reflecting the need for organizational learning. Top management strategist, M. J. Kiernan, has placed organizational learning at the top of his list of seven core elements of strategic architecture and has made it a managerial imperative. He writes:

> Propelled by the competitive exigencies of speed, global responsiveness, and the need to innovate constantly or perish, and enabled by new information technologies, learning will become the only viable alternative to corporate extinction. (Kiernan, 1993)

Slow-learning companies that survived in the past will become extinct in the future just as the dinosaurs became extinct some 30 million years ago after having dominated the planet for over 100 million years. Organizations with brainpower the size of dinosaurs will not survive in the faster, information-thick atmosphere of the new millennium. Making themselves bigger, heavier, and with tougher "hides" will not be a substitute for bigger, agile, and creative learning capacity.

Put very bluntly, organizations must learn faster and adapt to the rapid change in the environment or they simply will not survive. As in any transitional period, there presently exists side-by-side the dominant, dying species (i.e., nonlearning organization) and the emerging, more adaptive species (i.e., learning organization). Within the next 10 years only learning organizations will survive. Companies that do not become learning organizations will soon go the way of the dinosaur: die, because they were unable to adjust quickly enough to the changing environment around them.

Why Organizational Learning Is So Critical

The demands put on organizations now require learning to be delivered faster, cheaper, and more effectively to a fluid workplace and mobile workforce more dramatically affected by daily changes in the marketplace than ever before. And what are some of these critical issues facing today's corporations?

- Reorganization, restructuring, and reengineering for success, if not just survival
- Increased skill shortages with schools unable to adequately prepare for work in the 21st century
- Doubling of knowledge every 2 to 3 years
- Global competition from the world's most powerful companies
- Overwhelming breakthroughs of new and advanced technologies
- Spiraling need for organizations to adapt to change

Dilworth (1998) remarks how "change now tends to outdistance our ability to learn." Existing knowledge tends to misdirect inquiry rather than facilitate problem resolution. People and organizations need to learn new ways of coping with problems. Only by improving the learning capacity of organizations can we deal with change dynamics.

Thus learning inside the organization must be equal to or greater than change outside the organization or the organization will not survive. Revans (1983) aptly notes that "in any epoch of rapid change, those organizations unable to adapt are soon in trouble, and adaptation is achieved only by learning — namely, by being able to do tomorrow that which might have been unnecessary today. The organization that continues to express only the ideas of the past is not learning. Training systems ... may do little more than to make organizations proficient in yesterday's techniques."

Corporatewide, systemswide learning offers organizations the best opportunity of not only surviving, but also succeeding. As foreseen by leaders of the Rover Automotive Group in England, "The prospect that organizational learning offers is one of managing change by allowing for quantum leaps. Continuous improvement means that every quantum leap becomes an opportunity to learn and therefore prepare for the next quantum leap. By learning faster than our competitors the time span between leaps reduces and progress accelerates" (Marquardt, 1996).

To obtain and sustain competitive advantage in this new environment, organizations will have to learn better and faster from their successes and failures. They will need to continuously transform themselves into learning organizations, to become places where groups and individuals continuously engage in new learning processes.

Zuboff, in her 1988 classic *In the Age of the Smart Machine*, observes how today's organization may indeed have little choice but to become a "learning institution, since one of its principal purposes will have to be the expansion of knowledge — not knowledge for its own sake (as in academic pursuit), but knowledge that comes to reside at the core of what it means to be productive. Learning is no longer a separate activity that occurs either before one enters the workplace or in remote classroom settings. Nor is it an activity preserved for a managerial group. The behaviors that define learning and the behaviors that define being productive are one and the same. Learning is the heart of productive activity. To put it simply, learning is the new form of labor" (p.395).

As we approach the 21st century, we are entering a new era in the evolution of organizational life and structure. The immense changes in the economic environment caused by globalization and technology have forced organizations to, in turn, make significant transformations in order to adapt and survive in this new world.

Paradigm Shifts in Today's World

Why is there so much change around people and organizations in today's world such that today's solutions will be totally inadequate for tomorrow's challenges? Sociologists and management specialists have identified seven dramatic, paradigmatic shifts causing the chaos in today's world and workplace (see Figure 1.1).

Paradigm	*Yesterday*		*Tomorrow*
Physics	Newtonian	➡	Quantum
Era	Machine/Industrial	➡	Technology/Informational
Economy	National	➡	Global
Production	Products	➡	Knowledge
Workplace	Physical	➡	Virtual
Focus	Worker	➡	Customer
Means of Production	Manufacturing	➡	Mentofacturing

Figure 1.1 Seven Paradigm Shifts

Newtonian to Quantum Physics

For nearly three centuries the world and the workplace have been built upon Newtonian physics — the physics of cause and effect, of predictability and certainty, of distinct wholes and parts, of reality being what is seen. Newtonian physics is a science of quantifiable determinism, of linear thinking, and of controllable futures.

In the Newtonian mindset, people engage in complex planning for a world that they believe is predictable. They continually search for better methods of objectively perceiving the world. This mechanistic and reductionist way of thinking and acting dominates life even though it was disproved over 70 years ago by Albert Einstein and others who introduced the scientific community to quantum physics in the 1920s. Margaret Wheatley (1992), author of *Leadership and the New Science*, rightly notes, however, that this old, disproved mindset in today's world is "unempowering and disabling for all of us."

Quantum physics, on the other hand, deals with the world at the sub-atomic level, examining the intricate patterns out of which seemingly discrete events arise. Quantum physics recognizes that the universe and every object in it are, in reality, vast empty spaces that are filled with fields and movements that are the basic substance of the universe. Thus relationships between objects and between observers and objects are what determine reality. The quantum universe is composed of an environment rich in relationships; it is a world of chaos, of process, and not just of objects and things. Quantum physics deals with waves and holograms, of surprises rather than predictions.

In understanding quantum physics, organizations realize that they cannot predict with certainty that chaos is part and parcel of reality. It forces us to change the way we think, the way we attempt to solve problems, and the way we deal with order vs. change, autonomy vs. control, structure vs. flexibility, and planning vs. flowing.

Machine/Industrial Era to Technology/Information Era

It was machine technology that created the Industrial Age that began in the late 18th century. And it is the new quantum leap caused by computer technology that has now created the Information Age. We are now in a world of teletraining, infostructures, and ubiquitous computers.

Alvin Toffler (1990) writes how the advanced global economy cannot run for 30 seconds without the information technology of computers and other new and rapidly improving complexities of production. Yet, today's best computers and CAD/CAM systems will be "stone-age" primitive within a few years. We are moving from information exchange to virtual organizations to Internet commerce that can transform every process of global business, including buying, selling, and information flow.

The world has indeed entered an era of ever-increasing technological advancement — with new technologies such as optoelectronics, cyberspace, information highways, DVDs (digital video disks), informating, local area networks (LANs), wide area networks (WANs), groupware, virtual reality, and electronic classrooms. The power of computer technology has progressed from mainframe to desktop to briefcase portable to user's hand. More and more of a company's operations are being totally automated and customized. The impact on organizational work and on learning has been overwhelming.

All of these technologies have helped to create the Information Age. Each has become necessary to manage the "data deluge" present in the fast-changing, turbocharged organizations of today. When working in a global economy in which "being informed, being in touch, and being there first" can make all the difference between success and second best, technology and information provide a big advantage indeed!

Also, the speed and impact of technology on creating and managing information continues to accelerate! Trying to figure out the capabilities and future directions of this rapidly changing Information Era is impossible. Let's look at just a few of the already existing powers of technology:

- Superconducting transmission lines can transmit data up to 100 times faster than today's fiberoptical networks. One line can carry 1 trillion bits of information a second, enough to send the complete contents of the Library of Congress in 2 minutes.
- "Neural networks" bring advances in computer intelligence that make process commands sequentially; this neural network uses associative "reasoning" to store information in patterned connections, allowing it to process complex questions through its own logic.
- Expert systems, a subset of artificial intelligence, are beginning to solve problems in much the same way as human experts.
- Telephones are being manufactured that are small enough to wear as earrings; cellular phones can now respond to e-mail.

One of the most amazing and transforming technological additions to ours lives is the Internet. The use of the Internet is one of the fastest-growing phenomena the business world has ever seen — building from a base of fewer than 1000 connected computers in the early 1980s to over 10 million host computers today. Internet commerce is projected to grow from a mere $8 billion in 1997 to over $327 billion in 2002 (Tapscott, 1995).

Some of the new high-tech learning machines have been called "the most powerful learning tool since the invention of the book." With virtual reality, the mind is cut off from outside distractions and one's attention becomes focused on the powerful sensory stimulation (light-sound matrix) that bombards the imagination. It becomes possible for ideas and mental images to float in and out of a person's consciousness.

Technology is becoming more and more a part of all products and the total GNP, including aerospace, advanced industrial systems, and automotive. Already, nearly 20% of an automobile's value is the electronics within it. The computer service and software market has grown to over $420 billion, an increase of 50% in the last 4 years! Information technology is expected to form the basis of many of the most important products, services, and processes of the future.

In addition, an array of technological developments has recently emerged for use in the home as well as the office, including:

- Integration of television, telecommunications, and computers through digitization and compression techniques
- Reduced costs and more flexible use and application of telecommunications through developments such as ISDN, fiberoptics, and cellular radio
- Miniaturization (tiny cameras, microphones, small, high-resolution display screens)
- Increased portability through use of radio communications and miniaturization
- Expanded processing power through new microchip development and advanced software
- More powerful and user-friendly command and software tools, making it much easier for users to create and communicate their own materials (Bates, 1995).

The commoditization of ultrahigh technology opens spellbinding opportunities for new knowledge-exchange products. British Telecom, for example, believes that future generations of portable phones could be installed right in one's ear. While talking, the user could also glimpse images or data that are pulled invisibly off the Internet and projected onto a magnifying mirror positioned beside one's eye.

The technology of the future will respond to our voices and extend our senses. It will simulate complex phenomena — weather patterns, stock market crashes, environmental hazards — solving problems and predicting outcomes at a price anyone can afford. Computers, or networks of them, will become ubiquitous as they are invisibly imbedded in other things. These machines will reconfigure themselves when new applications are required. A whole new metaphor for computing is taking shape, patterned on the natural resilience and elegance of biological organisms. They will learn to diagnose, repair, and even replicate themselves (Gross, 1997).

The impact of technology on organizations, on management, and on the community is mindboggling; and it has only begun. The emerging power and applicability of technology will turn the world of work on its head. Organizations will become more virtual rather than physical because of technology. People will be more linked to customers in Kuala Lumpur than to co-workers across the hall because of technology. Thus the 21st century leader will need to appreciate and understand the power and purposes of technology.

National to Global Economy

We have entered the Global Age. We are a more global people, we share many global values and practices, and we are more and more working for global organizations. Globalization has caused a converging of economic and social forces, of interests and commitments, of values and tastes, of challenges and opportunities. We can easily communicate with people 10,000 miles away because we share a global language (English) and a global medium for communications (computers and the Internet).

Four main forces have quickly brought us to this global age: technology, travel, trade, and television. These four Ts have laid the groundwork for a more collective experience for people everywhere. More and more of us share common tastes in foods (hamburgers, pizza, tacos), fashion (denim jeans), and fun (Disney, rock music, television). Nearly 2 billion passengers fly the world's airways each year. People are watching the same movies, reading the same magazines, and dancing the same dances from Boston to Bangkok to Buenos Aires.

Ever more of us speak English — now spoken by more than 1.5 billion people in over 130 countries (often as a second, third, or fourth language). The English language, like all languages, carries with it implicit and explicit cultural and social values (e.g., precision, individualism, active control, clarity). It has, despite the protests of the French, become the global language of the airlines, the media, of computers, of business, and of the global marketplace.

The signs of the global marketplace are all around us.

- U.S. corporations have invested $1 trillion abroad and employ over 100 million overseas workers; over 100,000 U.S. firms are engaged in global ventures valued at over $2 trillion. Over one third of U.S. economic growth has been due to exports, providing jobs for over 11 million Americans.
- 10% of U.S. manufacturing is foreign owned and employs 4 million Americans; Mitsubishi USA is America's fourth largest exporter and Toyota has displaced Chrysler as the third largest in U.S. auto sales. Foreign investment in the U.S. has now surpassed the $3 trillion mark.
- McDonald's operates more than 12,500 restaurants in 70 countries and is adding 600 new restaurants per year.
- Many Gulf countries have more foreign-born workers than native population. More than 70% of the employees of Canon work outside of Japan.
- Financial markets are open 24 hours a day around the world.
- Over half of the Ph.D.s in engineering, mathematics, and economics awarded by American universities in 1997 went to non-U.S. citizens.
- Global standards and regulations for trade and commerce, finance, products, and services have emerged.
- More and more companies — InterContinental, Xerox, Motorola, Honda, Samsung, Pentax — are manufacturing and selling chiefly outside their countries of origin. We hardly know if a company is French, Japanese, Swedish, or American.
- Coca-Cola earns more money in Japan than in the U.S.
- Over 70% of profits for the U.S. $20 billion music industry is from outside our country. Most big-bucks movies depend on global viewers for big profits.

The global marketplace has created the need for global corporations. These organizations, in turn, have created an even more-global marketplace. The growing similarity of what customers wish to purchase, including quality and price, has spurred both tremendous opportunities and tremendous pressures for businesses to become global. More and more companies, whether small or large, young or old, recognize that their choice is between becoming global or becoming extinct (Marquardt, 1999).

Global organizations are companies that operate as if the entire world were a single entity. They are fully integrated so that all their activities link, leverage, and compete on a worldwide scale (Marquardt and Snyder, 1997). Global firms emphasize global operations over national or multinational operations. They use global sourcing of human resources, capital, technology, facilities, resources, and raw materials. They deem cultural sensitivity to employees, customers, and patterns as critical to the success of the organization (Adler, 1991). Globalization of an organization has occurred when the organization has developed a global corporate culture, strategy, structure, and communications process (Rhinesmith, 1993).

The global economy has created a level of complexity that most organizations are not prepared to understand, let alone deal with. Organizations must now relate to the ever-growing complexity of multiple relations in their environments — foreign markets, partnerships, and growing and failing economies, to mention a few.

Products to Knowledge

The wealth and GNP of nations will depend increasingly on knowledge-based, high-tech industries in areas such as biotechnology, health, environmental products and services, tourism and hospitality, telecommunications, computer software and software applications, financial services, and entertainment (film, television, games). Knowledge has quite suddenly become the world's most important resource (Sveiby, 1997). It now plays the prima donna role in world history that physical labor, minerals, and energy once played.

Simply put, knowledge has become more important for organizations than financial resources, market position, technology, or any other company asset. Knowledge is seen as the main resource used in performing work in an organization. The organization's traditions, culture, technology, operations, systems, and procedures are all based on knowledge and expertise. Knowledge is needed to increase the abilities of employees to improve products and services, thereby providing quality service to clients and consumers. Knowledge is necessary to update products and services, change systems and structures, and communicate solutions to problems.

"Cracking This Crazy Economy"

U.S. companies announced a record 678,000 job cuts in 1998, but the unemployment rate dropped to 4.3%, a 28-year low....It's the new economy. The U.S. economy has soared! Its health is increasingly dependent on the information industries, which have become the biggest job creators in the economy. In 1998, more the 37% of new jobs have come from information-related services, such as communications, education, software, and financial services (up from only 16% in 1995). While old-time industrial companies such as Caterpillar, International Paper, and Proctor & Gamble languish, big gains are coming from Intel, Microsoft, and Yahoo (Mandel, 1999).

Brainpower is becoming a company's most valuable asset and is what conveys a competitive edge in the marketplace. Stewart (1997) asserts that, "Brainpower ... has never before been so important for business. Every company depends increasingly on knowledge — patents, process, management skills, technologies, information about customers and suppliers, and old-fashioned experience. ... This knowledge that exists in an organization can be used to create differential advantage. In other words, it's the sum of everything everybody in your company knows that gives you a competitive edge in the marketplace" (p. 44).

Because the new global economy is based on knowledge work and innovation, there is a convergence between work and learning. While you perform knowledge work, you learn; and you must learn minute by minute to perform knowledge work effectively. Learning is becoming a lifelong challenge as well as a lifelong process. Most knowledge has a shelf life of 3 years or less, and knowledge continues to double every 18 months!

Physical to Virtual World of Work

The world of work and the workplace is being dramatically transformed. Workers no longer work in an office. Corporations collaborate and compete with one another at the same time. Customers provide supervision as well as dictate services. Fellow employees work closely with each other while never ever having met one another. Companies have temporary, part-time CEOs and permanent, full-time janitors. Corporate headquarters staff may consist of less than 1% of the company's workforce, if there is a headquarters.

Organizations have moved from the quality efforts of the 1980s through the reengineering processes of the 1990s to the radical transformation of the workplace itself as we enter the 21st century. They have moved from focusing on the reduction of defects and the streamlining of business processes to totally new forms that enable organizations to manage continuous, white-water change, creating "high-performance work organizations" in which work is reorganized, redesigned, or reengineered to improve performance.

Decades of breaking work into ever-smaller tasks are coming to an end. Instead teams of employees will be responsible for key business processes from beginning to end. Impatience with the rate of change will cause many organizations to reengineer (start from scratch) their key processes.

Companies will focus on and organize around what they do best. Therefore, they will structure according to core competencies instead of according to product or market. The organizational architecture of companies will evolve around autonomous work teams and strategic alliances. In such companies, "noncore" work will be outsourced or done by temporary and contract workers as needed.

Advances in information technology described above are providing faster transmission of data and expanded storage capacity as well as clearer, more complex links among users and greater computer power. Such innovation will permit greater control of more decentralized organization, while permitting the information flow needed to give local managers substantive decision-making authority.

Because of this technology, corporations will become cluster organizations or adhocracies: groups of geographically dispersed people — typically working at home — that come together electronically for a particular project and then disband, having completed their work. More organizations will be comprised of a minimal core of permanent employees supported by independently contracted professionals.

As more companies realize that the key resource of business is not capital, personnel, or facilities, but rather knowledge, information, and ideas, many new ways of viewing the organization begin to emerge. Everywhere companies are restructuring, creating integrated organizations, global networks, and leaner corporate centers. Organizations are becoming more fluid, ever shifting in size, shape, and arrangements.

Organizations are also becoming more and more virtual. A virtual organization is a temporary network of independent companies, suppliers, customers, even rivals linked by information technology to share skills, costs, and access to one another's markets. In its purest form, a company decides to focus on the thing it does best. Then it links with other companies, each bringing to the combination its own special ability. It will mix and match what it does best with the best of the other companies. For example, a manufacturer will manufacture while relying on a product-design outfit to sell the output.

The virtual corporation will have neither central office nor organization chart, and no hierarchy or vertical integration. Teams of people in different companies will routinely work together. After the business is done, the virtual organization disbands.

Increase in Temporary and Telecommuting Workers

Another new element of today's and tomorrow's worker is the presence of temporary and part-time workers. More and more companies are depending heavily on temporary help, and their employment is rising annually at 17% and over $50 billion in revenue. Businesses have made temp help an integral part of the hiring process as well as overall human resources policy. The hiring of temporary workers allows for greater flexibility for organizations, but at the expense of worker loyalty and knowledge retention.

Telecommuting, thanks to digital phone lines, affordable desktop video-conferencing, and wide-ranging cellular networks, is out of the experimental stage. By means of local phone companies offering Integrated Services Digital Network (ISDN) lines that can transmit voice, data, and video simultaneously, telecommuting has become easy and highly productive.

The over 15 million telecommuters in the U.S. represent the fastest-growing portion of workers. The entire 240-member core sales staff at American Express Travel Related Services Co. are telecommuters. Ernst & Young has implemented "hoteling" in which up to ten people share a single desk in a fully equipped office on an as-needed basis. Employees must reserve space and equipment in advance. Over the past 3 years, the accounting firm has slashed its office space requirements by about 2 million square feet, saving roughly $25 million a year.

Worker Focus to Customer Focus in the Marketplace

Customers will more and more determine how organizations set strategies and carry out operations. Customers rather than workers will become the focus of leadership attention organizational priorities. How to better serve customers through continuous innovations will become a prime focus of the 21st century workplace.

On a worldwide scale, customers will continue to push for new performance standards in quality, variety, customization, convenience, time, and innovation. They will increase the rapidity with which companies are compelled to move beyond domestic markets. Organizations will have no choice but to shop the world for customers, people, resources, technology, markets, and business partners. These new demands for quality, the constant change of taste, the existence of global fads, and short product life cycles are forcing new global partnerships and alliances.

Global communications and marketing have also increased consumers' awareness about possible products and services. Global competition has offered customers a more varied and higher quality of choices. What has been created is a "convergence of consumer needs and preferences." Consumers are now able to choose the products and services they want based on the best:

1. Cost — what is the least expensive and most economical
2. Quality — no defects; meeting and exceeding the customer's expectations
3. Time — available as quickly as possible
4. Service — pleasant and courteous; available immediately on products that are reparable or replaceable
5. Innovation — new, something not yet envisioned by the customer when produced (e.g., Sony Walkman)
6. Customization — tailored to very specific needs

Jorma Ollila, CEO of Nokia, adds that 21st century customers will be much more accustomed to information, and will be technologically more connected, more culturally conscious, and more international by nature.

Manufacturing to Mentofacturing as Means of Production

Knowledge is now providing the key raw material for wealth creation and is quickly becoming the fountain of organizational and personal power. Manufacturing work (working with our hands) has been replaced by knowledge work (working with our minds, i.e., mentofacturing). Brains have replaced brawn as the most important means of increasing productivity and profits.

Mentofacturing is needed to create and understand and manage the company's knowledge. It has become absolutely critical for the survival of organizations competing with the world's brightest companies.

Mentofacturing capacity and products (i.e., valuable knowledge) have become more important for organizations than financial resources, market position, technology, or any other company asset. Better mentofacturing and knowledge will increase the abilities of employees to continuously improve products and services, to adapt structures and systems, and to become world class.

Organizations must employ more and more knowledge workers. Not only senior executives, but employees at all levels must be highly educated, highly skilled knowledge workers. In the new postmanufacturing society, knowledge is not just another resource alongside the traditional factors of production, land, labor, and capital. It is the only meaningful resource in today's workforce. In an economy based on knowledge, the knowledge worker is the single greatest asset and mentofacturing its most important activity.

As society moves from the industrial era to the knowledge era, job requirements are changing. Employees are moving from needing repetitive skills to knowing how to deal with surprises and exceptions, from depending on memory and facts to being spontaneous and creative, from risk avoidance to risk taking, from focusing on policies and procedures to building collaboration with people. Work will require "higher-order" cognitive skills — the ability to analyze problems and find the right resources for solving them, and often with both limited and conflicting information.

The workforce is rapidly changing. By the year 2000, over 80% of all jobs in the U.S. will be in knowledge/service industries. Many of the new jobs will require a much higher level of technical skill than the jobs they are replacing, especially in manufacturing and resource-based industries. People will retain existing jobs only if they are retrained to higher standards.

Knowledge workers have already discovered that continual learning is not only a prerequisite of employment, but a major form of work.

United Way Of America — Learning, Unlearning, and Relearning

United Way of America (UWA) is the national service and training center which supports member United Ways by helping them pursue dual strategies of adding value to the community and conducting cost-effective, donor-oriented fundraising to increase financial resources. Nearly 1400 United Way organizations are members of UWA. Its mission is to increase the organized capacity of people to care for one another and together advance the nation's health and human service agenda by expanding resources and applying them effectively to build more self-sufficient communities.

The United Way of America recognizes the importance of organizational learning as a key to its survival and success:

The United Way, like every other institution in American life, confronts a future in which the rate of change will be a blur. Forces of change are requiring organizations to transform at tempos not considered realistic, or even possible, just 20 years ago. Organizations that thrive, not just survive, will be those that choose not to simply manage change, but to lead it.

Our challenges faced include the challenge of complexity, the consequences of citizen withdrawal, competition in the nonprofit sector, the curse of collective cynicism, and the need to confront the status quo.

UWA can best lead change by being bold in learning, unlearning, and relearning:

- Bold in learning to deal with the emerging truths from diverse communities.
- Bold in unlearning old myths and methodologies. "We've always done it that way" is only a statement of history, not one of predestination. In fact, having "always done it that way" may be the very best reason to change.
- Bold in relearning what we have known all along: there is strength in unity (1997 Annual Report).

Only through learning as an organization can UWA achieve the continuous improvement, trust, and teamwork needed to successfully lead its members into the 21st century.

Organizational Learning Becomes a Necessity for Survival

Albert Einstein once wrote that "No problem can be solved from the same consciousness that created it; we must learn to see the world anew." The paradigm shifts described above have altered the world of work so dramatically that old "dinosaur-like" organizations are no longer able to respond to these changes, to handle these new challenges. As Einstein had forewarned, these new problems won't be able to be solved using the same structures, mindsets, or knowledge that had worked for organizations in the past.

These seven paradigmatic shifts have created ever more change, chaos, and complexity. They have transformed the lives in which we live and the world in which we work. Organizations are forced to continually adapt and change if they seek to survive in this new environment.

Today, there are a growing number of organizational people who are becoming increasingly aware that the knowledge, the strategies, the leadership, and the technology of yesterday will not lead to success in tomorrow's world. It has become obvious to them that companies have to increase their corporate capacity to learn if they are to function successfully in an environment that includes continual mergers, rapid technological changes, massive societal change, and increasing competition.

To obtain and sustain competitive advantage in this new world, companies realize that they have to transform the way they work and, even more importantly, transform the way they learn. They will need to develop a higher form of learning capability, to be able to learn better and faster from their successes and failures from within and from outside their organizations. They would need to continuously transform themselves into organizations where everyone, groups and individuals, would quantumly increase their adaptive and productive capabilities. Only if they increased their capacity to learn would they be able to avoid the fate of the dinosaur, a creature that had not been able to adapt to the changing environment.

How can organizations better adapt to an ever more rapidly changing environment? How can they better capture, convert, and create knowledge? What are the best systems for learning? What is the best model for organizational learning? These are the questions that this book will seek to answer. However, before answering these questions it is important to clarify several key issues related to organizational learning — the subject of Chapter 2.

References

Adler, N., *International Dimensions of Organizational Behavior*, PWS-Kent, Boston, 1991.

Bassi, L., Chenny, S., and van Buren, M., Training industry trends, *Training and Development*, 51 (11), 46–59, 1997.

Bates, A.W., Technology, *Open Learning and Distance Education*, Routledge, London, 1995.

Dilworth, R.L., Action learning in a nutshell, *Performance Improvement Quarterly*, 11(1), 28–43, 1998.

Drucker, P., The new society of organization, *Harvard Business Review*, No. 5, 95–104, 1992.

Gross, N., Future of technology, *Business Week*, p. 72, June 23, 1997.

Kiernan, M., The new strategic architecture: learning to compete in the 21st century, *Academy of Management Executive*, 7(1), 7–21, 1993.

Mandel, M., Cracking this crazy economy, *Business Week*, p. 39, January 25, 1999.

Marquardt, M., *Building the Learning Orginization*, McGraw-Hill, New York, 1996.

Marquardt, M., *The Global Advantage: How to Improve Performance through Globalization*, Gulf Publishing, Houston, 1999.

Marquardt, M. and Snyder, N., How companies go global — the role of the global integrators and the global mindset, *International Journal of Training and Development*, 1(2), 104–117, 1997.

Owen, H., *Riding the Tiger: Doing Business in a Transforming World*, Abbott Publishing, Potomac, MD, 1991.

Revans, R., *The ABC of Action Learning*, Chartwell-Bratt, Bromley, 1983.

Rhinesmith, S., *A Manager's Guide to Globalization*, Irwin Publishing, New York, 1993.

Senge, P.M., *The Fifth Discipline: The Art and Practice of the Learning Organization*, Doubleday, New York, 1990.

Stewart, T., Brainpower, *Fortune*, 123(11), 44–60, 1991.

Stewart, T., *Intellectual Capital: The New Wealth of Organizations*, Doubleday, New York, 1997.

Sveiby, K. E., *The New Organizational Wealth*, Berrett-Koehler, San Francisco, 1997.

Tapscott, D., *The Digital Economy*, McGraw-Hill, New York, 1995.

Toffler, A., *Powershift*, Bantam, New York, 1990.

Wheatley, M., *Leadership and the New Sciences*, Berrett-Koehler, San Francisco, 1992.

Zuboff, S., *In the Age of the Smart Machine: The Future of Work and Power*, Basic Books, New York, 1988.

2 Clarifying the Key Issues in Organizational Learning

For any organization to perform, to deal with the multiplicity of ongoing problems and issues, to adapt to environmental changes, to survive and prosper, implies that it must learn.

C.C. Lundberg, 1989

Moving from "Fad" to Foundations

Organizational learning as a concept has been teetering on the boundary between a useful construct (usually seen as the learning organization) and a "fad" that offers metaphorical insights, but fades as the newest quick fix arrives on the organizational scene. Much of this instability stems from two interrelated causes.

First, the popular literature represents primarily the author's suggested characteristics of a learning organization. For example, the learning organization *should* be experimental, it *should* open its communications and dialogue, it *should* maintain a vision that motivates its members and provides direction for the organization, and it *should* also promote and develop organizational learning disciplines (to include systems thinking). The problem arises when an organization decides that it wants to be a learning organization. It finds neither guidance for obtaining these preferred future states nor information that may provide insights to possible consequences, either positive or negative. There are few, if any, dynamic models that allow the organization to critically analyze its internal and external means as they strive to attain the learning organization status.

The second reason for the instability of the concept is a lack of field research that can inform the actions of the organizations choosing to move toward this new state. This lack of research is related to the above issue in that the absence of dynamic models, as opposed to the current static or descriptive models, inhibits the development of useful propositions linking the potential constructs and the generation of researchable questions. This in turn limits progress toward a pragmatic theory of organizational learning.

Many organizations see the learning organization as an entry portal to the knowledge age. However, upon entering, they have been frustrated in their attempt to understand and respond to the following five critical questions:

1. What is the relationship between organizational learning and individual learning?
2. Is organizational learning merely another term for organizational change?
3. What is the difference between organizational learning and the learning organization?
4. Why are there so many different models of organizational learning?
5. Does the way our organization view the world impact our understanding and practice of organizational learning?

In order for organizations to successfully cross the bridge from theory to practice, they must first address these five questions.

Organizational Learning and/or Individual Learning?

Can organizations actually learn? Or is this simply a metaphor for the cumulative learning of all the members of the organization? Many authors have approached the organizational learning construct using a common understanding of the learning processes that individuals employ. This is understandable if one examines how we learn as humans: we relate the unfamiliar to the familiar. So when we are confronted with a very ambiguous concept such as the "learning of the collective whole (or organizational learning)" we most readily relate it to our understanding of the individual learner.

We are told at a very early age that we, as humans, have a very unique attribute. This attribute is not shared with any other species, thus separating us from our fellow creatures and imposing on us a certain responsibility. This attribute provided the basis for our survival as a species and, depending on your view of evolution, has not only determined our individual fate, but also the fate of the human race. Of course, this attribute was the human's ability to reason, draw cause–effect relations, and to remember the knowledge that was associated with our actions. Our uniqueness has been related to our ability to learn. Our associated responsibility as human beings was to continuously contribute to knowledge creation through this learning process.

As time moves forward and we do use our unique learning capacity, we find that the knowledge we create produces a more and more complex explanation for our success in the evolutionary game. The ability to reason is not the only critical prerequisite attribute; we are also dependent on our biology. The presence of an opposable thumb and the placement of our eyes and other universal specifications have contributed to our survival as a species. We also discover that we may not be the only species that has developed these attributes and that they exist in other creatures in various stages of development. Thus our previously thought uniqueness, the ability to learn, has created knowledge that has increased the complexity of the nature of our existence. First, we are confronted with multiple cause–effect relations concerning our survival, which in turn makes us question our reasoning capacity. Second, we must also deal with our loss of uniqueness and the concept that we are not alone and that our survival may be connected to other factors outside of our species and, possibly, outside of our galaxy. Not only do these factors have implications at the level of evolutionary survival of the species, but they are also important concepts for our behaviors in companies and other social organizations that span the globe.

The purpose of individual learning seems to be very utilitarian in nature. The focus is on the use of learning as a mechanism for adaptation and ultimately survival of the individual. Many authors have defined individual learning in a functional manner.

Learning means change. It is not simply a matter of accretion, of adding something. There is always reorganization or restructuring. There may be unlearning. Learning involves a change in behavior; learning may make us respond differently. Learning may also involve a change in the organism, and over time in the personality (Kidd, 1959).

Inherent in this definition is the assumption that if a person learns there is a progression and/or a survival element that will justify the learning in some cause–effect relation. This is most often delineated in some kind of change to the person or the actions of the person. This thinking then lends itself to the assumption that organizational learning is merely a sum total of each individual member's learning. This idea has been categorically rejected by a number of theorists in the field (Arggyris and Schön, 1978; Fiol and Lyles, 1985; Hedberg, 1981; Huber, 1991; Shrivastava, 1983). These authors all conclude that a social synergy exists that adds value to the knowledge creation process. This added value cannot be achieved simply by summing the level of knowledge of each member of the organization. (Our use of the term "organizational learning" in this book represents a very complex interrelationship between people, actions, symbols, and processes within the organization.)

Discussions of individual learning often include both the process and purpose of learning, and the portrayal of learning as a linear process. The assumptions that support the linearity of the construct are based on observations of a linear sequence of events in the learning process: information intake, action and reflection, interpretation and integration, and finally storage of knowledge. This prevailing assumption of linearity limits the use of the individual learning process as an organizational learning model. The social dynamics of an organization require a nonlinear systems approach to explaining collective learning. Any knowledge contained in the individual, to be useful to the organization, must be developed and transmitted through a social network that is nonlinear. This means that we must consider all of the social dynamics associated with organizational behavior such as turf wars, communication breakdowns, and power struggles, and how they all relate to knowledge creation.

The use of the individual learning model for organizational learning also breaks down when we try to examine barriers to organizational learning. In the case of the individual learner, these barriers require a physiological cause–effect reasoning, such as loss of a human sense or mental capacity. Barriers to organizational learning stem from dynamic sociological actions. The use of a physiological learning metaphor conveys misconceptions of normal social dynamics and places them into inherent disabilities. Although this metaphorical representation may help us in our understanding, it can also decrease the validity of the social nature of the organizational learning construct as a real entity.

When we say individuals are learning, we speak as though we could actually see the process. When we speak of a person's memory, we assume the brain is a place where he or she stores accumulated knowledge. The application of similar assumptions and metaphorical descriptions concerning organizational learning results in confusion and even disbelief. It often appears that we are merely assigning an individual characteristic to the intangible concept referred to as organizational learning. This process of attributing human traits to non-human entities is referred to an anthropomorphism. It is one of the pitfalls of the overuse of metaphor. It leads to false assumptions concerning the simplicity of the social interaction of the organization that is required to produce the system knowledge for its survival.

Although there is a relationship between an individual member's learning and the learning of the organization, it is more a necessary condition, but not a sufficient one. The answer to the organization's frustration is "yes, there is a difference between individual and organizational learning." Individual learning is a necessary, but not sufficient condition for organizational learning to occur. In the individual, we assign the whereabouts of the learning process to the body and mind. However, in the organization, the location of the learning process is contained within the social dynamic actions and the complexity of the interacting components of the organization. It is this complexity that prohibits us from assuming that organizational learning can be represented by the sum total of the learning of the individuals within the organization. This same complexity makes requisite a "social systems" approach to understanding the organization's learning processes. This in turn leads us to the question of change, not just individual change, but organizational change.

Organizational Learning or Organizational Change?

Global societies have become very aware of the paradigm called organizational change. Each and every theory of social science deals with the concept of change. Sociologists are concerned with large social changes, anthropologists are concerned with changes in cultures, psychologists are concerned with individual human change, and, of course, business and management scientists are concerned with all of the above (which we label organizational change). We have knowledge about the types of change (e.g., political, organizational, social, technological), the methods of change (i.e., radical, planned, transformational, etc.), and strategies for dealing with change (i.e., restructuring, human resource development, education, communications, etc.). With all of this knowledge, however, we still seem to lack an understanding of how to successfully implement the actual process of change — the dynamic and interrelated nature of the actions that make up the change process.

There probably is no other word in the English language that has had more attention from organizational researchers and practitioners than the word "change." In fact, as Huber and Glick (1993, p. 3) characterized the situation, "During the 1980's it was tiresomely fashionable for the popular press and the business literature to report on business's turbulent environment." The 1990s are still characterized in this manner, except we are now using the term "hyperturbulant" to describe our environment.

When we connect the concept of change with the concept of learning, many people almost feel this may be a redundancy. After all, when we learn, do we not change? And when we change, haven't we learned? The answer for both individuals and organizations is "not always." Often the performance of organizations becomes different (they change), but the organization has no new knowledge. For example, a large public organization had employees that failed to obey sexual harassment laws; they were sued, they settled, and as part of that settlement the organization trained all employees as to appropriate behaviors. Two years later the same organization was found to be out of compliance with the settlement. Did this organization learn?

The above example is a case of an organization performing actions differently so one could say they had changed. However, the organization as an entity committed the same error again. They performed differently, but did not understand the dependency of their actions on the cultural values within the organization. They had not developed the knowledge of the link between organization cultural assumptions and their employee's behavior. This also provides a good example of an organization providing training for all its employees (individual learning), yet the organization still commits the same error (lack of organizational learning).

Therefore, the answer to the organizational learning question is "yes, learning and change can be related." However, there is an important difference between organizational learning and change. Change should therefore be defined as a function of both performance and learning. This definition originates from a sociological perspective and has been interpreted as Change = Performance + Learning. For our purposes we have defined this relation as Change = Performance × Learning.

This reformulation provides a more realistic description of the importance of learning to change. In the first relation, it is possible to allow learning to go to zero (Learning = 0) and the organization would still be able to attain change through performance only (Change = Performance). This is what happened in our sexual harassment example above. By using the second relationship, the organization cannot let learning go to zero because the multiplicative nature of the relationship would give us zero for the change (Change = 0). Thus learning becomes an organizational imperative. The second relationship also demonstrates the leverage that can be attained through considering, simultaneously, both the contributions of performance and learning. This formulation will be further developed in Chapter 3 when we examine both organizational learning and performing systems.

The dynamics of the Organizational Learning System Model incorporates the concept of the dependency of change on the capacity of the organization (the collective) to learn — to learn as an entity, not merely as the sum of the individual learning of its members. Effective organizational change can only occur when both performance and learning occur for the collective.

Organizational Learning or the Learning Organization?

The symbiotic relationship between the knowledge age and the globalization of organizations is seen not only in grand actions such as the movement of large amounts of capital across national boundaries, mergers, and partnerships — once thought of as disconnected industries. It is also observed in the actions within the boundaries of our organizations. For example, the long-honored chain of command of the military has now come under question since e-mail allows us to contact anyone.

Our ability to sit at a computer keyboard and communicate across levels of the organization, and even communicate across national boundaries, has created potential for interaction that we did not envision a few short years ago. In conjunction with this newfound potential, we are also confronted with new concerns and questions. We have concerns about the security of information and knowledge. We also have concerns about the processes and time it takes to change information into usable knowledge; the relative time it takes to reflect on the information and knowledge. We have concerns about the roles of individuals and positions within our organization. Speed and quantity of information and knowledge are now impacting these roles.

Finally, we have questions about the values and basic assumptions of organizations as they confront new moral situations caused by the processes of knowledge creation and organizational learning.

With the advent of the technology explosion which the world has experienced during the past 20 years, increasing interest has been generated with regard to the development and transfer of new knowledge within and across organizations. Accompanying this interest has also been recognition of the increasing complexity of organizational environments. These conditions have prompted questions about productivity, quality, and utilization of human resources including an interest in the ability of organizations to learn. As learning takes on new organizational legitimacy, the terms organizational learning and learning organization are becoming "household" words in organizational literature, business schools, and corporate board rooms as if they were grounded in a known and accepted theoretical base.

This is a book about dynamic organizational learning, a process that may or may not result in a desirable condition called the learning organization. Although many of us may use these terms interchangeably, there is a distinct difference in the two concepts represented by these two terms. There is an underlying assumption that we have a foundational theory of organizational learning. Thus the difference between these two terms "learning organization" and "organizational learning" can best be explained as a "process" vs. "product" argument. The learning organization is a representation of a desired end. Organizational learning is a representation of the dynamic human processes required to increase the cognitive capacity of the total organization.

Is it important that we make a distinction between these two terms? The answer to this question lies in our ability, or inability, as an organization to implement the actions required for reaching the end results — the learning organization. This has been one of the problems associated with the movement of the theory of organizational learning into the operations of a learning organization. When a manager reads a book on the learning organization, he or she immediately tries to implement the end result without having a bridge from theory to practice; he/she only has the vision of a learning organization, not an understanding of the dynamics involved with the process. We simply haven't had the comprehensive theory that links the learning processes of the organization to their performance actions. This has led to many descriptive models of learning organization rather than dynamic models of organizational learning.

Descriptive or Dynamic Models of Organizational Learning?

Members of organizations, especially managers, become very impatient with organizational "fads." Organizational fads are those ideas, plans, and advice that become the "cure of the month" for managers and members of organizations as the way to help solve their ongoing organizational problems. Unfortunately, organizational fads seem to be plentiful. In the past 10 years we have experienced total quality, quality circles, reengineering, just-in-time management, empowerment, and, of course, the learning organization. Many organizational theorists are very willing to say that the learning organization has now become a fad. This conclusion is supported by the migration of the attention of popular management literature to what is now called the "knowledge organization" and its reliance on knowledge for survival in today's global economy.

Much of the interest in organizational learning has been focused on describing organizations as learning or nonlearning with the idea this would lead to identifying more effective organizations. However, major efforts in the area appear to be primarily descriptive in nature (Huber, 1991; Senge, 1990; Shrivastava, 1983) and have resulted in an attempt to build taxonomies of organizational learning as opposed to the development of an action-theory base that would aid organizations when they begin implementation.

Without an action-based theoretical construct, we continue to try to answer the question "What is the difference between a learning organization and a non learning organization?" rather than the questions "What constitutes organizational learning?" or "How do organizations learn?" This is one of the primary reasons managers have discounted the idea of the learning organization.

The learning organization concept has been more descriptive than analytic. That is, the literature provides the "what should be" vision, or end result, but fails to provide a framework that explains the processes of complex social interaction required to reach those ends. In fact much of the literature is more "advocating" as opposed to "explaining." Answering the latter questions is the next step in operationalization of an organizational learning construct.

Worldviews and Organizational Learning

Organizations are confronted with ever-increasing complexity. The concept of complexity is closely related to the failure of the rational worldview model to completely describe the environments that organizations face in a global economy. Western societies have relied heavily on the assumption that we live in a very real and objective world. That is, the world can be explained by the use of rational cause-and-effect relationships. This philosophical undercurrent has been key to our framework for training managers in organizational behavior. The quest for managers has been to turn complex and ambiguous situations into rationally understood events that can be managed or controlled. Of course, this doesn't always happen. In fact, each time society increases our abilities to define a more rational world we end up creating more and more complexity, as illustrated in Figure 2.1. Each time we introduce technology that allows us to better control our perceived objective world, we create more ambiguous situations, which then contributes to the growth of complexity.

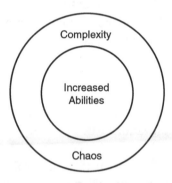

Figure 2.1 Small Increases in Rational World Abilities Result in Large Increases in Environmental Complexity

Each time we conquer the unknown with our rational model, we geometrically extend the world of complexity. For example, when Galileo first looked at the heavens he saw patterns of stars that could easily be counted. When he invented the telescope, which was a tremendous technical innovation, additional information appeared. He discovered thousands and hundreds of thousands of more stars that were not visible to the naked eye. In fact, he also found that not all objects were the same: some were planets, some were moons of planets, and some of the objects were not even in our solar system. An invention that was to reduce complexity by providing more information became an instrument that actually increased the complexity of our known world.

This phenomenon of ever-increasing complexity is also observable in organizations and their social dynamics. Concepts such as personal computers, the Internet, overnight mail delivery, and other innovations that we thought were developed to reduce complexity in reality have increased the complexity of our business environments by introducing high-speed communications and, at times, overwhelming quantities of data and information.

This new complex global environment has required managers to add new perspectives to the ways in which they view and perceive their environment. The nonlinear nature of the social learning system and the complexity of the environment have challenged the rational model of management. We are finding that the rational world represents only one worldview. As organizations become more global, they are exposed to very different worldviews.

Worldview differences provide us with a very useful frame of reference for the study of human actions, especially across international boundaries. As we move around the globe, societies and their cultures have established different assumptions concerning the relative subjective or objective nature of reality (sometimes referred to as ontology). Figure 2.2 illustrates the relative nature of these views by placing them on a continuum that stretches from the subjective view of reality that requires interpretation of socially constructed meaning to the objective view that relies heavily on natural laws to explain and predict social phenomena.

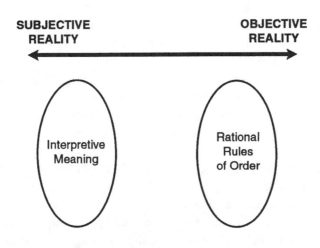

Figure 2.2 Realities Continuum

In their book, *Sociological Paradigms and Organizational Analysis,* Burrell and Morgan (1979) provide analyses of organizational theorists and the influence of worldview on the theories that drive our current interpretations of human systems. They make the point that the debate over what constitutes reality (subjective or objective) should not force us to choose one or the other; rather, it should inform our construction of theory and selection of methods of studying social phenomena. It is necessary that the rational and interpretive modes of understanding the environment (positivistic and anti-positivistic epistemological) and behavioral sciences be reflected in models of organizational learning. The model and theory discussed in this text provide common ground for the subjective and objective approaches to operationalize multiple worldviews.

The nonlinear and even chaotic nature of human systems makes it imperative that we formulate theory with a prerequisite understanding of both subjective and objective views simultaneously. To accomplish this, we may have to deal with more abstract ideas that are more holistic in nature. But to shy away from this abstractness would be misleading to the members of organizations that are in quest of an understanding of the complexity involved in the creation and management of knowledge in a global environment. Dealing with ambiguous ideas must become part of the learning capacity of all organizations. However, we know that this is very frustrating to organizational members who have relied on objective worldviews. This "non-real" appearance does lead to frustration initially.

Theorists caution us about the "nonreal nature" of the human systems models. They tell us that they are only metaphoric representations of the human phenomena under study. This is a caution against reification — the consideration of abstract representations as real things. This caution tends to move the researcher away from holistic models due to the fear that the metaphorical nature of the explanations is merely reification of the concepts. Therefore, the researcher and theorist move to a more analytical and reductionist focus so that they will be more apt to explain reality with accuracy. This reduces the potential for reification, but also reduces our potential understanding of the holistic nature of human interactions and how they relate to organizational learning and the production of knowledge.

This book offers a theory, a model, and examples of organizational learning that provide partial explanations for those phenomena that are observed in the social actions of organizations as they adapt to their environments through learning. From time to time the dialogue around the model may fall prey to reification; however, by incorporating research results and practical examples we believe the risk of reification to be minimal and the benefit to organizations in search of knowledge to be great.

Organizational Learning — Science Fiction or Reality?

The formulation of relativistic physics and space travel, specifically the phenomenon of time dilation, was first explained in terms of a story about one twin brother who traveled into space at the speed of light. Upon his return from his journey he found his identical twin had aged years, while he had aged only a matter of days. Science fiction or reality? Who knows? By understanding the key issues of organizational learning developed in this chapter, we hope to move to a greater understanding of the complex nature of the workplace as well as the global environment.

This chapter has raised several key issues associated with the concept and practice of organizational learning. We have shown that individual learning is only part of the organizational capacity to generate knowledge. We have seen that organizational learning is much more process oriented and highly dependent on the dynamic social forces within an organization. Finally, the worldview and organizational assumption of the organization will influence their ability to integrate the organizational learning process into its processes.

Chapter 3 will describe and analyze a number of world class theories that help to explain the dynamics of the organizational learning processes. By creating such a framework, we will be able to weave these concepts into a fabric that provides guidance to the questions that were posed in this chapter. We will then integrate these multiple theories into an integrated model of organizational learning, i.e., the Organizational Learning Systems Model which will be presented in Chapter 4.

References

Argyris, C. and Shön, D. A., *Organizational Learning: A Theory of Action Prospective*, Addison-Wesley, Reading, MA, 1978.
Burrell, G. and Morgan, G., *Sociological Paradigms and Organization Analysis: Elements of the Sociology of Corporate Life*, Heinemann, Portsmouth, NH, 1979.
Fiol, C. M. and Lyles, M. A., Organizational learning, *Academy of Management Review*, 10 (4), 803–813, 1985.
Gleick, J., *Chaos: Making a New Science*, Penguin Books, New York, 1987.

Hedberg, B., How organizations learn and unlearn, in *Handbook of Organization Design*, Nystrom, P. C. and Starbuck, W. H., Eds., Oxford University Press, London, 1981.

Huber, G. P., Organizational learning: the contributing processes and the literature, *Ogranization Science*, 2 (1), 88–115, 1991.

Huber, G. P. and Glick, W. H., What was learned about organizational change and redesign, in *Organizational Change and Redesign: Ideas and Insights for Improving Performance*, Huber, G. P. and Glick, W. H., Eds., Oxford University Press, New York, 1993.

Kidd, J. R., *How Adults Learn*, Association Press, New York, 1959.

Kiernan, M. J., The new strategic architecture: learning to compete in the twenty-first century, *Academy of Management Executive*, 7 (1) 7–22, 1993.

Lundberg, C. C., On organizational learning: implications and opportunities for expanding organizational development, in *Research in Organizational Change and Development*, Vol. 3, Woodman, R. W. and Pasmore, W. A., Eds., JAI Press, Greenwich, CT, 1989.

Senge, P. M., *The Fifth Discipline: The Art and Practice of the Learning Organization*, Doubleday, New York, 1990.

Shrivastava, P., A typology of organizational learning systems, *Journal of Management Studies*, 20 (1) 7–28, 1983.

3 | World-Class Theories of Organizational Learning

> There is nothing as practical as good theory.
>
> Kurt Lewin

Building Bridges from Theory to Practice

To fully appreciate and understand the Organizational Learning Systems Model (OLSM) that will be presented in Chapter 4, it is necessary to have a sufficient background in the theory and research that formulate the field of organizational learning. It is not our intent to produce a comprehensive review of the literature associated with organizational learning or the learning organization. However, we do not believe that the OLSM can be understood without relating it to the key foundations of knowledge that exist concerning the fields of human behavior, learning, and organizations.

The concepts of organizational learning have "circled the globe" and, in so doing, have accumulated multiple perspectives that reflect both Western and Eastern world-views. In addition, the history of organizational theory over the past 40 years has produced a framework of ideas and concepts that allow us to better understand the dynamic nature of social organizational learning. Both history and globalization have contributed to the building of the pillars for the bridge from theory to practice. These contributions make a good argument for a theoretical foundation and support our premise that organizational learning is here to stay and is not just the latest fad.

In this chapter we will present four major topics:

- Importance of developing organizational learning theory
- Historical overview of organizational learning theory
- Impact of theories of chaos, cognition, systems, and knowledge management
- Social action theory as the foundation of the OLSM

Importance of Developing Organizational Learning Theory

Theories of human behavior in organizational settings are plentiful. Because of the complexity of social interactions we require multiple theories to help explain the perplexing phenomena. Just as the physicist Stephen W. Hawking makes it clear that theory exists only in our minds for the purpose of explaining the world in which we live, this is true for both the natural sciences and the behavioral sciences. "Good" theory has two requirements that must be satisfied:

> It must accurately describe a large class of observations on the basis of a model that contains only a few arbitrary elements, and it must make definite predictions about the results of future observations. (Hawking, 1998, p. 9)

The social scientist, Bacharach (1989), reinforces Hawking's assertion by defining theory as a statement of relations between units observed or approximated in the empirical world. It is the observations of organizations and their behaviors, actions, successes, and failures that require a statement of relationship. These definitions emphasize the explanatory and predictive nature of theory as it relates to our empirical world.

Both Hawking and Bacharach are saying something very practical. Theory does not preexist for us to discover through research. Theory is created to describe and explain human and natural phenomena, and possibly predict their consequences and/or outcomes. Therefore, it behooves us to be familiar with and understand social science theory, not that it is the "law," but because it will provide a context for the plausibility of our actions.

The predominant contributors to our understanding of organizations and their behaviors have come from the fields of psychology and sociology. In recent years there have also been significant contributions from the field of culture that have been the domain of the anthropologist. However, if we examine the theory that is informing our practice we find a greater influence emanating from the field of psychology. In fact, many of the theories of group and organizational behavior are extensions of the individual psychology into a collective domain.

Only in the past 25 years have we seen an integration of psychology and sociology through works of Katz and Kahn (1978) and Weick (1979) in their use of systems theory. However, even with these significant works, our practice revolves around the use of operational variables that stem from the psychological field (i.e., motivation, personality preference, interpersonal relations, management styles, personal value orientation, theory-in-use/espoused, conflict, and locus of control are a few examples). The measurable nature of these psychological variables provides a pragmatic reason for practitioners to incorporate them in their diagnoses and interventions.

When practitioners or managers try to integrate the two paradigms (sociological and psychological) they encounter very practical questions. For example, "How do the concepts of social systems fit with the measure of individual motivation in the context of power issues and organizational structure?" This becomes a difficult question to deal with if we want to make measurements. In fact, the complexity of the interrelationships of the variables becomes overwhelming and we wonder if it isn't enough to just understand each of the variables separately. It is at this point that the manager and/or practitioner loses interest and decides to deal with only one of the variables in isolation (probably the motivational issue), and sets aside the variables associated with power and structure.

Unfortunately, this same scenario is being played out with the concepts of learning and organizational learning. Most of our knowledge concerning the learning process stems from the individual learning model which tends to be cognitively or behaviorally (or some combination) anchored. Thus, when it comes to asking questions about the collective (i.e., the organization), we extrapolate the sum of the individual learning or set aside the collective learning variables because it gets too messy or complex. Hopefully, the following discussion of theory dispels this aversion to complexity.

Forty Years of Organizational Learning Theory

The 1960s saw intense interest in the issue of organizational change. The attention of those interested in organizations was focused on the relative role of the "organization" as a system and the people that made up the organization. This was more than the classic "labor" and "management" struggle. It became apparent that the organizational goals, from a system's perspective, were many times in conflict with the goals of the individuals in the organizations. This led to the potential for lower effectiveness and productivity of the organization.

This interest in change became manifested in the introduction of organizational development strategies that attempted the integration of individual and organizational goals. It was also during this period that it became apparent that just concentrating on performance objectives was not enough. If organizations were to change and innovate, the cognitive or organizational learning had to be addressed.

In the 1970s, after surviving a decade of social tensions, the world of organizational theory turned to trying to better understand organizational learning and its importance to organizational survival in ambiguous environments. March and Olsen, publishing in the *European Journal of Political Research* (1975), developed their classic model of complete cycles of organizational choice (see Figure 3.1). This misconception of choice assumes a closed cycle of connections, namely:

- The cognitions and preferences held by individuals affect their behavior.
- The behavior (including participation) of individuals affects organizational choices.
- Organizational choices affect environmental acts (responses).
- Environmental acts affect individual cognitions and preferences.

Their model, although heavily dependent on individual cognition, allowed for analysis of several pathologies that were indicators of the break in complete cycles of choice. They linked individual beliefs to organizational behavior and concepts of information exposure, memory and retrieval, and communication structures. This type of model opened the door to exploration of learning, not only by individuals, but also by collectives.

The latter portion of the 1970s saw the advent of a school of thought that was characterized by the work of Chris Argyris and Donald Schön in

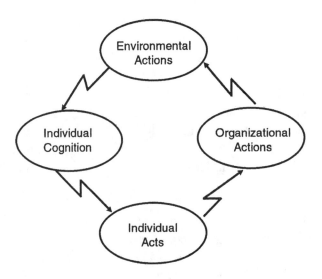

Figure 3.1 Cycles of Actions

their book, *Organizational Learning: A Theory of Action Perspective.* Unlike previous streams of thought concerning organizational learning, they saw a critical connection between the individual and the collective. However, the road to changing organizations was primarily one of working with individual actions and the inherent lack of congruency between their theory-in-use (often tacit) and their espoused theory.

Argyris and Schön introduced the concepts of single, double, and deutero learning as descriptions of types of learning that result from organizations detecting and correcting errors in organizational theories being used. They note that:

> In organizational single loop learning, the criterion for success is effectiveness. Individuals respond to error by modifying strategies and assumptions within constant organizational norms. In double-loop learning, response to detected error takes the form of joint inquiry into organizational norms themselves, so as to resolve their inconsistency and make the new norms more effectively realizable. In both cases, organizational learning consists of re-structuring organizational theory of action. When organization engages into deutero learning, its members learn about organizational learning and encode their results in images and maps. (Argyris and Schön, 1978, p. 29)

This body of knowledge led to highly interpersonal interventions. The processes of differentiating the theory-in-use from espoused theories were heavily dependent on interpersonal methods similar to those employed in sensitivity training during the 1970s. Later interpretation of this body of knowledge by Marsick and Watkins (1996) brought theory into the realm of workplace learning. They were able to link critical reflection to concerns about organizational structure, training, and culture.

During the mid-1980s the organizational learning literature, in an effort to define the construct, took a more descriptive approach to classification. Shrivastava (1983) summarized four "approaches" or views of organizational learning:

- Adaptive learning — adjusting goals to meet environmental change
- Assumption sharing — actions result from shared values
- Development of knowledge — knowledge is created in the process of comparing action with outcome
- Institutional experience — learning through experience and tradition

Shrivastava's review clearly sets the stage for the consideration of organizational learning as a complex social phenomenon with a heavy dependence on cultural variables, action orientation, and the linking of organizational process with its outcomes and its environment.

Building on the existing literature, Fiol and Lyles (1985) dichotomized the literature into an "either–or" framework in which organizational learning was defined in terms of either cognitive changes or behavioral changes. When considered as a separate function, only the cognitive change was seen as learning. It had the characteristics of relating action to process through shared schemes and projecting to the future. The behavioral changes were seen as adaptation. These actions were classified as incremental in nature and much more a response to short-term environmental fluctuations. Although little insight was provided as to the interrelationship between learning and adaptation, this work presented a view of organizational learning as a multidimensional and complex set of actions.

Daft and Huber (1987) viewed organizational learning from two basic perspectives: the systems-structural perspective and the interpretive perspective. Their constructs were primarily concerned with the acquisition, distribution, and interpretation of information from the environment.

> The systems-structural perspective emphasizes the acquisition and distribution of information as a resource that is necessary for an organization to learn about its external and internal environments...the interpretive approach focuses on the underlying purpose and meaning of messages. (pp. 5 and 8)

Although much of Daft and Huber's work was oriented toward the communication of information and media construction, their identification of the need for organizations to develop internal mechanisms for the distribution and interpretation of information emphasizes the systemic nature of the organizational learning process. In their work they apply their constructs to an empirical case study of a failed organization with the conclusion: "American La France failed because it was not designed to learn, yet it existed in an environment in which it needed learning and adaptation in order to survive." This conclusion generates these questions: "How does an organization both adapt and learn simultaneously? What are the dynamic systemic requirements?"

Variables that relate organizational learning and the environment (Hedgberg, 1981), organizational transformation and learning cycles (Lundberg, 1989), and organizational memory retrieval and storage (Walsh and Ungson, 1991) have contributed to our ability to postulate the organizational learning process. In a review of literature Huber suggests an organizational learning model as being described by four constructs: Knowledge Acquisition, Information Distribution, Information Interpretation, and Organizational Memory (Huber, 1991). His synthesis and the contributions of previous authors cited reflect a move toward interactive systems within the organizational learning construct.

A large amount of interest in organizational learning was generated by Peter Senge's book, *The Fifth Discipline.* Senge called for the focus on five areas he referred to as organizational disciplines:

- Systems Thinking — a conceptual framework for understanding patterns of events and behaviors to help see how to change them.
- Personal Mastery — discipline of continually clarifying and deepening our personal vision, of focusing our energies, of developing patients, and of seeing reality objectively.
- Mental Models — are deeply ingrained assumptions, generalizations, or even pictures or images that influence how we understand the world and how we take action.

- Shared Vision — the skills of building shared "pictures of the future" that foster genuine commitment and enrollment rather than compliance.
- Team Learning — starts with "dialogue," the capacity of members of the team to suspend assumptions and enter into a genuine "thinking together." It also involves learning how to recognize the patterns of interaction in teams that undermine learning (Senge, 1990, pp. 7–11).

Senge does not see the five component learning disciplines converging to create the learning organization; rather, he proposes a new wave of experimentation and advancement around these concepts. Although his focus is on characterizing the learning organization through the application of five disciplines, he addresses several "Systems Archetypes" which provide insight into systematic patterns that can inhibit the attainment of generative learning.

Nonaka and Takeuchi (1995) describe the knowledge-creating company as one that is recreating itself and everyone in it continually. Their approach relies on moving individual tacit knowledge into explicit organizational knowledge. They contend that the Western worldview of separating mind from object has had a delimiting influence on theoretical thinking and understanding of organizational learning.

> We contend that none of the (Western) thinkers has articulated the dynamic notion that human beings can actively create knowledge to change the world, implicitly suggesting that our view of knowledge and theory of organizational knowledge creation provide the fundamentally new economic and management perspective that can overcome the limitations of existing theories bounded by the Cartesian split. (p. 32)

Both Nonaka and Senge focus mostly on manager/leader behaviors and do not provide a very clear understanding of the dynamic social nature of the organization as a cognitive entity contained in a complex environment.

As the world is constantly and rapidly changing, the long-term success of organizations seem to rely on the understanding of their learning patterns in response to internal and external changes. To assume greater control of their own actions, organizations must be aware of how they, as a collective of individuals, learn to react to changes in the environment and how they come to question their own existing processes and procedures. The contemporary literature on organizational theory and practices has been increasingly concerned with the ability of organizations to learn to cope with the escalating dynamism and complexity of organizational environments.

Chaos Theory, Complex Systems, and Organizational Learning

The managerial sciences and their related fields such as human resource development and management, strategic planning, and organizational behavior are beginning to entertain the concepts associated with open systems and the new science (Gleick, 1987; Wheatley, 1992) through concepts such as complex systems and chaos theory. These theories assume a nonlinear open systems approach to the study of organizations as social systems of action. A premise of open systems, as stated by Bertalanffy (1980) in his discussion of entropy and open systems, is that they inherently evolve toward higher states of complexity. Therefore, if we adopt open systems thinking we must also assume that our social science models will have to deal with more complex issues requiring more complex theories. This is not unlike the hard sciences which have had to deal with the concept of time irreversibility and quantum phenomena not fitting Cartesian thinking and the Newtonian worldview (Prigogine and Stengers, 1984).

This confrontation with complexity, which in the past has been addressed through reductionist processes, is now being met with concepts of chaos theory, duality, spirituality, and self-organizing systems. Organizational sciences are only in their infancy with respect to this shift in worldview. With the advent of concepts such as organization configurations, managerial and organizational cognition, and organizational learning, we are embarking on a new era in investigation.

Emphasis is now being placed on the patterns which are seen from one perspective as chaos, but yet if focused on with a different lens or frame of reference appear to manifest commonalties or patterns. In this sense, we must consider organizational learning as a process manifested in patterns of actions and attributes of the social system, rather than causal relations between isolated variables.

Considering organizational learning from a configuration perspective mandates the simultaneous consideration of multiple organizational attributes and variables. Much of the current literature poses propositions that encompass questions concerning the organization's learning capacity as it relates to boundary spanning and strategy, managerial structures, and organizational culture. For example, Lyles and Schwenk (1992) select patterns called "knowledge structures" as their focus and pose nine propositions concerning the relationship between knowledge structures and strategic action. They suggest two general characteristics of organizational knowledge structures: (1) complexity (amount of information or number of elements) and (2) relatedness (linkages between elements). Through these characteristics they draw relationships between core and peripheral knowledge structures and their relative impact on the attention given by managers to their environmental queues.

How knowledge structures are formed and their usefulness and limitations are becoming a major path to the investigation into how the collective makes sense of its environment. Although there is interest in the collective sense making, much of the empirical research is centered on the mental models that managers bring to their position, their actions, and organizational renewal (Barr et al., 1992; Thomas et al., 1993). The role of the organization as an interpretive system has been seen as being dependent on organizational differences in environmental scanning, equivocality reduction, strategy, and decision making (Daft and Weick, 1984; Lant and Mezias, 1992). These authors provide us descriptions of organizational attributes that contribute to the organizational learning construct; however, what remains is the need to understand the synthesis of these multiple attributes into patterns that represent the organization's capacity to learn.

Social Action Theory and the Organizational Learning Systems Model

To understand how organizational learning works, it is important that one understands Social Action theory. The General Theory of Social Action posed by Talcott Parsons was based on his work with Shils and Bells (1953). This work, although criticized for its functional nature, dependence on the assumption of social equilibrium, and grand theory status, may be the first actual configuration theory of organizations.

Parsons' social action system theory suggests that both performance and learning processes have the capacity to change or disrupt the equilibrium in the organization-situation relationship. However, changes in the "social system" itself occur through the learning process and are related to the "latent pattern maintenance" function of the system. This concept is identical to that put forth by Edgar Schein in his discussions concerning the importance of cultural patterns and basic assumptions (Schein, 1992a).

Grounded in the Parsonian theory, the Organizational Learning Systems Model (as will be seen in Chapter 4) focuses on the learning aspect of an organization as a social system and explains how an organization learns so that it can survive in a changing environment. It provides a way of viewing organizational behavior in such a way that we can vividly see how people in an organization collectively engage in the learning process.

Organizational learning is defined as "a system of actions, actors, symbols, and processes that enables an organization to transform information into valued knowledge which in turn increases its long-run adaptive capacity" (Schwandt, 1993, p. 8). This definition is to be considered neutral with respect to the issue of "good or bad" knowledge. It is focused on the system's ability to adapt to its environment, which has a performance orientation; however, it represents a creative learning capacity through the transformation of information into knowledge.

The foundational theory used in Schwandt's formulation of learning patterns is rooted in Parsonian sociological constructs derived from the works of Pareto, Durkheim, Weber, and Comte. It is, therefore, difficult to escape the functional nature of the model and the associated assumptions about the world. Although these theorists maintained a functional approach, they were not necessarily positivist; they acknowledged the subjective nature of the human condition and its associated dualities of thought.

The logic behind the Organizational Learning Systems Model is founded on a sociological paradigm that has evolved over a period of 100 years. In 1893 Durkheim first defined the shared — hence social rather than individual — conceptions within a society as collective representation. For him, collective representations must be studied as social fact external to any one individual. Social behavior became more than just the summation of the individual behaviors within the collective. Parsons (1951) expanded on this concept in his formulation of social behavior as a system of actions (of both the individual and the collective). Thus, we have early recognition of the "added value" of the collective (which we now acknowledge as synergy) and the analytical potential of actions and systems of actions.

If we consider organizations as collective representations which are characterized by mutually dependent actions, then we can best describe their functioning through the concept of interrelated systems of actions emanating from the individual, group, and organizational levels. The use of a sociological paradigm as a basis for defining organizational learning not only allows us to classify the construct as a social phenomenon, but also provides us with the potential to explain the dynamic nature of the process using foundational sociological theory.

The primary purpose of the systems of actions in a collective is to provide the means through which the collective is able to survive in its changing environments.

> ...as the environments in which they exist become more and more complex and, consequently, more and more changeable, to endure, they must change often. (Durkhiem, 1895)

This adaptation function was further defined in Parsons' treatment of a General Theory of Action and subsequently he posed the need for "evolutionary universals" that are common to various systems that provide the capacity to cope with broad ranges of environmental factors and uncertainty. He defines the "evolutionary universals" as

> ... a complex of structures and associated processes the development of which so increases the long-run adaptive capacity of living systems in a given class that only systems that develop the complex can attain certain higher levels of general adaptive capacity. (Parsons, 1960)

Parsons goes on to discuss examples of these universals such as the human biological system's development of hands, eyes, and the brain. Corresponding to these biological examples, he adds the social system's "unique ability to create and transmit culture" through the use of symbols and language.

It is this unique capability that the organization develops so that it can interact with its environment and cope with the uncertainty that threatens its existence. It must maintain a level of readiness for change:

> ... the more obscure conscience is, the more refractory to change it is, because it does not perceive quickly enough the necessity for changing nor in what sense it must change. On the contrary, an enlightened conscience prepares itself in advance for adaptation. (Durkheim, 1895)

We postulate these sometimes-intangible series of actions we as the organization's ability to systematically integrate its social aspects with other objects and processes to form an organizational learning system. This system is so critical to its survival that it can be represented as an "evolutionary universal."

Using this logic, an operational definition of organizational learning will be developed in Chapter 4 that reflects both the systemic actions of the collective in adapting to their environment and the evolutionary universal nature of the concept of organizational learning.

Parsons' General Theory of Action

To analyze organizational learning as a system of actions, actors, symbols, and processes, we must draw on our knowledge of all the behavioral sciences to understand the nature of the system and to operationalize the construct. In this sense we require a unit of analysis that unites the knowledge associated with the multiple disciplines that make up the behavioral sciences. The common element for these disciplines is human action.

One of the most thoroughly developed integrative theories that emanates from the sociological perspective and incorporates the biological, psychological, cultural, and sociological concepts associated with human action is Parsons' General Theory of Action. This construct depicts organizations as systems of social interactions, or systems of social actions. He defines a social action (or unit act) as being comprised of

- A subject-actor — an individual, group, or collectivity.
- A situation — the physical and social objects to which the actor relates.
- Symbols — the means by which the actor relates to the different elements of the situation and attributes meaning to them.
- Rules, norms, and values — these guide the orientation of action — the actor's relations with the environment.

The complexity of Parsons' model becomes apparent as we add action upon action, much as a chain reaction occurs in a nuclear reactor. If we bring individuals together into a collective, their multiple actions constitute a "system of actions."

Using Parsons' symbolic representation of unit acts and system of actions, we can draw conclusions that have implications for the development of the organizational learning construct.

1. The unit act and system of actions are dependent on the knowledge that is available to the actor and a set of norms that allows for subjective interpretation of the situation and the ends.
2. When considering a system of actions, the relationship between actions becomes an important aspect of defining the system.
3. Parsons incorporated a "randomness" term in his derivations. This term represents the same concept as the Heisenberg Uncertainty Principle in the physical sciences; that is, an absolute measuring method with the actions themselves which will always create an effect that adds to our uncertainty of the action and its subsequent effects.
4. Parsons includes the full spectrum of world-veiws. Although he is clear in his disdain for the more subjective contributions to the unit act (which he refers to as "non-scientific"), he does make considerations of them in his formulation. This is in keeping with Parsons' post-positivist orientation to norms and values and with the understanding we have about the impact of organizational culture, and the high frequency of change that our organizations are experiencing. This doesn't negate the rational/positivistic interpretations; it merely means that the relative weighting of the elements and variables that make up the unit act may have to change from situation to situation.

These implications highlight for us the importance of understanding both the subjective and objective action variables simultaneously. This will enhance our ability to understand and possibly explain the complex nature of organizational actions as they pertain to learning and change.

The focus of Parsons' theory of action is the establishment of a systematic relationship between the "actions" of the actors and their ability to adapt to both their inside and outside environments. The unit act can emanate from the level of individuals, groups, organizations, or societies and is a function of the biological, psychological, sociological, and cultural systems. By using this frame of reference we are able to incorporate the entire range of behavioral sciences theories into our deliberations, thus providing a unifying theme for the behavioral sciences through the system of human actions. Parsons did not see this unification as a step to reduce the systems of actions to a one-dimensional entity describable by a single set of variables. Rather, he saw this theory providing an integrative medium in which the sum total of our knowledge in the behavioral sciences could simultaneously come to bear on the complex situations of the human condition.

Parsons' theory of action provides us with a starting point for understanding the actions of the collective as it changes through performing and learning. To further operationalize the concept of organizational learning as it stems from the General Action Theory, it is necessary that we understand its dynamic nature.

Dynamic Nature of the General Theory of Action

Parsons describes the General Theory of Action in terms of four subsystems: the biological organism (later renamed behavior), personality, culture, and social. Each of these subsystems of actions contributes to the survival of the total system of actions by carrying out a specific function that enables the system to adapt to its environment.

This theory not only provides a descriptive dimension of the system of organizational action, it also provides a conceptual framework that allows us to explain the operation or functioning of the subsystems with respect to each other and to the action system as a whole. Parsons defines the four prerequisite functions that are carried out by the respective subsystems, thus enabling the action system to adapt to its environment:

1. *Adaption* is the complex of unit acts which serves to establish relations between the system and its external enviroment. The comples consists of the exchange mechanism required to bring in the resources required by the system and the exploration of those things that help shape the environment for the system.
2. *Goal attainment* is the complex of actions which serves to define the goals of the system and to mobilize and manage resources and effort to attain goals and gratification.
3. *Integration* is the complex of actions, the purpose of which is to establish control, inhibit deviant tendancies, maintain coordination between parts, and avoid too-serious disturbances.
4. *Pattern maintanenace* is a complex of actions that accumulates and distributes energy in the form of motivation. It is the point of contact between systems of action and the symbolic and cultural universe (Rocher, 1975).

The relationship of these functions can be graphically depicted in Figure 3.2 by their relative "focus" (external or internal to the system) and by their relative "purpose" (instrumental means or consummatory ends) (Parsons, 1951).

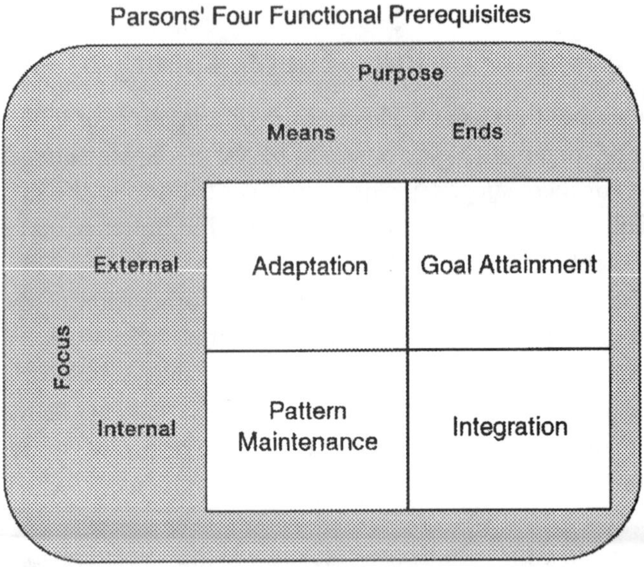

Parsons' Four Functional Prerequisites

| | Purpose | |
	Means	Ends
External	Adaptation	Goal Attainment
Internal	Pattern Maintenance	Integration

(Focus)

Figure 3.2 Parsons' Functional Prerequisites

The functional prerequisites can be generalized to all levels of analysis (individual, group, organization, society). They must be carried out or the system will not survive. This prerequisite relationship allows us to describe the purpose of each subsystem of any system as it relates to the whole and to each of the other subsystems. This dynamic relationship of a system of actions enables us to be more analytical in our approach to the organization. We observe organizations moving from periods of stability to periods of instability and back to some newly defined stability; in systems terminology we refer to this as homeostasis or dynamic equilibrium. By incorporating the General Theory of Action into our analysis we may better explain the dynamics of that observed change in terms of actions of the individual, group, or organization.

In his original theory, Parsons discussed two major processes that disturbed the equilibrium of the system of actions: performance and learning. This was Parsons' representation of change. Although his use of equilibrium as an unattainable and therefore unrealistic concept in the social sciences has been criticized, the concept provides a reference point for relative measures, just as the concept of absolute zero provides an unattainable reference point in the measurement of temperature in the theory of thermodynamics. Thus, we can use the concept of social equilibrium as a reference point to measure relative changes of the collective as a result of interactions in the system.

A question that must be answered by the foundational theory of action is, "How do the subsystems interact?" In other words, what is the relationship between the social and cultural subsystems that enables them to carry out their prerequisite functions? Parsons' theory incorporates a process of mutual exchange among the subsystems. He defines the elements of "input and output" as a **medium of interchange**. The function of this complex of media is to ensure the continual circulation within the action system of what Parsons calls "resources." He stresses the symbolic character of media and provides four general criteria, or properties, for judging the existence of a medium:

1. *Institutionalization.* A sense of legitimacy must be associated with the medium. Of course, there are situations in which the medium is used illegitimately.
2. *Specificity.* The medium must have specificity of meaning and efficaciousness in both evaluation and interchange.
3. *Circulability.* Medium should be subject to transfer of control from one acting unit to another in some kind of interchange transactions.
4. *Could not have a zero-sum character.* The medium cannot explicitly or tacitly assume that an increase in the amount of medium held by one group in a system ipso facto entails a corresponding decrease in the amount held by others.

An example of Parsons' use of the medium of interchange can be clearly seen in his discussion of the relationship between two subsystems of the General Action System: The Culture and the Social subsystems. The medium exchange theory predicts that the social subsystem, which is providing the Integrating function, generates influence, but requires commitment; and the culture subsystem, which is providing the Pattern Maintenance function,

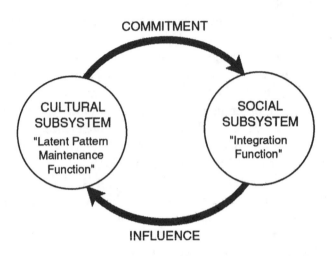

Figure 3.3 Interchange Media for Mutual Survival

generates commitment, but requires influence. Each subsystem is mutually dependent on the other subsystems to provide it with the needed inputs (medium of interchange) as shown in Figure 3.3.

In developing the concept of medium of interchange, Parsons not only provided a vehicle for the theoretical study of the General Theory of Action, but also brought a level of concreteness to a theoretically complex construct. The concepts of commitment and influence are quite familiar variables and are also observable in the actions of humans. It is the analysis of the exchange process that we will employ in the discussion of the organizational learning system and its associated subsystems in Chapters 4 to 8. In this chapter we have developed the key theories and foundations for the Organizational Learning Systems Model. Let us now look at the model itself in Chapter 4.

References

Argyris, C. and Schön, D. A., *Organizational Learning: A Theory of Action Perspective*, Addison-Wesley, Reading, MA, 1978.

Bacharach, S. B., Organizational theories: some criteria for evaluation, *Academy of Management Review*, 14 (4), 496–515, 1989.

Barr, P.S., Stimpert, J.L., and Huff, A.S., Cognitive change, strategic action, and organizational renewal, *Strategic Management Review*, 13, 15–36, 1992.

Bertalanffy, L., *General Systems Theory*, George Braziller, New York, 1980.

Czarniawska-Joerges, B., *Exploring Complex Organizations: A Cultural Perspective*, Sage, Newbury Park, CA, 1992.

Daft, R. L. and Huber, G. P., How organizations learn: a communication framework, *Research in the Sociology of Organizations*, 5, 1–30, 1987.

Daft, R. L. and Weick, K. E., Toward a model of organizations as interpretation systems, *Academy of Management Review*, 9(2) 284–295, 1984.

Durkhiem, E., *The Rules of Sociological Methods*, Free Press, New York, 1895.

Fiol, C. M. and Lyles, M. A., Organizational learning, *Academy of Management Review*, 10(4) 803–813, 1985.

Gleick, J., *Chaos: Making a New Science*, Penguin Books, New York, 1987.

Hawking, S. H., *A Brief History of Time*, Bantam Books, New York, 1988.

Hedberg, B., How organizations learn and unlearn, in *Handbook of Organization Design*, Nystrom, P. C. and Starbuck, W. H., Eds., Oxford University Press, London, 1981.

Huber, G. P., Organizational learning: the contributing processes and the literatures, *Organization Science*, 2 (1) 88–115, 1991.

Katz, D. and Kahn, R. L., *The Social Psychology of Organizations*, 2nd ed., John Wiley & Sons, New York, 1978.

Lant, T. K. and Mezias, S. J., An organizational learning model of convergence and reorientaion, *Organization Science*, 3(1) 47–71, 1992.

Lewin, K., *Resolving Social Conflicts*, American Psychological Association, Washington, D.C., 1997.

Lundberg, C. C., On organizational learning: implications and opportunities for expanding organizational development, in *Research in Organizational Change and Development*, Vol. 3, Woodman, R. W. and Pasmore, W. A., Eds., JAI Press, Greenwich, CT, 1989.

Lyles, M.A. and Schwenk, C.R., Top managment, strategy and organizational knowledge structures, *Journal of Management Studies*, 29(2), 1992.

March, J. G. and Olsen, J. P., The uncertainty of the past: organizational learning under ambiguity, *European Journal of Political Research*, 3, 147–171, 1975.

Marsick, V. J. and Watkins, K. E., Adult educators and the challenge of the learning organization, *Adult Learning*, 7(4), 18–20, 1996.

Nonaka, I. and Takeuchi, H., *The Knowledge Creating Company*, Oxford University Press, New York, 1995.

Parsons, T., *The Social System*, Free Press, New York, 1951.

Parsons, T., *Structure and Process in Modern Societies*, Free Press, New York, 1960.

Parsons, T., Shils, E., and Bells, R.F., *General Theory of Action*, Free Press, New York, 1951.

Prigogine, I. and Stengers, I., *Order out of Chaos*, Bantam Books, New York, 1984.

Rocher, G., *Talcott Parsons and American Sociology*, Barnes and Noble, New York, 1975.

Schein, E. H., *Organizational Culture and Leadership*, 2nd ed., Jossey-Bass, San Francisco, 1992.

Schwandt, D. R., Organizational Learning: A Dynamic Integrative Construct, unpublished manuscript, Human Resource Development, George Washington University, Washington, D.C., 1993.

Schwandt, D.R., Integrating strategy and organizational learning: a theory of action perspective, in *Advances in Strategic Management*, Walsh, J. P. and Huff, A. S., Eds., JAI Press, London, 1997.

Senge, P. M., *The Fifth Discipline: The Art and Practice of the Learning Organization*, Doubleday, New York, 1990.

Shrivastava, P., A typology of organizational learning systems, *Journal of Management Studies*, 20(1) 7–28, 1983.

Simon, H. A., *Administrative Behavior*, MacMillan, New York, 1947.

Thomas, J. B., Clark, S. M., and Gioia, D. A., Strategic sensemaking and organizational performance: linkage among scanning, interpretation, action, and outcomes, *Academy of Management Journal*, 36(2) 239–270, 1993.

Walsh, J. P. and Ungson, G. R., Organizational memory, *Academy of Management Review*, 16(1) 57–91, 1991.

Weick, K., *The Social Psychology of Organizing*, 2nd ed., McGraw-Hill, New York, 1979.

Wheatley, M. J., *Leadership and the New Science*, Berrett-Koehler, San Francisco, 1992.

4 The Organizational Learning Systems Model

Systems thinking is a discipline of seeing wholes. It is a framework for seeing interrelationships rather than things, for seeing patterns of change rather than snapshots, and begins by restructuring how we think.

Peter Senge
The Fifth Discipline

Creating the Map

We are now ready to examine the Organizational Learning Systems Model (OLSM), a model that builds upon the theories presented in Chapter 3. Making certain assumptions about organizations as social systems, we can create a framework (map) that allows the practitioner of organizational behavior to integrate multiple theories into a coherent picture of the dynamic learning of the organization. Before we create this map, we must state three of our assumptions about the organizational learning territory.

1. Organizations as human social entities are always learning — the process of learning is always going on. The results of this process can be

desirable; that is, they reflect success and survival of the organization. They can also be undesirable, ending in failure, learning the wrong things, and thus ending in failure or death of the organization.

2. Organizational learning is manifested through interrelated patterns of human actions, processes, and objects, and therefore constitutes a system — in fact, a system of human actions.

3. Because of the complexity of the human system, we must select a theory base for the framework that has the ability to integrate the psychological, social, and cultural aspects of organizational dynamics. Parsons' sociological theory of action and social systems best represents these facets.

If organizations critically think (reflect) as a social entity they will create a situation that is positive for the organization's survival. However, within the context of the organizational learning model, where reflection is a major function, we must also have supportive subsystems available to profit and support from the reflective/critical analysis. Therefore, capturing and transporting knowledge as well as maintaining an open interface to the environment must integrate with the reflection on organizational actions to allow for learning and for the organization to adapt to its environment. These elements constitute the terrain. How can we simplify this map?

The Failure of Linearity

Organizational learning represents a complex interrelationship between people, their actions, symbols, and processes within the organization. Traditionally, we have approached the organizational learning construct using our understanding of the learning process that individuals employ. This could be expected if one examines how we learn as humans — we relate the unfamiliar to the familiar. So when we are confronted with an ambiguous, or new, concept such as the "learning of the organization" we most readily relate it to our understanding of what we do know, the individual learner. This was the approach initially taken in the development of the linear model. It was seen as beginning with information intake, which triggers the combined processes of action and reflection, and concludes with interpretation and integration. Figure 4.1 depicts the linear model. Each element of the model represents an important function for the learning process and is reflective of the individual human learning.

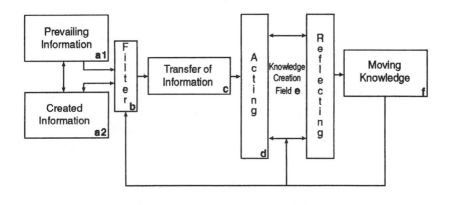

Figure 4.1 A Linear Model of Organizational Learning

The model consists of seven linear-sequential functions that could be described as ideal components of a learning system. The components are

(a1) **Prevailing Information.** The intake of information into the system is crucial. Information can be brought in through two major means [depicted as (a1) and (a2) in Figure 4.1]. The first intake happens as a result of the environmental fluctuations, and the organization has no control over this information — it just happens. Examples include world news, government interventions, etc.

(a2) **Created Information.** The second intake is through a set of activities designed to scan the environment for the organization. These activities are purposeful, that is, consciously directed by the organization, and include surveys, market information gathering, etc.

(b)   **Filter.** The information coming into the organization is filtered by a set of values and assumptions that the organization and employees hold to limit the influx of information. Filtering can be useful or harmful depending on the organization's need for information. It certainly can lead to tunnel vision and debilitating bias.

(c)   **Information Transfer.** Once the information enters the organization through the filter, it is distributed in accordance with a schema that the organization puts into place. This can be as simple as a routing slip or a mail system. The critical issue is to match the incoming information with those members of the organization who require it or must act on it.

(d) **Action and Reflection.** The central focus of the learning system is the conversion of information into knowledge. This is accomplished through a repetitive cycle of acting and reflecting on the information entering the organization. This process produces and stores knowledge in a "knowledge creation field."

(e) **Knowledge Creation Field.** The knowledge creation field is a complex and chaotic storage and retrieval center. It contains the values, basic assumptions, and artifacts of the organization that enter into the process of interpreting the information and creating knowledge. This field supplies the filter and the distribution systems with the values and assumptions they require to discern who gets organizational knowledge and what information is let in through the filter.

(f) **Distribution of Knowledge.** Finally, the learning system must also provide for the distribution and movement of the knowledge within the organization to the appropriate units and individuals.

Although the linear model appears to have a certain agreeable logic, in practice, we found that learning in an organization does not follow a sequential path such as depicted in Figure 4.1. The prevailing assumption of sequential linearity limits the use of the model as a mechanism for understanding organizational learning.

In an organization, the location of the learning process is everywhere, and therefore difficult to ascertain due to the complexity of the interacting units of the organization. The elements of the organizational learning system are not as definable as the boxes would lead us to believe. They are not clear functions of any one unit of the organization; they are functions that are most likely shared by all units. These model components may also vary in size and importance according to the situation. In addition, the model includes neither an indication of the dynamic nature of the system nor any connection with the human social dynamics of the organization. The operation of the learning system is vulnerable to power differentials, changing personnel and structures, lack of trust, and many other social forces. This complexity assures us that organizational learning cannot be represented by the mere sum total of the learning of the individuals within the organization. There is no repeated sequence of events that is indicative of this system. It is this nonlinear complexity of the organizational learning system that permits multiple barriers to block the learning process.

Because these anomalies cannot be explained by the linear model, it became apparent that the learning processes of an organization are dependent on the social actions of the organization, just as the performance of the organization is dependent on these actions. Therefore, the focus of our organizational learning system must be explainable in the context of the social system and its respective dynamic actions. It was in this shift of perspective that we employed the sociological paradigm to better explain the phenomena of organizational learning.

We started the development of the integrated model by thinking of the linear model as "sets of organizational actions" that the organization has to carry out in order to create knowledge about its goals and, therefore, survive in a rapidly changing environment. These actions, because they are mutually dependent on each other with nonsequential, multiple causal relationships, can be considered nonlinear systems of actions.

Actions as the Basis for Organizational Learning

The action system of the organization is composed of actions of the individual, the group, and the organization. They can be viewed from three different perspectives. The actions can be associated only with performance, associated only with learning, or they can be associated with both performance and learning simultaneously. The nature of human actions in the social context is very complex and not easily separated into learning or performing. However, this is in keeping with Parsons' premise that change occurs through both performance and learning actions of the system of actions. To simplify this conundrum, we can, for the purposes of analysis, assume that we can separate these actions into two independent subsystems — performance and learning.

If we could hold up a mirror to the system of actions, it would reflect two images — the performance system and the learning system (Figure 4.2). The image we see in a mirror is the reflection of the object; it is not real. It moves when the object moves and is identical in appearance. This image in the mirror we call "virtual." Using this example as an analogy, we propose a similar phenomenon for the organizational performance and learning systems; they are reflections of the real object which is all of the integrated actions of the organization.

The systems of action describing organizational performance and learning carry out their respective functions using different relational combinations of the same actions. For example, the organizational acts associated with the production of an annual report are designed to produce a document. This is surely performance. However, the same acts could contribute new information

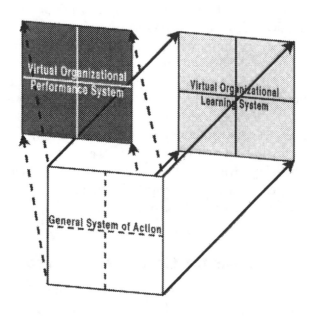

Figure 4.2 Learning and Performance — Virtual Images of the General System of Action

to the executive team concerning the processes used to judge their organization's productivity. From this perspective, the actions can be considered actions associated with organizational learning. These two systems, working together, allow the organization to change and adapt to its environment.

Parsons postulated the change of social systems through not only performance actions, but also through a process of learning. His work with learning was not as completely developed as other areas of the action theory. He postulated that information, once internalized (knowledge), changes the conditions of the actions and the actions themselves. This explanation applies not only to individuals but also to the organizational collective.

It is difficult to actually see an organization in the act of learning. It is similar to actually trying to see an individual learn. In both cases we see results of the learning process, as opposed to the process itself. In the case of the individual we may see cognitive or behavioral changes that indicate the person has learned. We can also look for changes in the organization. Unfortunately, the time required to exhibit a change in organizational behavior or actions is, in most cases, long, thus making it difficult to relate specific organizational learning processes to change. This time delay provides further rationale for depending more on the performance system to achieve faster change, what we now refer to as "short-term" thinking.

Performance — The "Other" System of Learning

As previously stated, change is a function of both learning and performance. Just as Parsons explained the system of actions in terms of subsystems, the organizational learning and performance systems are made up of subsystems of actions. Before we concentrate on the learning system, it is important that we at least delineate the subsystems of the performance system and show that it is indicative of our traditional approaches to organizational dynamics (see Figure 4.3).

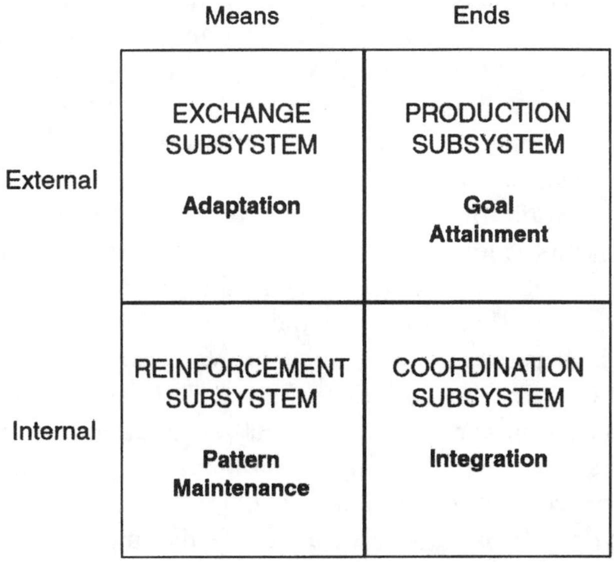

	Means	Ends
External	EXCHANGE SUBSYSTEM **Adaptation**	PRODUCTION SUBSYSTEM **Goal Attainment**
Internal	REINFORCEMENT SUBSYSTEM **Pattern Maintenance**	COORDINATION SUBSYSTEM **Integration**

Figure 4.3 Performance Subsystem Functional Prerequisites

A system of organizational actions can produce change through performance. Performance consists of all behavior by which the organization disrupts its situation to a greater or lesser degree. This statement of performance is general in nature and includes all actions of the organization. To analyze the relationship between organizational actions and their product it has normally required the employment of a performance management system. The performance system is also dependent on four primary subsystems that are each respectively responsible for accomplishing one of the four functional prerequisites of the Parsons' action system. These functions are portrayed in Figure 4.3 and described below.

> *The Exchange Subsystem* provides the performance system with the *adaptation* function. In its simplest sense, it is responsible for obtaining, selling, screening, and expelling human and material resources in an effort to respond to the needs of the organization as it achieves its goals.
>
> *The Production Subsystem* provides the human performance system with the *goal attainment* function. This subsystem is highly complex because it incorporates all of those actions and processes that the organization must perform to achieve a product or reach a goal. This subsystem has traditionally been the major focus of management efforts. It includes the application of knowledge, skills, and abilities to processes of manufacturing, service, marketing, sales, procurement, research and development, management, finance, planning, and quality assurance.
>
> *The Coordination Subsystem* provides the human performance system with the *integration* function. This subsystem is critical in that its elements and actions represent the process for linking human actions and skills with the requirements of the task and the standards of performance required so that separate acts can be integrated into the collective effort. This subsystem includes management control processes, job design, training, career development, job enrichment, organizational development, employee assistance processes, and planning.
>
> *The Reinforcement Subsystem* provides the human performance system with the *pattern maintenance* function. It is comprised of those elements that contribute to the maintenance of standards and values that the organization uses to make judgments concerning its performance. This subsystem is comprised of actions associated with appraisal, rewards, compensation, quality standards, feedback, mentoring, and coaching.

These four subsystems and their respective functions describe the organizational performance system. Each subsystem must be operable for the organization to change and be able to adapt to its environment. However, the performance system is not the only virtual image of the action system. In rapidly changing global environments the second system of actions has become as prominent, that is, the organizational learning system.

The Learning System

As the environment grows in complexity, it is becoming more apparent that the rate at which the organization learns may be the deciding factor in its ability to survive or adapt to its environment. By describing the organization as a social action system and extending Parsons' General Theory of Action, we can pose questions concerning the processes used by the organization to understand its external and internal environments. It enables us to relate organizational actions to a learning system composed of subsystems carrying out Parsons' functional prerequisites. These functions allow the organization to:

- Survive as a viable system of actions; to take actions different from past actions
- To know if present actions are different from the past or not, and to understand the reasons for this difference
- To allow the collective to retain its knowledge over a period of time
- To ensure that knowledge is available to inform the actions of the entire organization

It is this sensemaking that constitutes the purpose of the organizational learning system. We define this learning system as "a system of actions, actors, symbols and processes that enables an organization to transform information into valued knowledge which in turn increases its long-run adaptive capacity." We can now formulate the dynamic descriptions of the functions of this learning system.

Functions of the Organizational Learning Subsystems

One of the characteristics of optical virtual images is that they obey the same natural laws as do their objects. Thus, if one jumps in front of a mirror, the image in the mirror will also appear to jump. So it is with the learning system; it must also carry out the same functions as its object — the organizational system of action. However, the learning system deals

	Means	Ends
External	ENVIRONMENTAL INTERFACE	ACTION/ REFLECTION
Internal	MEANING AND MEMORY	DISSEMINATION & DIFFUSION

Figure 4.4 Organizational Learning Subsystems

with those actions that are focused on the organization, transforming information into valued knowledge, which in turn increases its long-run adaptive capacity. By relating the learning subsystems to Parsons' concept of prerequisite functions, we are able to describe how the four subsystems — Environmental Interface, Action/Reflection, Dissemination and Diffusion, and Memory and Meaning — support the organizational learning process (see Figure 4.4).

The Environmental Interface subsystem represents the Adaptation function. This subsystem contains those aspects of the action system that are aimed at allowing and/or disallowing information to enter the learning system. It is also directed at "manipulating" the characteristics of the learning system's external environment. This function is manifested in organizational actions that scan or test their environment and select inputs to the organization.

The Action/Reflection subsystem represents the Goal Attainment function. This function refers to those organizational actions that are aimed at satisfying learning needs or goals of the learning system. This function is manifested in organizational actions such as experimentation, research, evaluations, critical thinking, decision-making and problem-solving processes, and clarifying discussions. Its major concern is the production of knowledge that will add to the survival of the organization.

The Dissemination and Diffusion subsystem represents the Integration function. This function refers to those organizational actions directed at coordinating the elements of the learning system. This function is manifested in the implementation of organizational roles, leadership processes, structural manipulations, and communications that enhance the movement of information and knowledge.

The Meaning and Memory subsystem represents the Pattern Maintenance function. This function refers to the aspect of actions that aims at or consists of maintaining the general learning system's patterns of actions; as such it forms the fundamental source of tension, the "code" which gives rise to learning and action. It creates and stores the meaning or sensemaking control processes for the learning system. This function is manifested in organizational actions such as reasoning processes, comparisons, making of policy and procedures, creation of symbols reflecting organizational values, language, artifacts, basic assumptions, and the storing and retrieval of knowledge.

Each of the organizational learning subsystems represents one of Parsons' functions that must be implemented in order for the organization to learn. These functional prerequisites provide us with the ability to describe the learning system in terms of concrete organizational actions associated with Action Theory (see Figure 4.5). They also allow us to formulate analytical questions concerning the "health" of the learning system. Health of the organizational learning system is relative to its capacity to carry out its purpose — which is to transform new information into valued knowledge that in turn adds to the organization's capacity for long-term adaptation and survival.

If all learning subsystems are functioning, the learning system should be in good health and the organization will maintain a high capacity to learn. Each learning subsystem does not have to function at full capacity all the time. At any one instant we may find a need for much more action associated with Acting and Reflecting than with Dissemination and Diffusion. In the next instant we may find the reverse. The organizational learn-

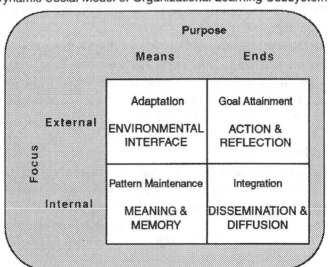

Dynamic Social Model of Organizational Learning Subsystems

Figure 4.5 Learning Subsystems and Functional Prerequisites

(From Schwandt, D. R., Organization learning, in *Advances in Strategic Managment,* Vol. 14, Walsh, J. P. and Huff, A., Eds., JAI Press, Stamford, CT, 1997. With permission; "Learning as an Organization," by David Schwandt from *Learning Organizations: Developing Cultures for Tomorrow's Workplace,* edited by Sarita Chawla and John Renesch. Copyright (c) 1995 by Productivity Press, P.O. Box 13390, Pòrtland, OR 97213–0390, (800) 394-6868. Reprinted by permission.)

ing system is dynamic in nature. This continuous changing of emphasis among the learning subsystems is the major reason a linear model had to be rejected.

The actions of the organization are based on a combination of the functions carried out by the actors, actions, symbols, and processes in a manner such that they will allow the system to survive (or prosper). It is this combination that we are defining as the organization's ability to learn. This being the case, it stands to reason that the unit of analysis of learning should be the actions of the organization and their cause-and-effect relationships. Thus, the use of Parsons' theory of action allows us to theoretically describe organizational learning using a unified theoretical base that can incorporate the broad nature of the behavioral sciences.

International Association of Machinists and Aerospace Workers — Implementing the Model

Under the leadership of Jim Leslie and Chris Wagoner, the International Association of Machinists and Aerospace Workers (IAM) has used the OLSM as a foundation for building organizational learning not only within the Union, but also within the companies served by IAM members.

IAM has nearly 500,000 members active in more than 200 basic industries. The Union's commitment to organization-wide learning is demonstrated by the state-of-the-art William W. Winpisinger Education and Technology Center, where union workers and employers participate in a "unique kind of learning program," with its emphasis on the sharing of experiences and seeking to create a culture of organizational learning.

The core of learning at IAM is built around the High Performance Work Organizations (HPWO) programs which were created as a partnership agreement between the IAM and employers to jointly redesign and operate the workplace. At its core, the program envisions a significant expansion of the issues over which the union engages employers, as well as a change in the nature of the relationship with the employer. Relationships change from an assumed adversarial to an interdependent partnership of equals.

All four subsystems of the Organizational Learning Systems Model are incorporated in the HPWO meetings. The meetings' primary focus is on dissemination and diffusion of information, knowledge, and values throughout IAM and the companies participating in the program. However, the collaborative learning process dynamically incorporates the other three subsystems. Both internal and external information are utilized (Information Interface). This environmental information is carefully related to the development and implementations of the HPWO partnership (action and reflection). Finally the results of all meetings are electronically stored and made available to all members of the community (memory and meaning). A number of principles and practices have emerged since introducing the OLS model and attempting to put it into practice at IAM:

- We learn from each other — what works and what doesn't work.
- We create a collaborative learning community across organizational boundaries.
- We utilize electronic meetings to look at environmental impediments.

- Data are shared from meeting to meeting.
- We continuously look for best practices through environmental scanning and visiting each other's sites.
- Lessons learned are put into software and carefully communicated.
- Trust is the key to building a learning organization.

The Dynamic Nature of the Organizational Learning Subsystems

In a pragmatic approach, we can now use the organizational learning system to profile learning capacity and to analyze potential strengths or weaknesses in each of the subsystems. The first step is to understand the relationship between each of the subsystems so that we can, for example, predict the impact of a weak Memory and Meaning subsystem on the other three subsystems. In order to do this we must turn to answering the questions, "What is the nature of the relationships between subsystems?" and "How do the subsystems relate to each other?"

One answer to the posed questions has been provided. Each subsystem carries out a prerequisite function for the total organizational learning system. However, this answer merely sets the stage for asking two questions of increasing complexity. The first is, "If these are subsystems of a larger system, what is the nature of their mutual dependence?" The second is, "How do these subsystems operate?" The second question requires a more complex theory of human interaction. At present, the subsystem's operations must be considered "black boxes." We do not have a sufficiently developed and unified theory of behavioral science to understand the chaotic nature of the simultaneous interaction of the multiple sets of human actions. In Chapters 5 to 8 we will to turn to empirical studies and other theories to begin to generate a clearer understanding of these "black boxes" (the four subsystems of actions). Knowing that this task is in front of us, we will now focus on answering the first question.

If we continue to borrow the idea of the "black box" from the field of physics, we are able to draw an analogy with the early work in atomic and nuclear science. If one is prevented from looking into the black box, one turns to observing inputs and outputs of the box and inferring what happens inside. In the case of the nucleus we bombarded it with gamma radiation and observed the incoming energy vs. the exiting energy and were able to draw certain models of interaction and operations of the nucleus and its component particles. This analogy serves our purpose well in the social sciences. We are not able to "see" inside the organizational learning subsystems of actions; however, we can develop a theory of mutual dependence and interaction among the four subsystems by assuming each provides a needed substance for the other subsystems. By examining the exchange of these substances, we can interpret what is happening in the subsystem of actions (black boxes) without having to track all the actions in the subsystem.

To answer the question "How do the organizational learning subsystems relate to each other in carrying out their functions?", we postulate that the subsystems relate through interchange processes. Each subsystem is dependent on the others for a critical "input" element that enables it to carry out its function with respect to the organizational learning system. In addition, each subsystem provides an "output" which is critical for each of the other subsystems. These inputs and outputs are the product of the actions associated with the subsystem of origin. This concept is in keeping with Parsons' sociological theory of Symbolic Media of Interchange.

Organizational Learning System Media of Interchange

By postulating the presence of interchange media in defining the relationship among the organizational learning subsystems, we are extending the General Theory of Action even further as an explanation of organizational learning. In defining the learning interchange media we are not negating the presence of those media postulated and explained by Parsons; we are merely adding to those media additional media that now more fully explain actions in terms of their organizational learning contributions.

When one moves from theory into practice with the organizational learning system and its component subsystems, it remains very conceptual in nature, and even to some extent abstract. In delineating the four subsystems of the learning system, we make them more concrete by assigning the subsystems the functional prerequisites. For example, it is reasonable that the Dissemination and Diffusion subsystem must carry out the function of integration through very concrete objects such as organizational roles, leadership, and movement of knowledge with the purpose of supporting the learning goals of the organizational learning system. It is also reasonable that the other subsystems must receive these products so that they in turn can carry out their respective functions.

The media of organizational learning interchange allow us to move to an even more concrete level in the construct of organizational learning. From this perspective we develop the potential to measure media of interchange and form the basis for obtaining empirical evidence of the usefulness of the model in the study of organizations' learning capacity.

Each of the organizational learning subsystems generates media that symbolically represent its functional product. The symbols that represent this output/input relationship are concrete and discernible through empirical methods of inquiry. Figure 4.6 schematically represents the relationship between the four subsystems and the interchange media.

The following discussion defines the four media, *New Information, Goal Reference Knowledge, Structuring,* and *Sensemaking,* and suggests the symbolic interchange variables indicative of the interdependent relationships established by the organizational learning subsystems. Each medium is subjected to an evaluation using Parsons' four characteristics of interchange media as criteria.

New Information

New information is the interchange medium output of the Environmental Interface subsystem. The learning system must have access to new information both from its environment and from within itself. The subsystem's function is adaptation, thus it is the window through which new information must come in from the outside and by which information leaves the organizational learning system.

The Environmental Interface subsystem must have the ability to secure (and influence) the data from its environment both internally and externally. In this process, that data must become **new information** for the learning system to disseminate/diffuse, create meaning and test against its memory, and to act-reflect on.

Information differs from data in that it has an ordering and it differs from knowledge in that it has not been valued by the organization. For example, performance data on company X becomes information to company Y when it is placed in a report format concerning market share, and becomes knowledge for company Y when company X is seen as a competitor in the market.

The medium of interchange, new information, meets the characteristics that Parsons believed were necessary for an interchange medium:

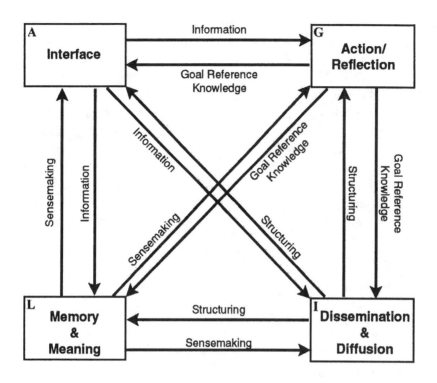

Figure 4.6 Learning System and Interchange Media

(From Schwandt, D. R., Organization learning, in *Advances in Strategic Management*, Vol. 14, Walsh, J. P. and Huffs, A., Eds., JAI Press, Stamford, CT, 1997. With permission; "Learning as an Organization," by David Schwandt from *Learning Organizations: Developing Cultures for Tomorrow's Workplace*, edited by Sarita Chawla and John Renesch. Copyright (c) 1995 by Productivity Press, P.O. Box 13390, Portland, OR 97213–0390, (800) 394-6868. Reprinted by permission.)

1. Institutionalization — New information has become highly legitimate over the past three decades. Organizations recognize the importance of continuously gathering new information for the system. It is this outward focus that is now evident in strategic scanning and networking processes that are prevalent in modern organizations. Of course, there is the illegitimate dimension of information that is characterized by the use of "disinformation."

2. Specificity — New information must generate in the learning system the requisite acting-reflecting, and the organization must have the

ability to differentiate the new information from the knowledge that it maintains in memory. Thus, new information is discernible from existing knowledge based on its value or lack of value. However, if the medium looses this characteristic or if new information is not recognizable or discernible from knowledge, the subsystem functions and the learning system may become dysfunctional.

3. Circulability — The nature of new information, whether verbal, written, visual, or electronic, makes it very circulable across organizational boundaries, if those boundaries are permeable.

4. Nonzero-sum character — New information can be held by all units within the organization simultaneously. Although new information possesses this characteristic, it does not preclude the withholding or misguiding of new information which makes it appear to be zero-sum.

Goal Reference Knowledge

Goal reference knowledge is the interchange media output of the Action/Reflection subsystem. We must be careful here to differentiate between two sets of goals: (1) goals associated with the actions of the organization's performance system and (2) goals associated with the organization's learning system. In a general sense, the objective of both sets of goals is identical — the changing of the organization with the purpose of survival. However, the goal of the learning system is to adapt through learning, while the goal of the performance system is to adapt through performance.

Goal reference knowledge is a product of those acts that are oriented toward the attainment of the goal of the organizational learning system, that is, through both action and reflection. This is defined as the transforming of information into valued knowledge which in turn increases the adaptive capacity of the organization in a changing environment. The actions that are taken by the actors in the organization must be accompanied by a reflection process so that goal reference knowledge can be produced. The referencing of the knowledge is to both the organization's performance goals and its learning goals.

An example of goal reference knowledge can be seen in the completion of a test, or pilot, of an organizational production process. The evaluation of the test by the organization constitutes the collective's reflection on the production process (action). This in turn creates knowledge that is referenced to both the goals of the performance system and the goals of the organizational learning system. This knowledge is needed by the other learning subsystems for dissemination-diffusion, meaning creation and memory storage, and to enable the interface with the environment.

We can judge the appropriateness of the goal reference knowledge as an interchange medium through the application of the Parsons' characteristics of symbolic interchange medium as criteria:

1. Institutionalization — All knowledge emanating from the action/reflection process by its nature (goal referenced) allows for its legitimacy for the organization. This is predicated on the legitimacy of the goals themselves.
2. Specificity — Those members of an organization who share its goals and the meaning of those goals will allow the goal reference knowledge to achieve efficacy.
3. Circulability — The nature of goal reference knowledge, whether verbal, written, visual, or electronic, makes it very circulable across organizational boundaries, if those boundaries are permeable.
4. Nonzero-sum character — Goal reference knowledge can be held by all units within the organization simultaneously. Although it possesses this characteristic, goal referenced knowledge does not preclude the withholding or misguiding of knowledge, which allows it to appear to be zero-sum.

Structuring

Structuring is the medium of interchange produced within the Dissemination-Diffusion subsystem. The nomenclature selected for this medium is indicative of its dynamic nature. It is more than a structure of the organization; it is an integration of organizational structures, roles, policies, objects, and processes that provide a dynamic quantity called structuring. It is through the structuring media that the organizational learning system is able to integrate the other three subsystems. It is the structuring mechanisms that allow for information and knowledge to move within the learning system and the organization itself. The actions associated with the movement of information and knowledge, in and of themselves, become part of the structuring process. Structuring symbolizes connection and order that facilitate the learning of the collective.

An example of structuring can be found in the role definition of leader or manager. If the role is defined as one of facilitator and teacher, rather than controller or monitor, the integrating capacity of the learning subsystem will be increased. This is an example of positive structuring which is input to the Meaning-Memory subsystem to aid in creating meaning and to the Action/Reflection subsystem to aid in reflection and the movement of goal reference knowledge.

We can judge the appropriateness of structuring as an interchange medium through the application of the Parsons' characteristics of symbolic interchange medium as criteria:

1. Institutionalization — All organizations accept and legitimize some form of structuring. They wouldn't be an organization if they didn't. However, the extent and methods of structuring will vary, and it is this variation that can either help or hinder the movement of information and knowledge within the learning system.

2. Specificity — Structuring represents order and connection. Both of these concepts are understood within an organization and mediate the movement of information and knowledge. Structuring is characteristic of the dynamic nature of the dissemination-diffusion processes.

3. Circulability — Structuring can be exchanged via the movement of roles and the relative arrangement of roles. Transfers are made, new policy is enacted, and reorganizations are possible. Thus structuring components are rarely held within one unit.

4. Nonzero-sum character — Structuring can increase or decrease without affecting the total amount of structuring available to any one segment of the organization. An example of this is simply changing the role implementation process of one manager. The style that he/she employs in moving knowledge may change the structuring and increase the organizational learning capacity, yet will not detract from other units' total structuring.

Sensemaking

The sensemaking medium is a product of the Meaning and Memory subsystem which carries out the function of pattern maintenance. The sensemaking produced and transferred from this subsystem is the product of sets of actions within the organization collective and is symbolically represented by its language and symbols. It is this medium that the organizational learning system relies on to make sense of its actions in reflection; it is this medium that is required to move and classify goal reference knowledge into stored memory; and it is this sense-making medium that is required by the Dissemination-Diffusion subsystem to generate appropriate structuring.

Language and symbols provide the means through which the Meaning-Memory subsystem communicates with the other subsystems within the organizational learning system. Language and symbols can be described as the specific words, signals, schemes (interpretive guidelines), and scripts (stored response routines) used by members of the collective in the action-taking process. Language and symbols are the outputs upon which the exchange process is dependent in order to produce useful information, goal reference knowledge, and structure for the organizational learning system.

An example of this medium can be found in the healthcare industry. Many hospitals are implementing a new form of patient-care delivery called "patient-focused care" which is designed to locate all patient ancillary services (pharmacy, radiology, nutritional care, respiratory therapy, etc.) on traditional nursing service floors. This would consolidate and change all patient care delivery roles. Refocusing the meaning of hospital care to patient-focused care required the organization to make new sense out of its services, structure, and roles. In turn, the changing of roles, titles, and structures changed the language and symbols associated with patient care (i.e., patient-focused care).

We can again apply Parsons' characteristics of symbolic interchange medium to judge the appropriateness of the sensemaking as an interchange medium:

1. Institutionalization — The language and symbols can be accepted and understood by the organizational collective for it to be useful to the organizational learning process. This medium is indicative of the culture of the organization. Therefore, the medium and the process of legitimization become one and the same.
2. Specificity — Language and symbols are created by the actors within organizations and represent essential common meanings. However, they may have mixed connotations across unit boundaries.
3. Circulability — Language and symbols can be termed the "currency of interaction" within organizations and are readily exchanged between individuals and units as a normal way of doing business.
4. Zero-sum character — Since new words and new symbols are constantly created within the units of action, language and symbols do not take on a zero-sum character.

To move the concept of organizational learning to a level of application that has pragmatic value, we must be able to translate the abstractness of the learning subsystems into the concrete measurable variables. The interchange media and their interaction with the learning subsystems provide the framework or map that one can use to measure the health of the organizational learning system, or the learning capacity of the organization. Table 4.1 summarizes the interchange media and some corresponding concrete variables that can be used to describe the outputs of the organizational learning subsystems.

Table 4.1 Variables Associated with the Media of the Interchange for the Learning Subsystems

Interchange Media	Variables[a]
New information	Internal and external data
	Customer feedback
	Employee survey
Goal reference knowledge	Results of an experiment
	Evaluation results
	Decision-making processes
	Knowledge structures
Structuring	Organizational roles
	Leadership
	Policies
	Organizational structure
Sensemaking	Schemas
	Language and symbols
	Values and assumptions

a. This list of variables is not meant to be complete, only representative. From Schwandt, D. R., Organization learning, in *Advances in Strategic Management*, Vol. 14, Walsh, J. P. and Huffs, A., Eds., JAI Press, Stamford, CT, 1997. With permission.

An example of the media of interchange as dynamic linking mechanisms can be seen in Figure 4.7. This is an illustration of an organization that has created knowledge concerning the treatment of people. Although this particular example is indicative of a pathology that can hamper learning and lead to harmful bias, it does demonstrate the mutual dependence of the subsystem of actions on the interchange media.

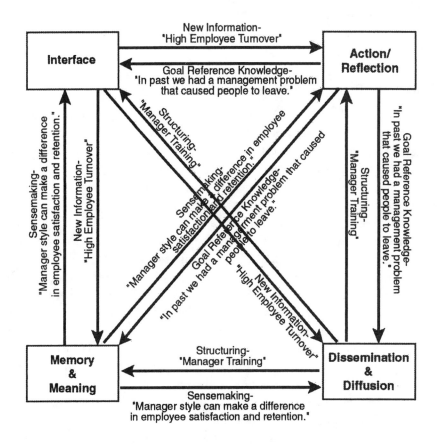

Figure 4.7 Example of Dynamic Learning Model

In terms of the organizational learning model, the Environmental Interface subsystem works in response to the demand for new information from outside and inside organizations. The Diffusion and Dissemination subsystem serves to create consistency and harmony among all parts of the organization by circulating necessary information and knowledge via structuring mechanisms. Of all four subsystems, the Action/Reflection subsystem appears to act as the knowledge creation center of the organization. With the pooled external information and internal conceptual bases, this is where organizational goal-specific knowledge is generated for the organization's effective operation. The knowledge then is transmitted and integrated into the whole by the Diffusion and Dissemination mechanisms. The most critical subsystem, however, is the Meaning and Memory subsystem. It exerts the control over the functioning of organizations through the shared organizational interpretative systems that allow the organizational members to make sense of their actions and the actions of the organization.

Patterns of Learning Media Interchange

The learning subsystems are not independent. Dysfunction in one learning subsystem will jeopardize the effectiveness of the whole system. The learning subsystem requires inputs (New Information, Goal Reference Knowledge, Structuring, and Sensemaking) from the three other subsystems to fulfill its own prerequisite function and to help the system accomplish its goal of creating knowledge. They are constantly interchanging their outputs with one another.

The learning patterns are configurations of the media of interchange (Table 4.1) that are based on an organization's choices along a "performance-learning continuum of interchange media." The organization's interchange patterns can be characterized as a point on a spectrum of patterns anchored on one end by a set of media variables that enhance organizational learning and at the other end by a set of media variables that enhance learning. Thus, the organization's choice (either purposeful or by default) of interchange variables will create patterns that favor either learning or performance, or some balance of the two. Table 4.2 illustrates the four learning interchange media patterns and their associated continuums, and their respective end-point anchors. These anchors were empirically derived from in-depth case studies and represent the organization's orientation to performance and/or learning.

These interchange media form patterns that, when congruent, support the organization learning system. If they are not congruent, the organization will experience a lower, or dysfunctional, learning capacity.

Pattern Congruency

The concept of congruency has been an underlying theme for many explanations of social interaction. For example, organizational theorists used the concept when explaining the matching of leadership styles to the contextual variables of the organization (i.e., production processes, employee maturity). In these comparisons we address congruency as the "best fit"; that is, do participatory leadership styles fit with employees who do not know the goals of the organization?

Most uses of the concept of "best fit" are reflections of our need to reduce ambiguous phenomena by establishing cause–effect relations between

Table 4.2 Interchange Media Continuum

Interchange Media	Continuum of Patterns	
	Heavy Performance ◄—————————————► Heavy Learning	
Sensemaking	Reasonable ◄——► Inquiry	
	Accurate	Plausibility
	Present Orientation	Future Orientation
	Pragmatic	Receptive
	Cynical	Theory
Goal reference knowledge	Routine ◄——► Experimental	
	Action based	Reflectivity
	Reductionary	Available
	Useful	Risk
	Applicable	Untested
New information	Nonequivocal ◄——► Equivocal	
	Rational	Nonrational
	Discernable	Ambiguous
	Predictable	Random appearance
	Justifiable	Chaos/complexity
Structuring	Closed ◄——► Open	
	Tightly coupled	Loosely coupled
	Directive	Developmental
	Controlling	Facilitating
	Rules	Guidance
	Rigid	Flexible

subjective measures of social variables. Many times congruency is used in situations where the variables cannot be measured precisely enough or where we do not have sufficient theoretical relations that allow for the prediction of cause–effect.

Learning Interchange Patterns

Our ability to predict cause–effect relations has been limited by the complexity of the social action system. There are simply too many variables to control for and their nonlinear nature creates highly complex relations. This section of the chapter presents an alternate approach to understanding

Table 4.3 Interchange Patterns

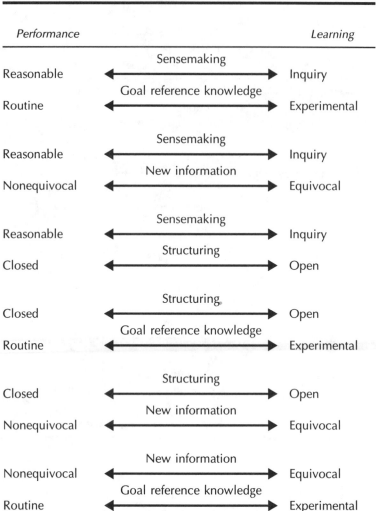

Performance		Learning
	Sensemaking	
Reasonable	←→	Inquiry
	Goal reference knowledge	
Routine	←→	Experimental
	Sensemaking	
Reasonable	←→	Inquiry
	New information	
Nonequivocal	←→	Equivocal
	Sensemaking	
Reasonable	←→	Inquiry
	Structuring	
Closed	←→	Open
	Structuring	
Closed	←→	Open
	Goal reference knowledge	
Routine	←→	Experimental
	Structuring	
Closed	←→	Open
	New information	
Nonequivocal	←→	Equivocal
	New information	
Nonequivocal	←→	Equivocal
	Goal reference knowledge	
Routine	←→	Experimental

organizational learning through the postulation of six configurational patterns of interchange media. Table 4.3 delineates the six patterns of learning interchange media.

The configurations allow us to better understand the dynamic nature of organizational learning and to identify pathologies associated with the organization's learning capacity. The actions within each subsystem of the model sustain a learning capacity through the dynamic balancing of the configurational patterns of interchange media. The organization's actions associated with each pattern must maintain congruency between the interchange media to achieve a high level of learning or performance capacity. Non-congruency reduces the functional nature of the subsystem of actions, which in turn reduces the organizational cognitive capacity (and /or the performance) of the collective.

To operationalize this model, Table 4.4 provides three examples of possible congruency of interchange media. Example A portrays high congruency between the interchange media of sensemaking and structuring. This particular pattern would be indicative of the actions of an organization prone to performance more than learning. Example B portrays the same configuration of interchange media, but now there is a congruence pattern oriented more toward plausibility and developmental actions. This pattern would be more indicative of learning than performance. Example C portrays the same configuration in an unbalanced pattern that lends itself to neither learning nor performance.

Table 4.4 Configurational "Fits" of Interchange Media

Examples of Configurational Patterns

Example A — Configuration

Reasonable	—X———————	Sensemaking	————————— Inquiry
Closed	—X———————	Structuring	————————— Open

Example B — Configuration

Reasonable	———————	Sensemaking	——————X— Inquiry
Closed	———————	Structuring	——————X— Open

Example C — Configuration

Reasonable	—X———————	Sensemaking	————————— Inquiry
Closed	———————	Structuring	——————X— Open

The following case of an organization that intended to reap benefits from the merger of two units illustrates these patterns of learning interchange media.

The Case of the Nonmerger

Units within a major healthcare organization were merged to achieve economies and effective customer relations. Six months after the merger the new organization was not functioning in a unified manner. The presenting problems of the merger were a lack of leadership, the lack of vision or strategic goals, and barriers created by cultural difference between units. All of these conclusions held some validity, but yet not any single issue appeared significant enough to hinder the merger's effectiveness. In addition, the efficiency objectives of this organization were being achieved on a day-to-day basis. The new unit was not emerging and this would eventually limit the growth and effectiveness expected of the unit. In the short term, the performance goals were being met; however, from a long-term perspective, it was necessary to ask if the organization had the capacity to adapt to its new environment — both internal and external.

Our study of this merger began with the collection of data through interviews and observations that would give us information concerning the four organizational learning subsystems and their respective functions. What respondents provided were not the descriptions of the organizational learning subsystem per se; rather, they provided descriptions of the more concrete variables that formed interchange media emanating from the actions associated with the organizational learning subsystems.

The analysis resulted in the description of interchange media, which included data and comments around roles, information, organizational structure, values, time for reflection, etc. Using the model as a lens, we formulated the results in terms of double interchange patterns — "interchange patterns." Each of the six products represents patterns of interaction between two interchange media (see Table 4.5). These six patterns (or interchange products) form the configuration indicative of the organizational learning system. The six sets of interchange media form a configurational learning pattern for the organization that did not allow the organization to successfully merge, even though it was successfully performing its mission. Its learning capacity was being hindered by a lack of congruency in the media of interchange that resulted in destructive learning system patterns.

The patterns of collective learning after the merger were characterized by rumor, doubt, focus on immediate performance of task, a lack of reflection on actions, and reinforcement of past routine processes dependent on pre-merger cultures. However, the organization was still performing at an acceptable level. The learning patterns were not affecting the performance system;

Table 4.5 Organizational Learning System Configurations

Interchange Media	Study Results
Set I: New information and goal reference knowledge	The absence of reflection on their actions provided no opportunity for the units to question their actions. The knowledge produced was primarily a passing through of the new information the organization received and was acted on in a routine manner, thus reinforcing the routine. Therefore the goal reference knowledge resembled the new information and vice versa.
Set II: Structuring and goal reference knowledge	The lack of leadership and nondefined organizational structure allowed the knowledge, or information, to be moved in the premerger modes. This confusion can stem from the ineffective communication between top and lower management and the maintenance of territorial boundaries.
Set III: Structuring and new information	Because of the lack of reflection this pattern of media is identical with Set II above. This is most obvious in the reported sluggish decision-making process which respondents saw as a contributor to the confusion. Organizational members were not able to draw distinctions between new information and goal reference knowledge.
Set IV: Structuring and sensemaking	The differences in values of the two units under study accentuated their differences and amplified the need to maintain their separate identities, separate databases, etc. The lack of leadership enabled the separatedness to be the default for guiding the routine actions of the respective units and the constant conflict and confusion.
Set V: Goal reference knowledge and sensemaking	The inability to reflect on the new information created conditions which simply reinforced the separateness of the two merged units and reinforced their present set of assumptions concerning their situations. Therefore, they were sending signals that did not even indicate a difference, or the need to reflect. Not understanding the agency's goals allowed the two units to maintain a "no difference" perspective.

continued

Table 4.5 (continued) Organizational Learning System Configurations

Interchange Media	Study Results
Set VI: New information and sensemaking	The basic assumptions held by the two merged units provided the guidance to the interface actions of both units. The emphasis on the boundary spanning mission and the interpreted criticality to the agency acted as a filter of the new information received. Thus, even the goal the agency had for the customer relations was never received so that it could be reflected on.

From Schwandt, D. R., Organization learning, in *Advances in Strategic Management,* Vol. 14, Walsh, J. P. and Huff, A., Eds., JAI Press, Stamford, CT, 1997. With permission.

however, the long-term merger plans of the new organization were not being realized. Although the purpose of this study was not to draw cause–effect relationships, one could make an argument that if the learning subsystem had a higher capacity, the merger would have been more successful. There should have been an understanding of "what could be," as opposed to "what was." This is reflected in the poor fit between structuring and sensemaking.

Let's now look at another merger that worked, thanks to an application of many of the elements of the OLSM.

Whirlpool — A Successful Merger that Applied Organizational Learning

Founded in 1911 in Benton Harbor, Michigan, Whirlpool Corporation is the world's leading manufacturer and marketer of major home appliances. The company manufactures in 11 countries and markets products in more than 140 countries under brand names such as Whirlpool, KitchenAid, Roper, Estate, Bajknecht, Ignis, Laden, and Inglis. Whirlpool has over 40,000 employees worldwide; 1998 revenues exceeded $10 billion.

For the past several years, Whirlpool has been pursuing a strategy of international growth, purchasing part of Philips in Europe in 1989, SAGAD of Argentina in 1992, and Kelvinator of India in 1994. For a long time number one in the U.S. and Canada, Whirlpool is now the third largest appliance marketer in Europe and number one in Latin America. And with sales in Asia expected to grow three to four times faster than in the U.S. in the next few years, Whirlpool has stepped up its operations, especially in China and India.

Whirlpool has become a global leader not only in home appliances, but also in corporate-wide learning. Corporate analysts attribute much of Whirlpool's success to its global vision and global strategy, areas in which *Business Week* declares, "They are outpacing the industry dramatically" (November 28, 1994, p. 98). The beginnings of this vision and strategies to accomplish it emerged as a result of a brilliantly designed global planning conference in Switzerland in 1990.

In 1989, Whirlpool acquired the $2 billion appliance division of Philips, headquartered in the Netherlands. In one fell swoop, Whirlpool had gone from an almost exclusively domestic company to a 40% global corporation, and in the process had become the largest household appliances company in the world.

The significance of becoming a global company was quickly seen by Whirlpool. Learning as an organization would be needed if the company were to successfully adapt and transform itself to compete for customers in the new global environment; and Whirlpool had a far distance to go — many of its U.S. senior managers didn't even have passports. Integrating the American and Dutch companies would not be easy.

CEO Dave Whitwam asked the human resources staff to develop policies and programs to help the company globalize. He wanted to avoid the problems noted in the case above, i.e., a lack of leadership, the lack of vision or strategic goals, and barriers created by cultural difference between units. Thus, within 6 months of the acquisition, Whirlpool brought 150 of its senior managers from 16 countries to Montreux, Switzerland for a 1-week global conference. The theme of the conference was "Winning through Quality Leadership: One Global Vision." Four major goals were identified for the conference:

- Advance a unified vision of the company's future
- Instill the idea of embracing the future as one global company
- Establish a keen sense of responsibility within the leadership group for creating the company's future
- Identify and initiate explicit steps toward integrating various activities and ideas throughout Whirlpool's worldwide operations into a uni-

fied whole, thereby creating a common vision (key for developing the Meaning and Memory Subsystem)

Encouraging cultural mixing among the 150 managers was deemed crucial for action learning to take place. The typical behavior of international managers gravitating toward their own "cultural cocoons" was avoided by planning activities and events that pushed managers beyond their own national backgrounds and people of their own language.

The well-planned structure of the conference freed the managers to be creative, reflective, and open to new possibilities. Emphasis was on meeting, getting to know and trust, working with, and learning with and from their new global colleagues (Dissemination and Diffusion). Together they could better focus on critical, challenging issues such as the Whirlpool vision, strategic planning, and quality. These efforts led to a better sharing of information (Environmental Interface) and more reflection and knowledge creation (Action/Reflection).

One element which built powerful learning among the global participants was the conference "ground rules." Attendees were encouraged to be active themselves and to help others participate as well, in both the meetings and informal activities. They were challenged to get beyond their comfort zones with these guidelines:

- Create situations in which you can meet everyone.
- Promote an atmosphere of worldwide learning. Remember that the only problems we cannot solve are the ones we don't identify.
- We are all responsible for making the week productive.
- Be a good listener.

Whirlpool managers themselves prepared and conducted the various workshops. This tactic began the process that continues today of managers of the new Whirlpool being learning facilitators and trainers as well as managers.

During the week-long event, managers were invited to identify which major areas of the company's operations could be improved. From an original list of 200 areas, 15 key issues were identified. Each of these issues became Whirlpool's One-Company Challenges. The challenges ranged from global management reporting systems to global quality initiatives, from development of a global corporate talent pool to consumer-product delivery cycles.

Fifteen cross-functional and multinational groups, called "Whirlpool One-Company Challenge Teams," were then formed to examine these 15 topics (Action/Reflection) and present their recommendations at the following global conference in Washington, D.C. Team members met regularly and reported their progress in *The Leading Edge*, the corporate newsletter for Whirlpool's worldwide leaders (Dissemination and Diffusion).

Listen to how Whitwam describes the role of Whirlpool staff in developing and implementing the new company vision:

> We made those 150 people accountable for educating all of our 38,000 people around the world. When going global, you have to communicate to everyone what the company vision is and what the long-term goals are. And then you have to follow through and design processes that force the interaction to continue. Every single employee must believe that there is great value in managing the company in an integrated way. To do that, you have to bring people together on real projects that tackle real problems or that explore opportunities on a cross-border basis.

The learning and change that this global conference achieved was so significant that Whirlpool people felt it launched the company ahead in time by 3 to 5 years in the integration of its global management team, and also saved the company millions of dollars in the process. It was at this conference that the vision of a global learning company and the importance of organizational learning began to emerge.

Advantages of the Social Systems Approach

The advantage of the broad social systems approach to dynamic learning allows us to integrate existing social theories of culture, leadership, cognition, sensemaking, and many others into the fabric of the Organizational Learning Systems Model. To illustrate the power of the Organizational Learning Systems Model, we will now focus in more depth on each of the four subsystems of actions and their dynamic interchange media. The four subsystems — Environmental Interface, Action/Reflection, Dissemination and Diffusion, and Memory and Meaning — are vital to maintaining a learning capacity that will contribute to the organization's long-term survival. In Chapters 5 to 8, we will develop each of the four learning subsystems of actions, including an in-depth discussion of the actions associated with the subsystem and the nature of the interchange media. Case studies exemplifying key aspects of the Organizational Learning Systems Model will be interspersed throughout these pages.

References

Luhmann, N., *Social Systems*, translated by Bednarz, J. and Baecker, D., Stanford University Press, Stanford, 1995.

Parsons, T., *The Social System*, Free Press, New York, 1951.

Schwandt, D. R. and Gundlach, A. M., Organizational Learning: The Development and Implementation of an Operational Systems Model, George Washington University, Washingon, D.C., 1992.

5 | The Portal for New Information: The Environmental Interface Subsystem

In new theories of evolution and order, information is a dynamic element, taking center stage. It is information that gives order, that prompts growth, that defines what is alive. It is both the underlying structure and the dynamic process that ensures life.

Margaret Wheatley
Leadership and the New Science

Seeking, Scanning, and Screening Information

The environmental interface subsystem performs as a collection of interdependent activities and actions that respond to signals from both the inside and outside of the organization determining the information it seeks and disperses. Its primary purpose is to function as the informational portal for the organizational learning system. The conceptual basis for this subsystem is one of intake and output, therefore, cause–effect relationships center around the actions the system uses to secure, filter, and expel information. This can be in proactive or reactive modes. The processes used by the subsystem will range from those designed to purposefully gather information based on internal criteria (e.g., market surveys, customer requirements, employee focus groups) to those which receive information such as regulations and economic indicators imposed on the organization from the external environment.

This subsystem includes actions associated with public relations, research efforts, lobbying, and other means of scanning the environment. It also includes activities that provide screening of information and data, such as monitoring news broadcasts and printed literature. Some of these acts are reactive, passive, and adaptive to the environment, while others are proactive and directed at creating the organization's environment.

Information as the Energy to Survive

Like any system, the organizational learning system must import energy to survive. New information is the energy required by the organizational learning system. One of the most basic differences between organizational learning and individual learning is the complexity of the system's boundary-spanning mechanisms that are required to bring new information into the system. The difference lies in the complexity of actions and dynamic structures that are required for the organizations to accomplish this functional prerequisite.

The actions associated with the Environmental Interface subsystem can be as simple as attending a Rotary Club meeting or as complex as the actions involved with negotiations of mergers of two large corporations. The actions can differ from very aggressive, intrusive ones to those that are more passive and only heighten our awareness to what is going on in external and internal environments. They can be actions associated with cornering the market on needed manufacturing information to nonintrusive surfing the net for information. They can be actions associated with gathering internal information from employee surveys to surveying external customers.

This exchange of information can be a two-way street. It is also promoting, selling the products, and influencing the environment to be more favorable to the organization's position. This is a difference in how organizations may have seen themselves in the past. Many firms have taken the position of "responding" to the environment; that is, coping with the constraints that are placed on the organization by its external environment (i.e., competitors, government regulations, etc.). The organizational learning system possesses the possibility of a more proactive approach. By extracting information from the environment, using the learning system to turn it into knowledge, and then exporting knowledge as information for use by the external environment, the organization can influence or enact its views and possibly shape its environment.

It is sometimes easier to see the effects of enactment at the industry level. For example, the early 1990s saw the insurance industry, primarily the health insurance industry, become very active in trying to influence the federal government's attempt to intervene at limiting healthcare costs. Their actions, through public forums and other legislative processes, prevented, in their eyes, a very harmful regulatory move by the federal government. A more negative example can be seen in the tobacco industry's efforts to promote the use of tobacco products. In this case, the industry relied on massive public relations and advertising to rebut, and in some cases suppress, evidence that the use of its product could be harmful to human health. In both of these examples, the organizations were enacting their environments through their actions in the Environmental Interface subsystem.

Organizations can also take on either an enacting or passive mode of scanning their internal environments. They can let information "perk up" through or "trickle down" through the organization. Or they can actively scan their own internal environments for information that can be reflected on and converted to usable knowledge. An excellent example of the latter is 3M Corp. and its ability to ascertain information from the bench scientists within the organization. Their encouragement, through the use of flexible structuring and reinforcement of the values of sharing work data, has provided them a wealth of information that has been converted into innovative knowledge and marketable products.

Gathering Knowledge at PricewaterhouseCoopers

On July 1, 1998, Price Waterhouse and Coopers & Lybrand merged to form PricewaterhouseCoopers (PWC), the world's largest professional services organization with over 140,000 representatives in 152 countries. PWC estimates that up to 99% of its revenue is generated from knowledge-based professional services and knowledge-based products. Its employees spend up to 80 hours/year "creating and sharing knowledge" (American Productivity and Quality Council [APQC]). Why is knowledge management so critical to PWC? Among the driving forces are

- The geographic dispersion and need to serve global clients requires a timely coordination and sharing of information among the different subsidiaries.
- Information about tax polices, legislation, banking, financial requirement, etc. changes so rapidly that it needs to be quickly captured and disseminated.
- Employee turnover of 15 to 25% per year necessitates systems to capture this knowledge or it will be lost.
- It is important to discover and constantly share best practices throughout the firm.
- Employees must know about former projects and projects conducted in other parts of the clients' organization.
- The tendency to have "islands of knowledge activity" creates inefficiencies and duplication.

KnowledgeView, PWC's proprietary best-practices repository of information, has been gathered from more than 2200 companies worldwide and contains over 4500 entries, with references to more than 350 internal and external benchmarking studies. The goal of KnowledgeView is to "support the firm's core competency of being business advisors: including the accumulation, analysis, creation, and dissemination of value-added information and knowledge that PWC professionals can use to improve business performance of clients, and ultimately increase the value of PWC's services" (APQC).

KnowledgeView is Lotus Notes-based rather than CD ROM-based, thereby allowing daily information updates as well as the capacity to access and share knowledge "instantaneously on a worldwide basis." The databases in KnowledgeView incorporate the following information:

- Best practices as identified in PWC and non-PWC programs
- Benchmarking studies from internal and external sources
- Expert opinions synthesized by industry or process subject matter experts
- Abstracts of books and articles on business improvement
- PWC staff biographies with resumes database according to country, industry, skill, language, etc.

■ Views and forecasts of PWC's own experts on important topics

KnowledgeView is classified according to industry, process, enabler, topic, and measurement so that PWC consultants can target and find the knowledge for which they are searching. An important feature of KnowledgeView is the format used for containing the information. For example, in the "best practices" database, the format is established to answer the following questions:

■ What caused the change?
■ What old process needed improvement?
■ What is the new process?
■ What is the new performance and how is it measured?
■ What were the lessons learned?
■ What are the future directions?

KnowledgeView is maintained and updated at four Knowledge Centers located in Dallas, London, Sydney, and Sao Paulo. Through these regional centers, local staff has more immediate access points as well as help in stimulating knowledge sharing. In 1996 Price Waterhouse received the "Best Practices Award" from *PC Week* magazine for its KnowledgeView technology.

The Hubble Disaster — Taking the Environment for Granted

It is important for managers and members of organizations to understand the potential barriers to organizational learning. In very complex global environments, it is this learning capacity of the organization that will provide a margin for survival. The lack of understanding was very evident in the initial costly failure of the NASA Hubble telescope project. This failure provides an excellent example of an organization that did not obtain new information that was vital to its long-term knowledge production.

In October 1993 Norwalk-based work in Perkin-Elmer Corp. and Hughes Danburry Optical Systems agreed to pay the government $25 million to avoid a lawsuit over the flawed Hubble space telescope. The settlement, the largest out-of-court agreement ever reached with a contractor by the NASA inspector general's office, concluded a 3-year investigation into the scientific debacle. Investigators for NASA confirmed that the null corrector, an optical instrument used to guide the polishing and serve as a principal test device, had been assembled incorrectly. They also concluded that the mirror flaw had surfaced on three occasions and was discounted, and that schedule and budget problems and lax supervision by NASA and Perkin-Elmer contributed to the failure to catch the error (Capers, 1994, p. 68).

If one reads this abstract, it sounds like many failures we have all experienced in various quality assurance processes. Two major changes occurred for which the organization was not prepared because the nature of its new information did not change. First, the U.S. Government environment and its political implications changed. No longer did the system tolerate the underbidding of federal contracts that allowed for cost overruns and continuous appeals for unplanned funds. This had been the nature of past Perkin-Elmer experiences. However, since the "six hundred dollar toilet seat," the public outcries drew harsh reforms. Second, the political environment was demanding that NASA run itself like a business, not a scientific research facility. This was translated into motivations that stressed deadlines and costs over scientific quality.

The narrow scope of Perkin-Elmer's environmental scanning was based on their past experiences and resulted in ignoring the new information in their environment. They continued with "business as usual" — cost overruns and slippage in time lines. This aggravated their environment and led to more pressure, which then resulted in the lack of reflection, breakdowns in supervision, and nonattention to test results, all of which resulted in failure of the project.

Could this "debacle" have been averted? Yes, we think so. If the management of Perkin-Elmer had examined the systemic nature of their learning system and the actions associated with ensuring the presence of new information for the system, this series of events could have been changed.

New Information — Output of the Environmental Interface Subsystem

As we noted in Chapter 4, new information is the interchange media of the Environmental Interface subsystem. The organizational learning system must have access to new information to disseminate/diffuse, to create meaning from and test against its memory, and to reflect upon (see Figure 5.1).

The relationship between the organization and its environment, both internal and external, is very important to the survival of the organization and the effective utilization of the learning system. Three major issues must be considered when looking at the actions associated with this subsystem of

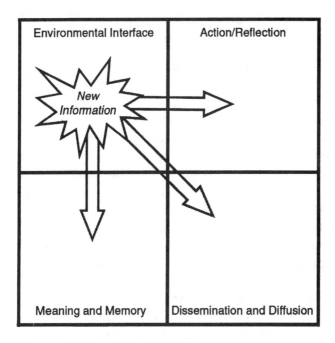

Figure 5.1 Environmental Interface Output is New Information

actions and its interchange media. First, how does the organization perceive its environment and what influence does this have on the choice of environmental sectors to be scanned for information. What is the ecology of the learning system?

The second issue to consider is what mechanisms can the organization employ that will result in environmental interface actions that will result in new information entering the organization. In addition, what are the implications for these mechanisms in a global economy?

The third issue deals with the nature of possible pathologies that involve all the interchange media in patterns that may cause this subsystem to be dysfunctional. These pathologies can provide organizations with guidance that could derail actions that are diminishing their capacity to create knowledge.

In the sections that follow we will discuss each of these issues and the body of knowledge associated with these actions. We will also provide examples of how organizations can manipulate the actions associated with the environmental interface subsystem and in turn influence the effectiveness of obtaining new information for the learning system.

Andersen Consulting — Acquiring Information

Andersen Consulting has placed a high priority on developing and utilizing a "Global Best Practices" knowledge base. This knowledge base identifies and describes best practices, best companies, engagement experiences, studies and articles, performance measures, diagnostics, process definitions, and process experts.

In 1994, the firm opened the Andersen Consulting Center for Strategic Research in California's Silicon Valley, intentionally near other technology innovators, thereby quickening the ability of Andersen to influence and apply the latest developments from these leading technology and research organizations. An initiative already under way is "Infocosm," which is the creation of a working model of the information highway.

To facilitate the exchange of the firm's knowledge capital, Andersen developed a team to create and implement a knowledge capital delivery system. Expected to be one of the largest Knowledge Exchange applications ever developed, the system will store and disseminate Andersen Consulting's methodologies, industry best practices, and reference materials.

More than 1000 CD-ROM discs of the knowledge base have been distributed worldwide. Global Best Practices workshops have been conducted for Andersen staff in offices around the globe. This base represents a powerful tool for learning for Andersen staff as well as a valuable service for clients.

Andersen also seeks to partner with "knowledge" firms so as to enhance their industry expertise. Recently Senn-Delaney, an international firm specializing in retail profit improvement, and Venture Associates, which specializes in the utilities industry, were contracted to work with the firm.

Andersen has a deliberate strategy to gain knowledge through training, research, and participation in professional and trade associations as well as producing publications for internal and external use on such topics as Retail Customer Satisfaction and Merchandizing, Physician Health Integration, and Vital Sign: Using Quality Time and Cost Performance Measures to Chart Your Company's Future.

In order to maximize the in-house transfer of conference participation, Andersen strives to have at least three staff attend seminars or conferences identified as valuable for the firm. Serving as presenters at conferences is promoted not only for reputation acquired, but also "pushing" the person toward quality preparation, research, and learning.

The Ecology of Learning

The "environment" is no longer seen as something "outside of" the organization's boundaries. Strategies for organizational survival are now finding ways to not only coexist with their environments, but to become one with their surroundings. This ecological approach to boundary spanning is especially viable to the organizational learning system's need for new information. The metaphors for today's global organizations have changed from "conquering" the environment or "beating" the competition, to "creating" partnerships and producing environmental "harmony." This frame of reference requires organizations to examine their understanding, not only of their external, but also internal environments.

Examining the environment is not just simply an antecedent to interpretation of information by the organization. We must remember that the organizational learning model and the Environmental Interface subsystem are a set of actions that span across and within the organization to "scoop up" or "generate" information. These actions are bounded by the assumptions and values the organization holds with respect to its environment. The actions and methods employed by the organization to achieve the interface function are dependent not only on how they perceive their environment, but also on the type and intensity of the actions the organization is willing to support.

Daft and Weick (1984), in their now-classic argument that organizations can be seen as interpretive systems, postulate a model for classifying research and observations made about how organizations interact with their environments. They hypothesize that organizations can be differentiated based on how they scan their environments and how the obtained information moves into the formulation of strategies for the organization. They define interpretation as the process of translating events, of developing models for understanding, of bringing out meaning, and assembling conceptual schemes among key managers. They see the process as a circular flow among the actions associated with scanning, interpretation, and learning. The role of the culture of the organization is heavily manifested in the values and assumptions the organization holds concerning its environment and its role with the environment.

Daft and Weick's model uses two key dimensions to differentiate types of organizations based on interpretation patterns: "(1) management's beliefs about the analyzability of the external environment and (2) the extent to which the organization intrudes into the environment to understand it" (Daft and Weick, 1984, p. 287).

These two dimensions provide a classification schema for the interpretive actions of an organization. The assumptions about the analyzability of the environment range from the environment being concrete with events that are measurable and determinable to it being unanalyzable, and therefore not measurable and requiring interpretation processes that are more personal, more ad hoc, and less structured.

The second dimension deals with different interpretation systems as to the extent to which organizations actively intrude into their environments. "Organizational search may include testing or manipulating the environment. Forceful organizations may break presumed rules, try to change the rules, or try to manipulate critical factors in the environment" (Daft and Weick, 1984 p. 288). On the other hand, passive organizations accept whatever information the environment gives them. They do not actively search for the solutions. (As a notable exception to this passivity, see the case of Matsushita — the "possibility-searching company" — in Chapter 6.)

Daft and Weick's analysis results in four patterns that organizations may exhibit in their environmental interactions:

1. The *enacting* mode reflects bold and active, intrusive strategy and the assumption that the environment is unanalyzable. These organizations construct their own environments. They gather information by trying new behaviors and seeing what happens. They experiment, test, and stimulate, and they ignore precedent, rules, and traditional expectations.

2. The *discovering* mode also represents an intrusive organization, but the emphasis is on detecting the correct answer already in an analyzable environment rather than on shaping the answer. Carefully devised measurement probes are sent into the environment to relay information back to the organization. This organization uses market research, trend analysis, and forecasting to predict problems and opportunities.

3. Organizations characterized as *conditioned viewing* (Aguilar, 1967) assume at an analyzable environment and are not intrusive. They tend to rely on established data collection procedures, and the interpretations are developed within traditional boundaries. The environment is perceived as objective and benevolent, so the organization does not take unusual steps to learn about the environment. The viewing is conditioned in the sense that it is limited to the routine documents, reports, publications, and information systems that have grown up through the years.

4. *Undirected viewing* (Aguilar, 1967) reflects a similar passive approach, but these organizations do not rely on hard, objective data because the environment is assumed to be unanalyzable. Managers act on limited, soft information to create their perceived environment. These organizations are not conditioned by formal management systems within the organization, and they are open to a variety of cues about the environment from many sources (Daft and Weick, 1984).

Daft and Weick's patterns provide two very important insights. First, ways in which organizations perceive their environments can influence the type and quality of new information the learning system imports. Therefore, the organization must be aware of these idiosyncratic patterns and the impact on their ability to judge (reflect on) information in the context from which it emanates. Second, Daft and Weick do not see organizations "cemented" in a certain pattern. The process of interpretation, or the actions of the Environmental Interface subsystem, can change (and probably should) as environmental conditions change. Thus the scope of the scanning processes should err on the side of more variety in environmental sectors and modes of interaction rather than on less variety. This will reduce the potential pitfalls of limited types of new information (similar to the Hubble problem).

Capturing Learning at Canadian Imperial Bank of Commerce

Canadian Imperial Bank of Commerce (CIBC) is a highly diversified Canadian financial services company operating on a global basis with more than 6.5 million individual customers and 10,000 commercial customers. The bank has more than 47,000 employees and invests over $40 million in employee development each year.

CIBC has recently undertaken a major effort to develop the tools and techniques to capture the intellectual capital necessary to succeed as a bank. The criterion for success is to "ensure that the rate of learning by individuals, teams, and the corporation as a whole must equal or exceed the pace of change in the external environment."

Michele Darling (1996), executive vice president of human resources, notes that much of CIBC's corporate knowledge is not collected. "It rests in people's heads. It is more than just facts; it includes experience and instinct, management style and the corporate culture. Organizing it — mapping it, making it available to others, seeking ways of increasing its usefulness — begins with lining up all the corporate systems against that goal, many of them logically rooted in human resource management and development."

The purpose of all knowledge management is improving output for the customer. It is not knowledge for knowledge's sake. At CIBC there are four levels for gathering knowledge and learning:

1. Individual Learning: The responsibility for continuous learning has to be placed on the individual. To assist, CIBC has mapped the knowledge requirements of each position in the organization — the theoretical understanding, skill sets, and experience required for each job — and electronically posts the requirements of all job vacancies. We provide a huge variety of methods for learning these requirements such as classrooms, correspondence courses, seminars, video and audio aids, reference material, and external courses. Employees choose the method most suited to their individual needs.

2. Team Learning: Task-focused employee groups also have to take responsibility for their learning. This means structures have to change; management responsibilities and styles are shifting from command-and-control to coaching, mentoring and advising, brokering team knowledge, and assessing the knowledge needs across the organization. Compensation systems have to reflect team success as well as individual success. Teams are expected to find ways of making sure the knowledge and ideas of all members are known and shared.

3. Organization Learning: Particularly across a large, multinational organization, "silos" of knowledge develop — useful to those inside them, but unknown and unavailable to others. Team successes and achievements — one team's potential contribution to another — have to be shared through learning networks.

4. Customer Learning: The organization and everyone in it need to know more about the customer and his or her evolving needs. For business customers, it means understanding their industry, their strategy and agenda, and providing solutions to their problems, rather than selling previously defined products and services. The process works both ways; customers need to know more about what banks can provide. For example, derivatives are a complex and valuable set of risk management tools, but often not well understood, even by

sophisticated corporate-finance managers. In the last year, more than 3400 clients have attended a formal derivatives school organized and run by CIBC Wood Gundy.

The Actions of Scanning and Importing New Information

Scanning the environment refers to those actions that organizations carry on that can be planned and/or unintentional. Important questions associated with scanning actions include what are the modes of scanning, who does the scanning, and under what conditions. Perceiving and choosing the sectors of the environment to be scanned are highly dependent on the organization's assumptions concerning their environment. However, as we move to a dynamic analysis of the processes, more concrete factors must also enter into our analysis of actions. One of these factors is the key relationship between executives/managers and their needs for information and the nature of the situation (as perceived by the executives/managers).

Martin's (1993) review of organizational scanning resulted in several relationships that are indicative of Daft and Weick's concerns of analyzability and intrusiveness. Table 5.1 delineates more specific potential causal relationships between managers' behaviors, the organization's need for information, and the nature of the perceived environment. From this summary table we see that the actions of those responsible for obtaining and interpreting information are a highly dynamic interaction governed by the assumptions of the organization.

Table 5.1 Managerial Scanning Behaviors: Indicators from Research

Analyzability	
Daft, Sormunen, and Parks, 1988	Strategic uncertainty is a predictor of the frequency with which top executives scan sectors.
	The perceived importance of an issue affected scanning behavior of executives.

continued

Table 5.1 (continued) Managerial Scanning Behaviors: Indicators from Research

---

Analyzability

Daft, Sormunen, and Parks, 1988 (continued)	Strategic uncertainty was a predictor of the frequency of scanning and the higher the uncertainty in the environmental sector the more frequently executives rely on personal modes both within and outside the organization (p. 133).
	In high-performance firms' chief executives increase their scanning through personal modes more than through written modes as strategic uncertainty increases (p. 134).
West, 1988	High-performance firms in both differentiation and low-cost strategies conducted greater amounts of scanning than low-performing firms.
Thomas, Clark, and Gioia, 1993	Top managers' attention to higher levels of information during scanning was related to their interpretation of strategic issues as positive and as implying potential gains; attention to a wide array of information tends to influence the interpretation of strategic issues positively (p. 258).
Aguilar, 1967	Information was obtained by and circulated among members of top management, that the information tended to be concerned with the immediate industrial environment; and that it was largely collected in the course of normal business operating activities (p. 148).
	Managers with different functional specialty showed a degree of specialization with respect to their use of outside sources. For example, marketing managers relied heavily on customers for external information; production managers relied heavily on suppliers; and so on (p. 95).
	In considering sources by level of responsibility, findings indicated that first-line managers had a high preference for nonmembers when compared to lower level managers; subordinates were regarded more highly as root sources of information at each higher level of responsibility; and at each higher level of responsibility, managers gained less important information from publications when compared to other sources; managers in large companies relied more heavily on internal sources than those in smaller companies.

Table 5.1 (continued) Managerial Scanning Behaviors: Indicators from Research

Analyzability	
Aguilar, 1967 (continued)	Information from outside sources was more unsolicited and information from inside sources was solicited. It was found that managers from larger companies were more active in soliciting external information from the outsiders. Larger organizations showed an increase in use of staff, internal communications, and institutionalized search units.

Knight-Ridder — Scanning to Meet the Challenges of Change

Knight-Ridder, with over 20,000 employees worldwide, is the nation's second-largest newspaper publisher, with products in print and online. The company publishes 31 daily newspapers in 28 U.S. markets, with a readership of 9.0 million daily and 12.6 million Sunday. To demonstrate the internal and external environment that Knight-Ridder is seeking to create for organizational learning, the following excerpts have been taken from the company's Web pages:

- Change is accelerating and the transformation of Knight-Ridder must keep pace. Our abundant challenges are more than matched by opportunities that dwarf our past. Our future is bounded only by our ambition. The commitment we make is to provide the highest standards of service to our customers and communities and to assure continued prosperity for our company and shareholders.
- Our success will stem from providing innovative and essential content and services to readers and advertisers. These strategies require a company with capacities for rapid change, flexibility, creativity, market focus, strategic thinking, and strong marketing and technology skills. We stand for excellent service to customers and communities, and a respectful and safe learning environment for all our employees.

All staff are expected to develop and display the following attributes in building organizational learning at Knight-Ridder:

1. External focus for gathering information: use market information to create tools for information gathering and analysis. Build relationships and form partnerships with current and potential advertisers, readers, and other information consumers — general market or business. Be personally involved in community activities or interaction with the community and use that knowledge to inform business strategy.
2. Strategic business knowledge: continually scan business and identify global and market trends.
3. Collaboration: ask for and hear feedback and data from others that challenge assumptions and behaviors.
4. Sharing learning: take responsibility for acquiring and sharing new skills, behaviors, and competencies. Coach others through the development process, share learning broadly throughout the organization, and vacillate learning from new opportunities and settings.
5. Nurturing innovation: foster an environment that inspires others to deal creatively with business and people problems. Reward and recognize innovation; develop capacity for identifying effective solutions.
6. Urgency: demonstrate sense of purpose by taking prompt action as issues emerge, pushing for closure and results. Share information while ideas are evolving.
7. Communicate vision: provide clearly articulated goals, values, and performance expectations that are integrated across levels, function, work processes, and other boundaries.
8. Flexibility: modify behavior effectively in new, changing, or ambiguous situations as needed.

The higher the variations in the environmental situation, the more we see variations in the modes of scanning and behaviors by manager and executives. However, the selection of sectors is also impacted by management cognition. We have to be aware that the interaction that we are proposing is not only dependent on organizational assumptions about the environment, but also may be dependent on the individual's (executive, manager, worker) orientation to their role within the organization (Figure 5.2).

A possible avenue for understanding this interaction is through the concept of human attribution. In one domain of attribution research, social

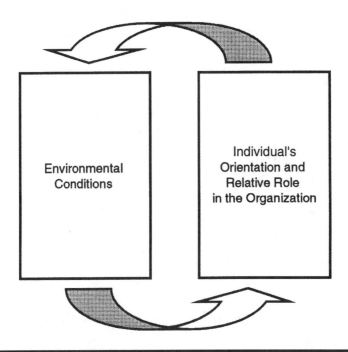

Figure 5.2 Interaction of Roles with the Environment

psychologists have focused attention on the tendency of people to attribute instances of personal success to internal, personal causes, and to attribute instances of personal failure to external, situational (environmental) causes. "Researchers describing the motivational underpinnings of self-serving bias have suggested that people attribute success more than failure to personal factors because they are motivated to protect the feelings of self-esteem, maintain a sense of mastery over their environment, or project favorable self-images to others" (Wagner and Gooding, 1997, p. 276).

An example of this phenomenon can be seen in the research of Wagner and Gooding. Their study of attribution of managers found that managers receiving equivocal information about the performance of an organization described as their own credited positive outcomes to organizational strengths and blamed negative outcomes on environmental threats. In contrast, managers receiving equivocal information about an organization described as managed by others associated positive outcomes with environmental opportunities and linked negative outcomes to organizational weaknesses. Both self-serving and actor-observer attribution patterns were thus detected (Wagner and Gooding, 1997).

Thomas and co-researchers (1993) also found that the type and quality of the information can influence the interpretation of strategic issues.

> Top managers' attention to higher levels of information during scanning was related to their interpretation of strategic issues as positive and as implying potential gains. Such information use during scanning was also associated with a heightened interpretation of strategic issues as controllable. These results, taken in tandem, imply that high information use strongly influences strategic interpretation; attention to a wide array of information tends to influence interpretation of strategic issues positively. (p. 258)

These results suggest that organizations must not only continuously examine how managers are noticing changes in their environments, but that noticing may have to lead to new understandings or changes in the personal schema of the managers themselves (Barr et al., 1992).

State Rehabilitation Service Agency — Perspectives Can Change

The connection between organizational scanning, environmental sector selection, and cultural assumptions can all be seen in the following study of a state rehabilitation service agency. The mission of the agency was to provide services to individuals with disabilities to assist them in achieving employment. The services included vocational counseling, personal counseling, education or retraining, medical and health services, and job placement assistance. Martin observed this organization during the reauthorization of the federal law under which the organization was authorized to provide these services. The new federal legislation required the organization to change its focus from primarily determining rehabilitation needs to one that demanded more involvement of the total rehabilitation-employment system. This created a large amount of perceived uncertainty in the agency's environment (Martin, 1993, p. 179).

> The findings of this study suggest that the themes of Inclusion, Recognition, Services (Employment and Timeliness), and Regulations are related to the scanning activities of the executives. It appears that these themes were related to the executive's scanning of the Customer Sector. The executives describe the federal act as meaning greater involvement

of persons with disabilities in the agency's planning and policy development processes, and greater involvement of clients in determining rehabilitation goals and selection of vendors for training and physical and mental restoration services.

The executives describe the importance of scanning the Customer Sector and receiving input from individuals with disabilities and clients. The findings also suggest that the Meaning and Memory Subsystems Interchange Media was influencing the Environmental Interface and selection of sources of information. The themes of Inclusion and Recognition were related to the executive's preference for personal sources. The executives spoke of the extensive use of persons with disabilities and advocates as sources of scanning information. The meaning schema ascribed by the executives to the 1992 Amendments to the Rehabilitation Act also included the theme of Service and its subtheme of Employment. The executives describe the act as meaning a "refocusing on employment" and they spoke of importance of scanning the employment sector. It appears that the Meaning and Memory Subsystem's Interchange Media, the meaning of Services (Employment), was affecting the direction that the organizational learning system was seeking to attend to and acquire information about in the external environment.

The sectors of the external environment that were identified by the executives as important for the organization to scan were the customer, employment, services, and regulatory sectors. Martin's identification of the organization's sensemaking patterns included the schema of inclusion, recognition, services, change, and regulations. These became the values and assumptions that the agency used in determining the environmental sectors to scan for new information. Among the executives, the customer and employment sectors were described as being the most important sectors for the organization to scan.

Figure 5.3 illustrates the relationship between the external environment sectors, actions of environmental interface subsystem of the learning system, and the sensemaking patterns emanating from the Memory and Meaning subsystem. Because the information from the Rehabilitation Act emphasized involvement and employment of the agency's clients, the relative criteria for environmental sector selection began to shift. The environmental sectors of customer and employment became dominant. This is a good example of learning. The organization was able to shift its attention and its values to sustain this change and deal with the uncertainty.

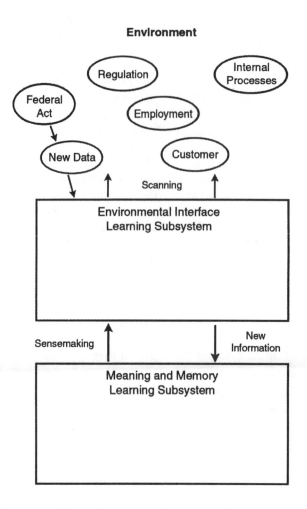

Figure 5.3 Learning System Interaction with Environment

If we consider Martin's analysis of the variations of the interactions between the scanners and the environment and the possibilities associated with attribution theory (Wagner and Gooding, 1997), we begin to understand the vulnerability of organizations to the screening potential of the actions associated with the Environmental Interface subsystem. Organizations must be open to multiple ways of scanning and of testing the viability of the selection of environmental sectors that they are using as their focus.

This necessitates a closer look at the modes of selection that are available to us for scanning our organizational environment.

Selecting Modes of Interfacing with the Environment

The nature of the new information and the importing process, because of the interchange nature of the media, impact the functions of Reflection, Dissemination and Diffusion, and the Memory and Meaning subsystems. Huber (1991), in creating a typology of organizational learning, put forth five basic categories of information importation:

> *Congenital* — this input process concerns existing information and transfer through the simple mechanisms of hereditary processes. In some cases, founding individuals account for this process of preexisting information.
>
> *Experimental* — these processes include things such as organizational experiments, organizational self-appraisal, unintentional or unsystematic processes that are often haphazard and multifaceted.
>
> *Vicarious* — these processes are directed at accumulating information through secondhand experience concerning other organizations, especially other technologies also included in the concept of imitation. Channels for bringing information into the organization include consultants, professional meetings, trade shows, publications, vendors and suppliers, and, in less competitive environments, networks of professionals.
>
> *Grafting* — these processes include mergers and acquisitions in which large amounts of information are brought in through the "capture" process. It also includes the acquisition of information through individuals and the hiring of expertise for consulting activities.
>
> *Searching and Noticing* — the processes involved in searching include scanning, focused search, and performance monitoring. Each of these becomes more specific with scanning certain sectors of the environment. Focused search is directed at more specifically defining problems that require solutions not within the existing knowledge. Finally, performance monitoring involves very specific information concerning the output and processes of the organization's operations.

Huber's classification emphasizes broad categories of action that organizations can employ to enhance their acquisition of new information. In the global environment we are seeing the increased use of what Huber may see as "grafting" modes of interface. The reliance on this mode of importing new information may be due to it having multiple advantages in attaining both information for the learning sustem and resources for the performance system simultaneously. However, the expediency of this process is not without difficulties; it is especially vulnerable to cultural barriers. We will discuss three of these modes of information importation: contingency work force, partnerships, and joint ventures.

Using Contingent Work for Importing New Information

One of the largest increases in the employment sector has been the use of contingent work. It consists of independent contractors, individuals brought in through employment agencies, on-call or day labor, and workers on site whose services are provided by contract firms, such as outsourced information technology workers.

Within this trend, contingent work in professional and technical functions is the most rapidly growing. Whereas 90% of firms use contingent work in some capacity, 43% use it in professional and technical functions that have the potential to impact core areas of the firm. Firms such as Microsoft outsource customer service and technical writing functions and use contingent work in the testing and debugging phase of its product development process (Cusumano and Selby, 1995).

Matusik and Hill (1998) see contingent work as an important mode for importing valuable performance, enhancing "public" knowledge into the firm. This serves to keep the organization connected to the "industrywide" information pool. Contingent work is a useful mechanism for bringing public knowledge into the firm and, therefore, of insuring that the firm has access to the same industry- and occupation-specific best practices as its informed competitors. We hypothesize that the magnitude of positive effect on public knowledge is determined by the individual worker's skill level and the firm's ability to integrate this knowledge. Thus, up to a point, the use of contingent work will increase the performance of the firm by virtue of the contingent worker's role as a conduit for bringing knowledge into the firm (Matusik and Hill, 1998, p. 687).

Positive effects of this mode of obtaining information are enhanced by the organization valuing the information and its usefulness. If people are not clear about the usefulness, then the transfer process will be hampered. Much of this receptivity to new information is dependent on the other subsystems of the organizational learning model (this will be addressed in subsequent chapters). This also reinforces the need to understand the nature of the environment. Matusik and Hill's work provides factors to consider as to when to use contingent work: (1) the value of flexibility in responding to changing market conditions and (2) the dynamics of the environment (competition, technology, etc.).

New Partnering Modes

The use of the partnering structure is not new to organizational theory. These partnerships range from the two individuals who join forces to achieve a mutual goal to the firm that has 1000 partners (for example, law firms and consulting firms). Many of these arrangements have been predicated on reasons that include resource needs, market control, risk dilution, and political advantages. More recently, these arrangements have also been based on organizational needs for information and knowledge that have to be met in very short time frames.

One way to expand boundaries of organizations is to form partnerships and then link the information from each individual into a common information system that can be used by all the partners. This type of construct forms the basis of many large consulting firms in which each partner enters information concerning his/her particular client encounters so that the information is available to other partners and their problem-solving needs. Although this concept of partnering appears to be an answer to the ever-increasing complexity of the environment, these firms are still dealing with Environmental Interface actions that will allow them to handle the equivocality of the large amount of information that is now available to the firm.

We are now finding that traditional partnerships that focused on the dividing of profits derived from a joint effort are now taking on new emphasis. "In a world economy manufacturers are fighting for their lives in many industries, and the reason for that is the manufacturer often doesn't know what the customer wants," says John Jack, vice president of corporate development and marketing for Minneapolis-based Business Incentives Inc., a full-service incentive house. "We haven't stopped to form alliances properly with the people who meet consumers face to face: the retailers. If you work properly with the retailer, you get closer to the customer" (Brewer, 1992, p. 15).

Inkpen and Crossan's classic study of American/Japanese joint ventures and their ability to exploit the learning opportunities reinforces the importance of the interchange media and its relationship to providing new information for the organization. The study included all North American/Japanese joint ventures located in North America that were suppliers to automakers in North America.

These new partnerships are comprised of organizations that occupy sequential steps in the chain of events that goes from product development to selling the product. They include supplier/retailer activities to increase the understanding of the mutual dependence that each has with the other. In addition, these partnerships allow for more accurate and abundant information about customers.

Cautious consumers are increasingly demanding more information from retailers about the products they sell. Many manufacturers are responding by training retail salespeople to be more knowledgeable about their inventory and more responsive to customer inquiries. The cornerstone of the relationship lies on a foundation of flexibility, shared information, thinking long term, and developing a trust between the parties. Manufacturers themselves are becoming far more informed than they have been in the past about consumer demands and buying habits (Brewer, 1992, p. 48).

Whirlpool — Building Learning Partnerships

To gain in its ability to delight the customer, Whirlpool has emphasized to staff the importance of learning from the customer. Success, according to Wigwam, means understanding better than anyone in the industry the present and future needs of consumers and trade partners. Whirlpool believes that its research in these areas is the most exhaustive in the home appliance industry.

By paying consumers to "play around" with appliances at its Usability Lab in Comerio, Italy, Whirlpool discovered that microwave oven sales would improve if it introduced a model that browned food. The result: Whirlpool developed the VIP Crisp. Now, it's Europe's best seller, and Whirlpool recently began making it in the U.S.

Whirlpool recognizes that to do business successfully in a geographic region requires a thorough understanding of consumers and the market as a whole. In Asia, for example, Whirlpool recently conducted focus group sessions with 1000 consumers in nine countries, surveys among 6500 households, 700 consumer discussions in four countries, and other extensive research through economic, diplomatic, and regulatory sources. Whirlpool has also benchmarked other Western companies that have been successful in the Asia region, among them Motorola, Proctor & Gamble, AT&T, Emerson, Westinghouse, Hewlett-Packard, and McDonald's.

Whirlpool has also developed close learning relationships with organizations in related businesses such as Proctor & Gamble and Unilever. In these and other partnerships there are exchanges of not only basic information and ideas, but also more intensive involvement at the development, engineering, and technology levels.

As Whirlpool enters into the People's Republic of China, it is prepared to share its expertise in technology, manufacturing, human resources management, innovative product designs, and such modern infrastructure support as information technology. Overall, the potential for long-term links between Whirlpool and the People's Republic of China is enormous and mutually beneficial.

As a world leader in establishing trade partnerships, Whirlpool has strategic agreements with three of the top four major domestic retailers in North America, three of the top five in Europe, and most leading retailers in South America. These partnerships have produced significant learnings and driven Whirlpool's business success.

These new types of partnering for information and knowledge are not limited to large consulting firms and manufacturing–retail chains; they also include education institutional partnerships, specialized centers and institutes, applied research initiatives, and employer-sponsored training programs and courses. One type of partnership relation that has received focused attention, especially in the global market, is the joint venture.

Joint Ventures as Environmental Interface Actions

The ambiguous nature of international ventures occurs not just because of the geographical constraints or the complexity of the substance of product; it is also hampered by the movement of information and knowledge. It is true that information flow can be hampered by geographical constraints and the complexity of the product. However, for many corporations, cross-cultural boundaries are now turning to join ventures as a mechanism to aid in solving both the performance and learning problems associated with international/global processes. Another mode of interfacing to increase the flow of information is the joint venture (JV).

JVs and alliances are becoming common as we begin to restructure for the global economy. The definition of a joint venture is "a means of performing activities and combination with one or more firms instead of autonomously. A JV occurs when two or more distinct firms (parents) pool a portion of their resources within a separate, jointly owned organization. This definition excludes other forms of cooperative agreements such as licensing distribution and supply agreements, research and development partnerships, or technical assistance and management contracts" (Inkpen and Crossan, 1995, p. 596).

Interviews were conducted with 58 managers associated with 40 JVs which represent a response rate of 80% of all ventures participating in the study. Broadly speaking, all of the JVs were formed to strengthen existing business. The Japanese partners were usually responsible for implementing the manufacturing process, installing the equipment, and supplying the product technology. Consequently, the JVs provide the American partners with a unique opportunity to study a new, state-of-the-art organization that would not have been possible without a collaborative relationship. Second, the JVs were often the American partners' initial experience in supplying Japanese automakers.

This study resulted in three key findings directly related to the JV as a mode for importing new information (Inkpen and Crossan, 1994):

1. Managers in the American parent companies frequently pointed to the poor financial performance of the JVs as evidence that learning was not occurring or could occur. The Japanese parents, on the other hand, generally had longer time horizons and different expectations regarding JV performance. More generally, a preoccupation with short-term issues was a common characteristic of the American partner (p. 612).
2. Thus a key factor in a firm's ability to absorb new skills is a sufficiently complex managerial belief system with which to notice and appreciate firm differences (p. 613).
3. Most of the American firms in the study formed their JVs with the objective of learning from their Japanese partners; their expectations

often were to learn "what" the Japanese knew, rather than "how" and "why" the Japanese firms new what they knew (p. 614).

Inkpen and Crossan found three types of mechanisms that can promote individual to collective integration of information:

- Personal facilitation by leaders to enhance the development of shared schema
- Shared common ground between partners to enhance trust and respect of one another
- Organization systems and structures to act as integrating mechanisms

This research again points to the importance of a role of managers as linking mechanisms with the environment. It is not only the manager's role, it is the general assumptions about the nature of the environment that influence all members of the organization. If the individuals perceive their environments as threats and complex (which is indicative of global, cross-cultural ventures), then the interpretation of information and the openness to multiple sectors in the environment will suffer. This in turn will lead to less, or poor, quality of new information and will lower the capacity of the organization to learn.

Scenario Planning and Collaboration at Royal Dutch/Shell

Royal Dutch/Shell, with a market capitalization of $178 billion, $128 billion in annual revenues, 101,000 employees, and operations in 130 countries around the globe, ranks as one of the world's largest and most successful companies. One perceived reason for Royal Dutch/Shell's superior performance is its use of strategic organizational learning tools such as scenario forecasting. Through use of such technologies, Royal Dutch/Shell has become known as a premier learning organization in its pursuit scanning for information and its understanding of trends in the global business/economic environment.

Arie de Geus, former coordinator of group planning for Royal Dutch/Shell and leader in the development of scenario forecasting, has described the process as one in which management teams change their shared mental models of their company, their markets, and their competitors. Graham Galer of Royal Dutch/Shell notes that "Sophisticated decision making and forecasting alone fail to perceive unexpected influences that come at a project 'sideways' — the unforeseen variables that do not arise in a standard mental model. Scenarios constantly rehearse possible pathways into the future and build sets of mental models through which managers can enrich the corporate one-track mind" (Brenneman et al., 1998). Through the use of scenario forecasting and planning, organizations have begun to view planning as learning and learning as planning.

Systemic plans, based on forecasts from history, can be accurate when times are stable. But since the world business environment is often turbulent and volatile, Royal Dutch/Shell developed "scenario planning," an alternative tool for looking at the future. Anticipatory planners write imaginary stories about the future concluding with multiple scenarios. Guided by such scenarios and aided by other organizational strengths, Royal Dutch/Shell comfortably survived the petroleum crisis of the 1970s.

In 1968, Shell undertook a study of the year 2000, analyzing the question, "Is there life after oil?" One scenario developed was the possibility of $15 for a barrel of oil, a seemingly disastrous scenario in a world of $28 to $30 for a barrel of oil. When oil actually dropped to the $15 level Shell weathered the storm better than their competitors because they had anticipated the possibility and made tentative plans for the downturn. Through scenario forecasting, Shell developed a team of highly diverse experts that brought varying knowledge to planning efforts.

Throughout the world Shell encourages decentralization and increased collaboration with operating companies, with global clients, and others with whom Shell can share technology. All Shell business lines with suppliers, clients, and/or significant shared technologies are in transition toward more active "interaffiliate" collaboration. That means increased intercultural and transnational interaction with increasingly shared (or understood and respected, if different) learning from culturally diverse experiences (Brenneman et al., 1998).

In 1998 when the APQC teamed with the American Society of Training and Development to conduct a "Global Best Practice Study of Leadership Development," it is not surprising that Shell was chosen as a model for its commitment to learning and its emphasis on applying learning tools to actual corporate challenges. Royal Dutch/Shell, the parent company, appears to be a model of a learning company, partially because it has survived for over 100 years, but more especially because it seems to be exemplifying some of the criteria that de Geus found present in similar long-lived companies. It is navigating the turbulent whitewater of environmental changes through its ability to gather and apply new information.

The Subsystem that Imports Energy

Like any system, the organizational learning system must import energy to survive. New information is the energy that is provided through the actions associated with the Environmental Interface subsystem of actions. The relationship to the other subsystems is accomplished through the use of the interchange media. We saw examples of this in the patterns established between the perceptions of the environment (sensemaking) and new information, and also the relationship between joint ventures (structuring) and new information. Organizations such as PricewaterhouseCoopers, Whirlpool, Andersen, Shell, Knight-Ridder, and Canadian Imperial Bank of Commerce have been cited as world leaders in developing and implementing this subsystem. We will now turn to a discussion of the Action/Reflection subsystem, the nucleus of the Organizational Learning Systems Model.

References

Aguilar, F. J., *Scanning the Business Environment*, Macmillan, New York, 1967.

Barr, P.S., Stimpert, J.L., and Huff, A.S., Cognitive change, strategic action, and organizational renewal, *Strategic Management Journal*, 13, 15–36, 1992.

Brenneman, W., Keys, B., and Fulmer, R., Learning across a living company: the Shell companies experience, *Organizational Dynamics*, 27(2), 61–69, 1998.

Brewer, G., Promoting partnerships, *Incentive*, March, p. 15, 1992.

Capers, R. S., NASA post Hubble: too little, too late?, *Academy of Management Executive*, 8(2), 68–72, 1994.

Coolidge, S. D., "Temping" is now a career — with an upside for workers, *Christian Science Monitor*, October 1996.

Cusumano, M. A. and Selby, R. W., *Microsoft Secrets*, Free Press, New York, 1995.

Daft, R. L. and Weick, K. E., Toward a model of organizations as interpretation systems, *Academy of Management Review*, 9(2), 284–295, 1984.

Daft, R., Sormunen, J., and Parks, D., Chief executive scanning, environmental characteristics and company performance: an empirical study, *Strategic Management Journal*, 9(2) 123–139, 1988.

Darling, M., Building the knowledge organization, *The Business Quarterly*, 61(2), 61–71, 1996.

Huber, G. P. and Crossan, M. M., Believing is seeing: joint ventures and organization learning, *Journal of Management Studies*, 32(5) 595–618, 1995.

Marquardt, M., *Building the Learning Organization*, McGraw-Hill, New York, 1996.

Martin, T. J., A Study of the Relationship of Organizational Meaning and Environmental Scanning. Case Study, Human Resource Development, George Washington University, Washington, D.C., 1993.

Matusik, S. F. and Hill, C. W. L., The utilization of contingent work, knowledge creation, and competitive advantage, *Academy of Management Review*, 23(4), 680–697, 1998.

Thomas, J. B., Clark, S. M., and Gioia, D. A., Strategic sensemaking and organizational performance: linkage among scanning, interpretation, action and outcome, *Academy of Management Journal*, 36(2), 239–270, 1993.

Wagner, J. A. and Gooding, R. Z., Equivocal information and attribution: an investigation of patterns of managerial sensemaking, *Strategic Management Journal*, 18(4), 275–286, 1997.

Weick, K., *The Social Psychology of Organizing*, 2nd ed., McGraw-Hill, New York, 1979.

6 The Dynamics of Knowledge Creation: The Action/Reflection Subsystem

Reflection is the capacity to "notice oneself noticing"; that is, to step back and see one's mind working in relation to its projects.

Peter B. Vaill

Linking Knowledge to Action

In the cover story of *The Straits Times*, the daily newspaper of Singapore, under the headline "Rise of the Knowledge Society" (Thompson, 1993), Peter Drucker, the famed management "guru," noted that the move from an industrial society to a knowledge society is characterized not by a loss in value of productivity or products, but by equally valuing knowledge and its potential in developing the society. "Knowledge today must prove itself in action." Knowledge in and of itself is important, but in this transformation from the industrial age to the knowledge age, it is even more important to see the link between knowledge and action. They are inseparable and equally important elements.

Actions and knowledge occur in context of both the global and a local society. The world is no longer looking at knowledge; it must look at "knowledges." This multiple, global perspective of knowledge requires a set of competencies from individuals and organizations to transform information into valued goal reference knowledge.

Knowledge creation is a very complex construct. It occurs at the individual, the organizational, and the societal level. At each of these levels we encounter human dynamics that are dependent on the type of information that the organization receives, the structure of the organization as it processes the information, and the culture as it makes sense and assigns meaning to the information. All of these dynamic processes result in the creation of knowledge that is linked to the organization's actions and goals that support its survival.

The Action/Reflection subsystem describes the organization's actions and examines those actions that enable it to assign meaning to new information, and in doing so creates Goal Reference Knowledge. Thus, the organization creates valued knowledge by reflecting on new information. This subsystem functions as the nucleus of the organizational learning system. The processes in this core function are heavily dependent on dynamic interactions of the organizational social system.

The organization can employ three different perspectives in its reflection: (1) it reflects on the processes used in their actions; that is the "how" we do things; (2) it reflects on the content or results of its actions; this requires the answering questions of cause–effect relations or the "what" we do; (3) the deepest perspective that organizations can reflect at is the underlying premise of their actions; this requires answering questions about "why" they do what they do (or did).

Each of these perspectives requires successively deeper introspection on the part of the organization. Each combines with a level of action to create knowledge that supports the learning process. Many organizations feel comfortable with inquiry into the "how" and "what" of their actions. However, the "why" questions require examination of the assumptions and values that underlie the actions of the organization. This is usually very difficult for the organization because it leads to questioning its cultural foundations and purposes.

Reflection by the organization means that some, or all, individuals in the organization review, judge, and decide on issues in the name of the organization. It doesn't always have to be the managers and executives — it can be at any organizational level. However, the need for the survival of the organization and the need to create knowledge that will help achieve its goals guide these processes and people.

Solving Problems via Action/Reflection at General Electric

Probably one of the most well-known and successful of all corporate action/reflection programs is GE's WorkOut, which began in 1989. Among the key goals of WorkOut are

- Solve critical systems-wide problems.
- Develop learning capacities of employees.
- Improve responsiveness to customers.
- Minimize vertical and horizontal barriers.
- Rid the company of boundaries and needless bureaucracy.

WorkOut is also seen as an opportunity to provide GE professionals with a broad array of functional experiences in organizational learning.

WorkOuts generally occur over a 3-day period and involve a group of 40 to 100 people who meet at a conference center or hotel. Sessions begin with a talk by CEO Jack Welch or another leader who roughs out a problem agenda for them to fix and then leaves. An outside facilitator breaks the group into action learning sets to tackle various parts of the agenda. Over the next 2 days the groups identify solutions and prepare presentations for the final day.

On the third day, the GE executive returns and takes a place in front of the room. One by one, the teams present their proposals. The rules of Work-Out require the executive to make only one of three responses: (1) agree on the spot, (2) say "no," or (3) ask for more information — in which case the person must charter a team to get it by an agreed-upon date. Almost always, the response is a "yes" since a "no" answer would need great reasoning and would destroy the tremendous power and value of the WorkOuts.

Goals of the Organizational Learning System

The goal of the organizational learning system is defined as transforming of information into valued knowledge. This in turn increases the adaptive capacity of the organization in a changing environment. Goal reference knowledge is the interchange media output of the Action/Reflection sub-

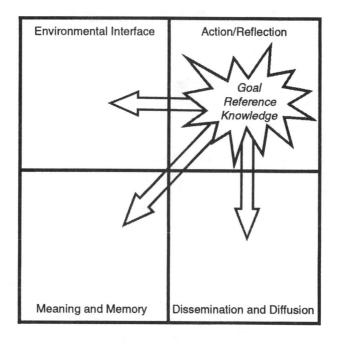

Figure 6.1 Action/Reflection Output is Goal Reference Knowledge

system of actions (see Figure 6.1). We must be careful here to differentiate between two sets of goals: there are those goals associated with the actions of the organization's performance system, and there are the goals associated with the organization's learning system. In a general sense, the objectives of both sets of goals are identical — the changing of the organization with the purpose of survival. However, the goal of the learning system is to adapt through learning, while the goal of the performance system is to adapt through performance.

An example of goal reference knowledge can be seen in the results of a test, or pilot, of an organizational production process. The evaluation by the organization of the test constitutes the collective's reflection on the production process (action). This in turn creates knowledge that is referenced to both the goals of the performance system and the goals of the organizational learning system. This knowledge is needed by the other learning subsystems for dissemination-diffusion, meaning creation and memory storage, and as a reference for the environmental interface subsystem to scan for new information.

The concept of knowledge and its continuous creation is vital to the survival of the organization. The ability to reflect on information is not only critical to the organization's performance, it is also the key to its self-regeneration. The Action/Reflection subsystem of actions provides the path for altering cultural values and assumptions so that the organization can achieve long-term adaptation. The remainder of this chapter will integrate the concept of knowledge, its types and modes of creation, with the dynamic actions of the organization.

"Knowledge by Any Other Name" — Types of Knowledge

The term "knowledge" can be used at various levels of action. It can be used at the level of routine actions that characterize the day-to-day operations of the organization. In many situations these are governed by standard operating procedures. Another level includes all other actions that have no routine nature and require unique actions. At this level actions are not very predictable, but yet they are perceived by the organization as having significant impact on their adaptive capacities and may be of major magnitude. Reflection on these actions exists at both levels, however, in different forms and intensity.

Routines Are Efficient ... But

The human mind is limited as to the number of variables that it can deal with simultaneously. Even when we put many individuals into an organizational structure, they are still limited. To simplify this complexity, organizations establish processes that have routine. These routines provide standard operating procedures because we have found that certain tasks are repetitive and do not require new or intensive reflection — "don't reinvent the wheel."

Normally, routine actions don't generate very much knowledge; they usually consume it. They do, however, require a minimum amount of reflection, but only at a low-level perspective (how or what). The use of routines is meant to purposefully limit our need for reflection on "everything," so that we can use our reflection power to focus on unique and major issues. As Winter (1985) proclaims, this is not always the case:

> Routinized competence clearly does not dictate inattention to considerations that fall outside of the scope of the routines; in fact, it should make possible higher levels of attention to such considerations. But the wider the range of situations subsumed by the routines and the better the routinized performance, the fewer reminders there are that something besides routinized competence might on occasion be useful or even essential to survival. (p. 111)

Routines can blind organizations to new options. They can even retard progress on important advances in a research environment.

Garud and Rappa (1994) describe the development of the cochlear implant, an electronic biomedical device that provides the profoundly deaf a sensation of sound. This case, not unlike many cases of discovery, hinged upon differences in approaches to the development of an implanted device for increasing the ability to not only understand differences in sound, but to recognize speech. The differences in the approaches consisted of the number of electrodes that would be inserted into the ear and the extent of physiological intrusion that was required to restore speech recognition as opposed to speech discrimination.

The research began in 1973 with two different research centers moving with two different sets of expectations of the cochlear outcome. They were also developing test routines that were specific to the design around the efficacy of their own expectations. It was not until 1988 that the National Institute of Health and the Food and Drug Administration held a consensus-developing conference in which the multichannel stimulation produced superior recognition performance compared with single-channel stimulation. Once this dialogue was achieved, progress in the development of the implant was attained.

> The authors draw some very important points about the roles of routines and their pitfalls. The evidence suggests that there is a reciprocal interaction between beliefs, artifacts, and routines that gives rise to two cyclic processes, one is a process of inversion at the micro level of individual cognition wherein evaluation routines designed to judge specific artifacts began reinforcing researchers' beliefs. Once evaluation routines become the basis for constructing individual reality, technological claims are perceived as relevant only to those who employ the same routines while becoming noise to those who employ different routines. The other is a process of institutionalization at the macro level of shared cognition. By institutionalizing we mean the development of

a common set of evaluation routines that can be applied to all technological paths. Commonly accepted evaluation routines represent a
shared reality that strongly shaped the direction of future technological
change (Garud and Rappa, 1994, p. 344).

These findings point to a disconnect. The research scientists must create
and believe in their own reality so that they can pursue the development of
the technology. But at the same time they must also be open to criticize their
own realities when new information becomes available. As we begin to examine the dynamic interaction of reflecting processes used to create goal
reference knowledge, we must be cognizant of the stress placed on the organization's readiness to question itself and its routines.

Levitt and March saw organizations as learning by encoding inferences
from history into routines that guide the organization's behavior. These
routines should change in response to direct organizational experiences
through trial and error and search for new routines. However, once an
organization has a routine and becomes very proficient at that routine that
it meets with success, it continues to use the same routine and may stop
searching; this in turn increases the use of the routine. Levitt and March
labeled this behavior the "competency trap:" " … competency traps can
occur when favorable performance with an inferior procedure leads an
organization to accumulate more experience with it, thus keeping experience with a superior procedure inadequate to make it rewarding to use"
(Levitt and March, 1988, p. 322).

We worked in an organization that provides an example of the competency trap. This organization, a large health insurance company, had all of
its management trained in a particular method of conducting meetings. The
method was very formal and required that an agenda (prescribed by a template) be prepared at the beginning of each and every meeting. The managers
became very good at this process. This routine became a habit for the managers. Even though many privately criticized the procedures, they continued
to apply it in all situations because "it's the way we do it here."

Although the highly structured meeting procedure surely had a time and
place, it also, if inappropriately applied, would curtail open thinking, creativity, and the creation of knowledge. The organization "becomes committed
to a particular set of routines; the routines to which it becomes committed
are determined more by early, relatively arbitrary, action than by information
gained from the learning situation" (Levitt and March, 1988, p. 324).

Organizational Learning at Spring Branch Schools

Surprisingly, schools often are the last places to implement organizational learning. The Spring Branch Independent School District, located within a 44-mile area of west Houston, is a startling exception. With an operating budget of over $200 million, 31,000 students, and 4000 employees, Spring Branch, like many school systems in the U.S., has witnessed tremendous changes in the past decade. While it has some of the wealthiest residential areas in the city, over half its student population is on free and reduced lunch. Almost half the district is Hispanic, and for many of these students English is a second language. Nearly one third of the children are economically disadvantaged.

Enrollment is increasing with three new elementary schools being opened in the past few years. Middle schools and high schools are quickly exceeding building capacity and new facilities will need to be created. Growing student needs are not able to be matched by corresponding financial resources (e.g., state funding per student has dropped by nearly 70% in the past 10 years). Becoming a learning organization has become essential, and thus Spring Branch recently established a learning organization initiative (LOI).

The LOI is a multiyear organizational development plan designed to build "a community of learners through individual learning, team learning, and districtwide organizational learning." The LOI fosters a work culture that:

- Reflects on its actions and learnings
- Empowers employees to learn and create
- Makes learning intentional at all times and in all locations
- Models trust in day-to-day operations
- Provides training opportunities for all employees

LOI moves the district beyond the individual successes of established practices to a more systemic approach by focusing on the collective learning and contributions of each district employee. Student success is the result of complex interactions of every part of the school system — districtwide and school leadership, bus routes, curriculum, food services, assessment, parental involvement, etc. All of these parts must be critically examined to determine the influence on one another and on student learning. Unless both individual learning and organizational learning are addressed simultaneously and support one another, the gains made in one area may be canceled by continuing problems in another area (Andersen and Boutwell, 1998).

The purpose of the LOI is to increase the district's ability to make the most of its employees' talents and resources, and to establish acceptance in the work culture of continuous change and learning in the way the district conducts its daily business. The district's ability to meet 21st century challenges will occur only if ongoing change in the work culture of the district is present. The district must "operate and think not only for today, but also for the changing world of tomorrow."

The learning organization initiative consists of five components:

1. An "Increasing Human Effectiveness" program designed to assist employees in realizing individual potential and personal growth. Skills being developed include goal setting, self-reflection, self-evaluation, and self-efficacy.
2. Steven Covey's "Seven Habits of Highly Effective People" program which fosters development of habits that assist people to move to collaborative interactions and effectiveness in the workplace. Capabilities being developed include self-direction, problem solving, and personal effectiveness.
3. Vertical leadership teams that include improved team thinking, evaluation and learning, and self-managed teams.
4. Senge's five disciplines of shared vision, mental models, personal mastery, systems thinking, and team learning.
5. A learning organization center that is a facility that houses learning laboratories designed to examine what it actually takes to improve work with a focus on organizational learning and applying systems thinking (Andersen and Boutwell, 1998).

Spring Branch recognizes that organizational learning is an ongoing journey that builds a community of learners through individual, team, and organizationwide learning. The final goal is a work and learning environment that will reflect:

- Individuals who feel valued and continuously adapt, improve, and learn
- Individuals who are responsible for their own learning and development
- High-performing teams that incorporate optimal strategies for learning
- A work environment that demonstrates and models a commitment to learning and success

As a result of Spring Branch Independent School District's efforts in organizational learning, it has received numerous awards and acknowledgments:

- World Initiative on Lifelong Learning award (1997)
- *Certificate for Achievement for Excellence in Financial Reporting*, the highest form of recognition in the area of government accounting and financial reporting
- Fifteen of the schools — recipients of the U.S. Department of Education's Blue Ribbon Award for being the Nation's Best
- Spring Branch Independent School District's Police Department recognized for safety and use of technology, with recognition by Sam Houston State University as one of the best districts in Texas
- Recipient of "What Parents Want" award from SchoolMatch
- In a recent communitywide survey, 85% rating the overall quality of their schools as excellent or good
- Numerous teachers named as Texas Teachers of the Year
- 27 National Merit Semifinalists in 1997–1998

Knowledge — Even If I See It, Will I Know It?

Before we move to actions that can help the organization increase its reflectivity, we must have a better understanding of what constitutes goal reference knowledge. We will now discuss different perspectives on what constitutes "organizational knowledge" beyond simple routines as well as examine why the process of reflecting is so difficult for organizations.

The title of this section is a play on Karl Weick's famous retrospective assignment of meaning phrase, "How can I know what I think till I see what I say?" (Weick, 1979, p. 5). This phrase signifies the complex, and sometimes ambiguous, nature of knowledge. It has a wide spectrum of meanings and attributions. It is enacted, retrospective, tacit, explicit, structured, socially constructed, useful, goal referenced, and culturally based, just to mention a few attributes. The thing that makes this so perplexing is that, at times, they are all accurate in their portrayal of organizational knowledge. To avoid some of this ambiguity, this section will discuss only three general dimensions of knowledge that are related to the dynamic actions of the organization and are associated with the interchange media: (1) tacit and explicit knowledge, (2) culturally based knowledge, and (3) knowledge structures and mapping.

Tacit and Explicit Knowledge

One of the major problems associated with knowledge creation and management is applying appropriate processes that will identify and objectify knowledge that is not apparent or visible; this means the movement of tacit knowledge into explicit knowledge. Michael Polanyi, although primarily focused on the individual level of analysis, provides us with one of the better definitions of these types of knowledge. His distinction between these two is that tacit knowledge is personal, context-specific, and therefore hard to formalize and communicate; explicit knowledge, or "codified" knowledge, on the other hand, refers to knowledge that can be transmitted by formal systematic language (Polanyi, 1966).

We will examine two approaches to the relationship between tacit knowledge and explicit knowledge. First we will examine Nonaka's transformational approach, and second we will discuss Spender's more specific analysis of knowledge with respect to the individual and the organization.

Nonaka's Knowledge Creation Model

Nonaka's central theme is that organizational knowledge is created through a continuous dialogue between tacit and explicit knowledge. He argues that while individuals develop new knowledge, organizations play a critical role in articulating and amplifying that knowledge.

The assumption that knowledge is created through conversion between tacit and explicit knowledge allows him to postulate four different "modes" of knowledge conversion.

- From tacit knowledge to tacit knowledge
- From explicit knowledge to explicit knowledge
- From tacit knowledge to explicit knowledge
- From explicit knowledge to tacit knowledge

Each of the four modes of knowledge conversion can create new knowledge independently. The central theme of the model of organizational knowledge creation proposed here hinges on a dynamic interaction between different modes of knowledge conversion. These interactions result in four types of knowledge for the organization:

- Externalization outputs "conceptual knowledge," such as using metaphor to encourage creative thinking.
- Socialization yields what can be called "sympathize knowledge" such as shared mental models and technical skills.
- Internalization produces "operational knowledge" about project management, production processes, new product usage, and policy implementation. This knowledge starts off very concrete, however may become more taken for granted as time moves on.
- Combination gives rise to "systemic knowledge" such as prototypes and new technology engineering — very concrete in nature (Nonaka and Takeuchi, 1995).

Knowledge creation centers on a building of both tacit and explicit knowledge and, more importantly, on the interchange between these two aspects of knowledge through internalization, socialization, combination, and externalization. There is a dynamic nature of the interactions between the tacit and explicit nature of knowledge. Although the focus of Nonaka's model is on the individual actions, he sees a continuous movement between the interactions that portrays the organizational level of analysis.

Matsushita — A Possibility-Searching Company

Matsushita Electric Industrial is the world's largest consumer electronics maker selling audiovisual and computer products, home appliances, household equipment, electric motors, and air conditioners in more than 180 countries. The Matsushita group includes more than 200 overseas affiliates in about 45 countries. In 1998 sales topped $59 billion with over 275,000 employees. Matsushita decided to become "a possibility-searching company" with goals in the following four areas:

1. Human innovation business — business that creates new lifestyles based on creativity, comfort, and joy in addition to efficiency and convenience
2. Humanware technology — technology for human innovation business
3. Active heterogeneous group — a corporate culture based on individuality and diversity

4. Multilocal and global networking management — a corporate structure that enables both localization and global synergy

Nonaka and Takeuchi (1995), in their classic *The Knowledge-Creating Company*, demonstrate how Matsushita took the knowledge it created in various projects and spiraled that knowledge throughout Matsushita. The learnings that took place in the Cooking Appliances division eventually affected corporate strategy. Matsushita was thus better able to (1) identify the type of knowledge required by the changing competitive environment and (2) enhance the enabling conditions continuously.

Nonaka and Takeuchi postulated that the company's success points out four key aspects of knowledge creation:

1. Leveraging the tacit knowledge base of an individual and making use of socialization to transfer it throughout the organization (for example, the head baker's kneading skill leading to the development of the bread-making machine) is a highly valuable activity. By its very nature, tacit knowledge is hard to communicate, but critical. Socialization is very important as a means to share tacit knowledge between individuals. Tacit skills are learned by observation and imitation, thus engineers had to experience the actual bread-making process to learn the kneading skill.
2. Amplifying knowledge creation across different levels in the organization led to the creation of "Human Electronics" and a series of successful products that embodied that concept. In order to make knowledge creation truly dynamic, knowledge created at one level needs to be amplified across different levels of the organization. Only by cross-leveling can companies obtain the true benefits of organizational knowledge creation. The knowledge created in developing the Home Bakery unit spiraled itself to create new knowledge at the corporate level.
3. Enhancing the enabling conditions promotes the four modes of knowledge conversion. Matsushita (1) increased redundancy and requisite variety by providing the R&D people with up-to-date sales information; (2) brought autonomy back to the divisions by restructuring organization; and (3) instilled intentions and creative chaos into the organization by setting challenging goals, represented by the sift to multimedia or the improvement of productivity by 30%.

4. Continuing to create knowledge continually requires continuous innovation. Because the competitive environment and customer preferences change constantly, existing knowledge becomes obsolete quickly. The continuous upgrading of organizational intention or values is important since new knowledge must be constantly justified against the latest intention.

Matsushita recognized the importance of self-organizing teams in the organizational learning process. Knowledge-creation started when members of each team shared tacit knowledge on what types of work employees at Matsushita should do and shouldn't do to utilize their creativity fully. The teams also analyzed existing work patterns and uncovered causes of inefficiencies. Matsushita realized that teams must be given full autonomy to better develop ideas for improvement. Redundancy helped members of the teams by providing common language about which to share their tacit knowledge.

Knowledge was also created when Matsushita installed a new communication infrastructure, called Market-Oriented Total Management System (MTM), that connected R&D, factories, and retail stores online. The company realized that the greatest knowledge-creation resides in the free flow and sharing of information among different functional groups. Under this system, the sales and manufacturing departments shared the same explicit knowledge (i.e., sales information at retail stores). MTM allowed product development teams to obtain instant feedback on how well a particular product or model sold at retail. Development people could thus develop a variety of "what if" solutions more precisely in anticipation of customer reactions.

Spender's Types of Knowledge

Spender's typology expands on the relationship between implicit and explicit knowledge by delineating them at both the individual and social (organizational) levels. Individual knowledge can be either conscious or automatic. Automatic knowledge is implicit knowledge that "happens by itself" and is often taken for granted or intuitive. Conscious knowledge may be codified, perhaps as a set of notes, and is potentially available to other people. Socially explicit knowledge is evaluated according to institutional standards of truth, such as the cochlear implants, and therefore becomes objectified. Collective, social implicit knowledge is of a social or communal nature and is exemplified in cultural assumptions and values.

Other organizational learning researchers (Tsoukas, 1996) have criticized the separation of explicit and tacit knowledge. "Knowledge types therefore must be classified on a continuum that ranges from explicit knowledge embodied in specific products and processes to tacit knowledge acquired through experience and embodied in individual cognition and organizational routine" (Inkpen and Dinur, 1998, p. 456).

Both Nonaka and Spender have spotlighted the dynamic social actions that the organization must possess so that it can bridge the gap between tacit and explicit organizational knowledge. Each of them see the individual and the organization involved in a very complex system of dynamic social interchange when it comes to creating knowledge. These interchanges result in different types of knowledge. This transformation process, and therefore the type of knowledge that results, is highly dependent on the cultural context of the reflection dynamics.

The "Secret" May Be in the Cultural Transformation

To increase the capacity of the organization's learning system, the social dynamics of the organization must encourage the evaluation and valuation of new information, both tacit and explicit. The secret to this process is locked in the cultural assumptions of the organization. Sonja Sackmann (1998) postulates existence of "commonly held cognitions which stimulate the form of cultural knowledge." From this perspective, she also defines four different kinds of knowledge that come together to form a cultural map that is indicative of a specific organization:

1. Dictionary knowledge — commonly held descriptions (labels and sets of words used in particular organizations); refers to the level of "what."
2. Directory knowledge — commonly held descriptive, not prescriptive, practices; refers to the level of "how."
3. Recipe knowledge — based on judgments, refers to prescriptions for repair and improvement strategies; refers to the level of "should."
4. Axiomatic knowledge — reasons and explanations of the final causes perceived to underlie a particular event; refers to the level of "why."

Using this classification framework, Sackmann's research revealed the presence of multiple cultures within one organization that can be identified by their different knowledge maps. One is then led to the question, "Does the type of knowledge create a set of cultural structures and assumptions, or does the culture determine the available knowledge?" Also, if the actions of reflection and other dynamics that influence the creation of knowledge are heavily rooted in the history and culture, we can see that the learning process may be very threatening because it may require deep change in the cultural assumptions.

The actions associated with the Action/Reflection subsystem are directed toward enhancing the movement of new information into goal reference knowledge. A resistance to confronting the present knowledge that is available to the organization can hamper this transformation process. This resistance is normally rooted in the organization's cultural assumptions and their manifestations in behavior toward new information. Therefore, many of the actions in this subsystem are also directed at protecting the present goal reference knowledge and its structure.

Knowledge as Structure and Maps

Knowledge structures are cognitive structures comprised of socially constructed guidance that governs the relationship among content, its interpretation, and the procedures for operationalizing the content within the interpretive context. They provide the organizational reference point for subcultural, group, and individual schema that are employed in the learning and performance of the organization.

Lyles and Schwenk (1992) select knowledge structures as their focus and pose nine propositions concerning the relationships between knowledge structures and strategic action. They suggest two general characteristics of organizational knowledge structures: complexity (amount of information or number of elements) and relatedness (linkages between elements). Through these characteristics they draw relationships between core and peripheral knowledge structures and their relative impact on the attention given by managers to their environmental queues. Their classification corresponds closely to Hannan and Freeman's (1977) discussion of "core" and "peripheral" organizational structuring.

How knowledge structures are formed and their usefulness and limitations are becoming a major path to the investigation into how the collective makes sense of its environment. Walsh uses the knowledge structure as a mechanism to represent managerial cognition. He also reflects the usefulness of the knowledge structure to bring sense to the manager's world, but also understands that they can work against the manager (and the organization) during change (Walsh, 1995, p. 281).

> The most fundamental challenge faced by managers, however, is that their information worlds are extremely complex, ambiguous, and munificent. Somehow they must see their way through what may be a bewildering flow of information to make decisions and solve problems. Managers (and indeed all individuals) meet this information challenge by employing knowledge structures to represent their information worlds and use, facilitate information-processing and decision-making. The intriguing problem for management researchers has been that while these knowledge structures may transform complex information environments into tractable ones, they may also blind strategy makers, for example, to important changes in their business environments, compromising their ability to make sound strategic decisions. A key point to recognize here is that this mental template consists of organized knowledge about an information domain. Hence, we must consider both the content and the structure of individuals' knowledge structure.

Walsh provides an example of the significance of managerial cognition and its relation to a collective knowledge structure in his review of the research of Barr et al. (1992).

> In a provocative study, Barr et al. (1992) traced the changes in the cognitive maps of the top managers of two railroads over a 25-year period. Interestingly, one railroad is still viable today (C & NW) and the other went out of business in the 1970s (Rock Island). The researchers found that the managers in both companies altered their cause maps in the face of environmental change, but only the surviving company showed evidence of continued experimentation, change, and learning in its maps. The defunct company made the change and never changed again. This study is important because it asks us to weave our understanding of cognition with our understanding of the organizational learning process. It also suggests that we need to consider issues of representation (for example, noticing a changed environment) and development (linking cognitive change to learning) as we strive to understand the basic issues of knowledge structure use (Walsh, 1995, p. 293).

Establishing a theory of knowledge structures is important, but the development of methods of observing them through individual and collection maps has allowed the comparison of organizational cognition and its potential relationship to outcomes and the survival of the organization.

Mauri Laukkanen, University of Vaasa, Finland demonstrated that patterns of industry-typical core causal thinking, manifestations of a dominant logic or recipe, can be located, operationalized, and comparatively analyzed with causal maps. He defines cause maps as directed graphs, which consist of nodes (terms) and arrows that link them. The nodes stand for concepts, phenomena, which their owners, such as managers, subjectively seem to perceive in their domains. The arrows represent their beliefs about efficacy (causal) relationships among the phenomena. The configuration of such interlinked concepts and beliefs can thus model patterns of causal thinking of a person or a group (Laukkanen, 1994, p. 323). Figure 6.2 represents two different maps concerning the relationship between employee satisfaction and customer satisfaction. The upper map portrays separate relationships linked to organizational performance, whereas the lower map is more complex because it represents an additional relationship that sees customer satisfaction also dependent on employee satisfaction.

Laukkanen's study found that managerial thinking was clearly not random, but internally and externally logical and consistent in the groups. He saw how the relevant action context must have been learned and internalized by the managers so as to later emerge in the cause maps. He conjectures, "that this is as if the cause maps were overt traces, "frozen dynamics," of past problem-solving processes performed many times over, thus providing a tentative explanation for the observed situational isomorphism of the underlying causal link assertions" (Laukkanen, 1994, p. 335).

Laukkanen sees cause maps useful to

- Analyze a discourse itself, especially for the causal estate dimensions
- Model a domain of reality, its entities, and its interrelationships, as represented in the knowledge/belief base of the respondents or of other researchers themselves
- Represent interlinked domain-related knowledge and/or belief base, e.g., an "ideology" or a "worldview" of a group as manifested in related communication
- Model the cognitive structures of the respondents, e.g., schemas, cognitive maps, or mental models
- Mirror cognitive processes such as generating algorithms or heuristics, which the respondents may use when they produce their oral responses or some text data (p. 337)

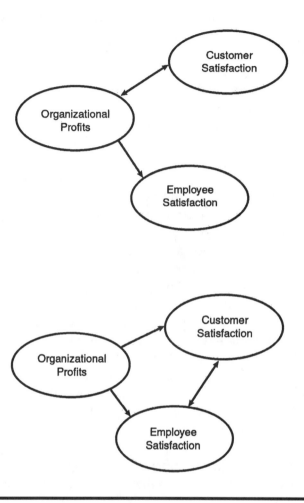

Figure 6.2 Cognitive Maps

There are questions about legitimacy of the technique of mapping. Lauk-kanen (1994, p 338) says, "today, a cautiously optimistic view has surfaced suggesting the validity depends largely on the type of cognitive elements acquired, and on the method's appropriateness. Despite such cheery notes, validity problems will stay with us."

Colin Eden, University of Strathclyde, Glasgow, Scotland has used the concepts of mapping in risk analysis interventions. He has employed computer analysis techniques to facilitate the development and delineation of the cognitive maps. He uses The Designing Explorer, a software package specifically developed for working with cognitive maps. It runs under Windows and allows for flexible graphical representation of maps and all of the analysis discussed above (Eden, 1997).

Knowledge structures and maps can exist at all levels of the organization and even at the industry level. "In the end, industry level cognitive representations are thought to both define the competitive playing field and supply the rules of the game" (Walsh, 1995, p. 297). Changes in these knowledge structures and maps require a dynamic interaction between the social and cognitive nature of the organization. This process is dependent on the type of new information that is available, the cultural assumptions that support inquiry and sense-making, and the structure placed on the organization by its management and other control mechanisms.

Organizations many times fail because their structures (leadership and management), reinforced by recollections of past successes, are circumscribed by their knowledge structures. Complaints, warnings, and policy disagreements should cause reflection that sometimes leads to reconsidering and possibly replacing old knowledge structures. Because these warnings contain new information that asserts that something may be wrong, managers and executives should respond by reflecting on their assumptions, beliefs, and practices. Nystrom and Starbuck call this "unlearning."

Short of replacing all the individuals in the organization, Nystrom and Starbuck (1984, p. 61) suggest that knowledge structures can be reexamined if managers:

- Assume that all dissents and warnings are at least partially valid.
- Evaluate the cost or benefits that would accrue if the messages turn out to be correct.
- Try to find some evidence other than the message's content about probabilities that messages might prove to be correct.
- Find ways to test in practice those dissent and warnings that might yield significant cost or benefits.

"Unlearning" processes are a subset of the possible actions that enhance, protect, or change the knowledge structures of an organization. Other actions can be employed by the organization to increase its learning capacity through reflection. The next section of this chapter turns to a more detailed examination of these actions and how they can be implemented by organizations.

Knowledge-Creating Actions of Organizations

James March's theory of organizational learning is based on a balance the organization has to maintain between information exploration and information exploitation. This is very similar to what we have been discussing as the balance between the Environmental Interface subsystem actions and the actions of the Action/Reflection subsystem.

> This balance is influenced by the state variables of the model. The level of knowledge the organization eventually achieves in a dynamic equilibrium depends on the state variables. Adjusting the state variables (guessing, group open-mindedness, updating the collective knowledge in the organizational code, self-confidence, socialization, individual open-mindedness which might be termed "organizational engineering") alters the context in which learning takes place and might be used to enhance organizational learning (Rodan, 1996, p. 2).

Simon Rodan, INSEAD, France conducted a simulation using four aspects of March's variables to manipulate and achieve a closer relationship between exploration and exploitation of information. The four characteristics he used were

- The pressure on individuals to adopt a position on issues about which they have (and know they have) insufficient knowledge
- Individuals' confidence in the accuracy of their intuition having made such decisions
- Their propensity to be persuaded from an existing belief to a new one at a single stroke by the prevailing collective point of view
- The willingness and ability of the superior group to change routines and operating procedures in which organizational beliefs are embedded at a single stroke

One of his results was that guessing in the absence of guidelines from the organization helps organizational learning. Guessing can be a very appropriate action to arrive at knowledge. However, most organizations can increase their reflective capacity in other, less "chance-driven" modes. March's state variables provide insight into possible interventions; however, one of the ways in which humans can interact and reflect, and hedge their bets on guessing, is through dialogue.

Dialogue — The Art of Fearless Listening

One of the better definitions of dialogue comes from the works of David Bohm (1996).

> ... when one person says something, the other person does not in general respond with exactly the same meaning as that seen by the first person. Rather, the meanings are only similar and not identical. Thus, when the second person replies, the first person sees a difference between what he meant to say and what the other person understood. In considering this difference, he may then be able to see something new, which is relevant both to his own views and to those of the other person. And so it can go back and forth, with the continual emergence of a new content that is common to both participants. Thus, in a dialogue each person does not attempt to make common certain ideas or items of information that are already known to him. Rather, it may be said that the two people are making something in common, for example creating something new together. (pp. 22–23)

He goes on to establish prerequisites for the dialogue to take place:

- People are able freely to listen to each other, without prejudice, and without trying to influence each other.
- Each person has to be interested primarily in truth and coherence.
- Each person must be ready to drop his or her old ideas and intentions and be ready to go onto something different if this is called for.

These criteria for success lead us back to the level of assumptions that govern the dynamic interactions of the participants. If dialogue does not meet these conditions, it can expose organizational members to anxiety, threats to self-esteem, holding back, making fools of themselves, and power roles of domination and weakness. The power-domination factors are directly related to the structuring and sensemaking interchange media involved in the actions of dialogue. The objective of a dialogue is not to analyze things, push your agenda, or exchange opinions.

> ... it is to suspend your opinions and to look at the opinions — to listen to everybody's opinions, to suspend them, and to see what all that means. If we can see what all of our opinions mean then we are *sharing a common content*, even if we don't agree entirely. It may turn out that the opinions are not really very important — they are all assumptions. And if we can

see them all we may then move more creatively in a different direction (Bohm, 1996, p. 26).

If the leadership style and even the physical organizational structure do not allow this exchange of ideas to happen, then dialogue becomes another activity, which in the long run can harm the organization because of unfulfilled expectations. The structuring interchange media are the most visible and changeable modes of increasing the probability of useful dialogue.

Regular meetings are useful, but shared understanding relies on continuous discussions over an extended period of time. It must also involve all levels of the organization — not just management.

Floyd and Wooldridge (1992, p. 39) provide an example where the prolonged dialogue worked.

> In the early 1980's executives at the Adolph Coors Company agreed about the need to reposition themselves as a national brand but disagreed about which specific strategy would best achieve this goal. As Richard Daft suggests, managers inside Coors knew what they wanted but "hadn't yet learned how to make the company a sophisticated competitor" (Daft, 1988, p. 382). Some managers argued for a national advertising campaign and price reduction; others thought corporate image building should take priority. Another suggestion was to attack the East Coast market head on. Initially these discussions created considerable confusion and resulted in a series of tentative efforts. Over time, however, the dialogue led to a national advertising campaign, the successful introduction of Coors Light, and the establishment of Coors as a leading national brewer.

The key to the success of this example was not only the quality of the dialogue, but also the time devoted to the actions and the diversity of the participants.

The Same, But Yet Different

The actions associated with knowledge creation are part of a dynamic nonlinear system. Therefore, it is not strange to find consensus and diversity occurring in the same dialogue. This counterintuitive idea is captured by the advice of Bill Starbuck et al. (1978, p. 123).

> One sensible operating rule is that once an organization adopts one prescription, they should adopt a second prescription that contradicts

the first. Contradictory prescriptions remind organizations that each prescription is a misleading simplification that ought not to be carried to excess.

Marlene Fiol (1994) found that in a new venture development process in a large financial institution, the venture team members developed unified ways of framing their unique arguments. Her findings include very interesting characteristics of diversity in a dialogue situation:

- There is a need to distinguish between personal, openly judgmental expressions of meaning from those couched in more "objective" terms.
- After a time, results began to clarify the role of consensus along different dimensions of meaning involving ambiguous group decision processes. Group consensus around one is not necessarily implied consensus around the other.
- There was aggressive agreement about how to tell the story, not about the underlying content or moral of the story. The converging language of the story, as it unfolded, became sufficiently shared to give the appearance of a unitary moral.
- Successful corporate innovation requires not only the overt decisions to embrace something new, but also the decision makers developing a new, collective understanding allows them to collaborate in implementing the innovation. It was not necessary to trade off unity and diversity of interpretations of the group's learning process.

Fiol's results reveal one way that organizations managed to combine the unity and diversity needed for collective learning. "To promote learning as a community, managers must actively encourage the development of different and conflicting views of what is thought true, while striving for a shared framing of the issues that is broad enough to encompass those differences" (Fiol 1994, p. 417). Although the structuring interchange media can enhance the dialogue through insuring diversity, the process of inquiry is still accomplished within the context of the organization's mission and goals. " ... collective mind calls for mindful attention to the system level consequences of each individual's contributing, representing, and subordinating behavior. Thus collective mind lay between rather than within the participating individuals" (Spender, 1995, p. 15).

The ability to use dialogue successfully does not come overnight. Organizations have to prepare themselves, and they must work at their readiness.

Readiness for Organizational Reflection

Donald Schon feels that the creation of knowledge in an organization is dependent on the organization understanding how it learns. This is a very difficult thing to do because it means the organization and the people that make up the organization must confront themselves as to the meaning assigned to their behaviors. He describes this as "deutero learning," a term that he obtained from Gregory Bateson's discussion of levels of learning in *Steps to an Ecology of Mind*. "This concept, learning to learn, encourages the individual to test their theories in use ("the theory constructed to account for a person's actions by attributing to him a complex intention consisting of governing variables or values, strategies for action, and assumptions that link the strategies to the governing variables"). Theory-in-use is distinguished from espoused theory, which is the individual's explicit version of his/her theory of action, that is observable by others. Theory in use and espoused theory need not be, and often are not, congruent" (Schon, 1975, p. 7).

Schon develops the concept of deutero learning at the organizational level of analysis. To increase the organization's readiness one most develop the capacity learning about learning. This can be done at several levels of policy, structures, and technique. It requires that interacting members of the organization continually be able to carry out tasks that cannot be carried out by top management or by organizational planners alone. Five of these tasks (Schon, 1975, p. 15) are

- Integrate scattered perceptions of organizational phenomena.
- Generate and test interpretations of the perceived phenomena and make ideas to generate action within the organization by bringing them into the open for discussion, or confirmation, of reputation.
- Conjure up new structures and policies designed to remedy dysfunction. These images must be generated out of a context of uncertainty. They must be drawn from past experience and projected into future behavior at a time when the relevance of past experience and predictability of future consequences are most in doubt. Hence they require a shared commitment to point of view beyond what the evidence available strictly would justify.
- Respond to conflicts in interpretation through inquiry rather than through bargaining.
- Experiment with new structures and policies. It requires, in particular, the ability to draw from experiments that are perceived as

failing a more precise and comprehensive representation of the organizational situation.

More explicit examples of Schon's tasks can be found in the readiness actions of R. J. Reynolds. They focused on empowering employees by enacting the slogan, "Ask for forgiveness rather than permission." Workers were encouraged to "take the initiative" and step out of the box. Critical to sustaining this learning environment were a group of approximately 30 facilitators. Each graduated from the R. J. Reynolds School of Innovation. These facilitators, representing all departments within the R & D group, facilitated meetings, developed teams, helped create vision/mission statements, provided workers with brainstorming interventions, and encouraged fellow employees to continue along their journey toward a new, innovative culture.

Another example included the Smithsonian support of risk-taking by establishing cross-functional teams to solve service and process issues and by implementing creativity through innovation training. Problem solving was encouraged at all levels of the organization and facilitators were also used to provide guidance to working teams. Overall, the Smithsonian supported the innovation culture of its organization through a philosophy of learning from the mistakes; blaming the process, not the person; and the adoption of a no-fault attitude (Andert-Schmidt and Dorsett, 1996, p. 2).

Watkins and Marsick encourage organizations to use their Human Resource Development professionals to enhance their readiness for inquiry. Systemwide skill assessments and training for strategically targeted skill gaps hold promise in enhancing the capacity of the organization to learn (Watkins and Marsick, 1995, p. 1).

These actions of reflection, or getting ready for reflection, can be implemented around the performance actions of the organization. Action learning techniques can be used to generate goal reference knowledge and solve pressing organizational concerns (Revans, 1980).

Action/Reflection Learning at Andersen Worldwide

In 1993 the Andersen Worldwide Organization became the world's largest firm in both accounting and in management consulting. Revenues now exceed $12 billion. Over 100,000 employees work at Arthur Andersen's 400 offices in more than 80 countries.

In 1989 Andersen reconfigured into two distinct units: (1) Arthur Andersen & Co., which provides auditing, business advisory services, tax services, and specialty consulting services; and (2) Andersen Consulting, which provides strategic services and technology consulting.

Action, Reflection, and Collaboration

Andersen has placed a high emphasis on learning from experience (including reflection) at all levels of the organization, even as the vehicle to build executive skills at the partner level. Throughout the organization there are efforts to move action learning from just the training environment to the work environment.

An example of ongoing action learning built into the Andersen process is the "Coaching and Continuous Learning Framework" taking place between the supervisor (coach) and employee (learner), as shown in Figure 6.3.

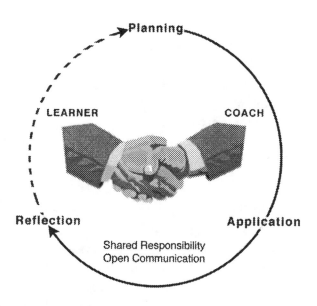

Figure 6.3 Coaching and Continuous Learning Framework

A number of important steps must occur at the planning, application, and reflection stages as follows:

1. Planning (between coach and learner, but as learner-driven as possible)
   Determine the gap between the learner's existing skills/knowledge and those demanded by the engagement (learning opportunity).
   Develop learning objectives and a plan to meet those objectives.
   Complete any pretask learning identified.
2. Application
   Coach's main responsibilities
   ■ Coach the learner based on the learning needs (job-specific, functional, adaptive).
   ■ Provide the learner with needed opportunities.
   ■ Make sure the learner has access to references and tools.
   ■ Provide guidance and feedback when needed.
   Learner's main responsibilities
   ■ Apply the skills/knowledge acquired.
   ■ Use the resources available.
   ■ Reflect on current task being learned.
   ■ Ask for assistance and feedback when needed.
3. Reflection
   Take the time to reflect on lessons learned.
   Determine how lessons learned can be applied in the future.
   Provide feedback on how well supervisors/supervisees did in regard to coaching and continuous learning.
   Discuss not only what can be done better, but recognize and/or reward what was accomplished.
   Share what has been learned with others who might find the insight useful.

Collaborative Learning

Andersen has implemented collaborative learning which consists of small group work where group members learn from one another by working together. This creates a rich learning environment in which the learner takes on various roles, including the role of the instructor. This approach promotes the sharing of ideas and knowledge and allows learners to review one another's work. It also allows them to coach, model, teach, and learn by using the abilities of team members and the team's synergy as part of the learning process.

The new learning model at Andersen recognizes that "learning the process of getting the right answer" is the most important issue. The critical task is now to make the learning more efficient and effective. This new model of staff development at Andersen centers on the learner who, as a decision-maker, chooses from among various available tools and resources to learn what he or she needs for success. The emphasis is on the learning needed by the learner. The former role of instructor/presenter has been shifted to one of a coach/mentor/facilitator.

According to Joel Montgomery, an education specialist at Andersen's Center for Professional Education, learners are now "much more active in the learning process, and are jointly responsible for their learning. Learners are asked to use what they have learned rather than repeating or identifying what they have been exposed to."

Andersen now designs its learning programs in a way that stimulates the learners to engage in activities that allow them to focus their learning on what they know they need. In the process, they are given the tool to reflect on what they are doing, to evaluate it according to some standard, and to give and receive feedback about what they are doing and learning. After they have gone through the process once, Montgomery notes, "we again stimulate them to reengage in learning, bringing with them what they learned the first time, again reflecting on, evaluating, and giving and receiving feedback on what they are doing and learning. This ensures a greater depth of learning" (Marquardt, 1996, p. 52).

This view of learning focuses on what happens to the learner internally, and encourages increased sensitivity to the learner while instruction takes place. The instructional approaches are adjusted to meet the individual learner's needs. This represents a paradigm shift from a "supply push" instructional approach to a "demand pull" approach.

Action Learning — A Key Action/Reflection Tool for Organizational Learning

Action learning is a dynamic process that involves a small group of people solving real problems while at the same time focusing on what they are learning and how their learning can benefit each group member and the organization as a whole. It is built on the application of new questions to existing knowledge as well as a reflection on actions taken during and after the problem-solving sessions (Marquardt, 1999).

Perhaps action learning's most valuable capacity is its amazing, multiplying impact to equip individuals, teams, and organizations to more effectively respond to change. Learning is what makes action learning strategic rather than tactical. The fresh thinking and new learning found in action learning are needed if we are to avoid responding to today's problems with yesterday's solutions while tomorrow's challenges engulf us (Dilworth, 1998).

Among the benefits of action learning are

- Shared learning throughout various levels of the organization
- Greater self-awareness and self-confidence due to new insights and feedback
- Ability to ask better questions and be more reflective
- Improved communications and teamwork

The action learning program derives its power and benefits from six interactive and interdependent components (see Figure 6.4). The strength and success of action learning are built upon how well these elements are employed and reinforced.

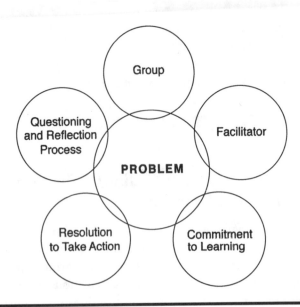

Figure 6.4 Six Elements of Action Learning

1 — Problem (Project, Challenge, Opportunity, Issue, or Task)

Action learning is built around a problem (be it a project, a challenge, an issue, or task), the resolution of which is of high importance to an individual, team, and/or organization. The problem should be significant, be within the responsibility of the team, and provide opportunity for learning. Why is the selection of the problem so important? Because it is one of the fundamental beliefs of action learning that we learn best when undertaking some action, which we then reflect upon and learn from. The main reason for having a problem or project is that it gives the group something to focus on that is real and important, and that is relevant and means something to the group's members. It creates a "hook" on which to test out stored-up knowledge.

Solving Problems at AT&T with Action Learning

AT&T's use of action learning occurs under its "Gap Group" program in which leaders of each AT&T group seek to identify and overcome the gaps in performance or output faced by the divisions. High potential managers bring in a key problem from their divisions. They then work with an action set of six to seven peers from other divisions over a period of 7 days, during which each person gets 1 day of air time that is dedicated to working on his/her business problem.

The problem-solving process is quite simple. Each leader (client) presents his or her issue to be examined that day. The set then wrestles with the problem and searches for agreement as to the true nature of problem. Possible alternatives and solutions are proposed. A set facilitator or subject matter expert guides the action learning process. When the group has agreed on a possible solution, the client develops an action plan for his/her problem and is accountable for producing the results in the time period designated. The action learning group may meet informally after an agreed-upon period of time to check progress.

Gap Groups are composed of as diverse a membership as possible. "We tried it once the other way," says Joe Dalerneau, executive education director at AT&T, "by having sets formed of people who were, for example, all from sales, and they would always say, 'I've tried that" to every suggestion that was raised" (Froiland, 1994).

2 — Action Learning Group or Team

The core entity in action learning is the action learning group (also called a set or team). The group is composed of four to eight individuals who examine an organizational problem that has no easily identifiable solution. Ideally, the makeup of the group is diverse so as to maximize various perspectives and to obtain fresh viewpoints. Depending on the type of action learning problem, groups can be composed of individuals from across functions or departments. In some situations, groups are comprised of individuals from other organizations or professions, for example, the company's suppliers or customers.

3 — Process That Emphasizes Insightful Questioning and Reflective Listening

By focusing on the right questions rather than the right answers, action learning focuses on what one does not know as well as what one does know. Action learning tackles problems through a process of first asking questions to clarify the exact nature of the problem, reflecting and identifying possible solutions, and only then taking action.

Action learning employs the formula: $L = P + Q + R$; i.e., Learning = **Programmed Knowledge** (i.e., knowledge in current use, in books, in one's mind, in organization's memory, lectures, case studies, etc.) + **Questioning** (fresh insights into what is not yet known) + **Reflection** (recalling, thinking about, pulling apart, making sense, trying to understand).

4 — Resolution to Take Action

For action learning advocates, there is no real learning unless action is taken, for one is never sure the idea or plan will be effective until it has been implemented. Therefore, members of the action learning group must have the power to take action themselves or be assured that their recommendations will be implemented (barring any significant change in the environment or the group's obvious lack of essential information). Action enhances learning because it provides a basis and anchor for the critical dimension of reflection described earlier.

5 — Commitment to Learning

Solving organizational problems provides immediate, short-term benefits to the company. The greater, longer-term, multiplier benefit, however, is the learning gained by each group member and how the group's learnings can be applied on a systems-wide basis throughout the organization. The learning that occurs in action learning has greater value strategically for the organization than the immediate tactical advantage of early problem correction.

In action learning, the learning is as important as the action. Action learning places equal emphasis on accomplishing the task and on the learning/development of individuals and organizations. Figure 6.5 captures the interplay between solving the problem and learning, as well as between self-development and organization development.

Figure 6.5 Seesaws of Action Learning

(Adopted from Weinstein, K., *Action Learning: A Practical Guide*, Gower, London, 1998.)

Learning to Act at U.S. Shell

The primary instrument of learning and change at U.S. Shell's Leadership and Performance (LEAP) project is action learning which reaches over 20,000 people per year. The strength of Shell's learning organization derives from the fact that action learning focuses on business results, the engagement of senior leadership, and the involvement of personnel at all levels. The work being done by these leadership champions is not only unique, but also extremely effective. There is also a felt need to include Shell contractors and suppliers in action learning programs.

Steve Miller, group managing director of the Royal Dutch/Shell group of companies, recalled how the company brought six-to eight-person teams from about six operating companies to a "retailing boot camp." In Malaysia, to improve service station revenues along major highways, the firm brought together a cross-functional team that was made up of a dealer, union trucker, and four or five marketing executives. "A new business model and leadership skills were developed to prepare participants to apply new tools to their local market." As one group of teams left, another group came in. For 60 days, the first set of teams worked to develop business plans to address their problems. They then returned to the "boot camp" for a peer-review meeting (Brenneman et al., 1998).

At the end of the third workshop each team sat with Miller and his team in a "fishbowl" environment to review its business plan as other teams looked on. At the end of the sessions, the teams returned home for another 60 days, during which they worked to put their ideas into action. At the end of the 60 days they returned to discuss not only their breakthroughs but their breakdowns. "Ultimately," said Miller, "these grassroots folks go back home and say, 'I have just cut a deal with the managing director to do these things …'"

Throughout the units reviewed there is strong emphasis on action learning, a systematic process that requires that project teams and other units not only solve problems and complete projects, but reflect on learning from each episode, and bank this learning in institutional memory. This will provide increased adaptability and the ability to learn and adjust.

Miller credits three major elements of the learning/leadership program with its success. First, executives ordinarily make presentations about things the company is doing, speaking in the third person — a safe way to talk and interact. Grassroots leadership calls for talking in the first person. For example, "I'm talking about my transformation," says Miller. "This creates a personal connection and it changes how we talk and how we work with each other." Second, the leader in the grassroots model must be a personal teacher and coach. "The scariest part," according to Miller, "is letting go. You don't retain the kind of control that traditional leaders are accustomed to, although you may, in fact, have more control in the form of more feedback and learning." Third, grassroots leaders rely on the "fishbowl" concept. Teams "on a hot seat" lay out business plans for Miller and peer teams. Miller says, "They think the pressure is on them, but the truth is, the pressure is on me." He explains that the fishbowl exercise forces him to be consistent — to call peer plans "a bunch of crap," if indeed they are, and reserve praise for truly worthy plans (Brenneman et al., 1998).

This kind of straight talk is a major culture change for Shell — persons at a lower organizational level speaking directly to a managing director, a candid interchange from a director, and the use of personal "I"-type conversations.

Lest readers conclude that LEAP is merely an "interesting" example of a current fad in organizational learning, we should point out that Shell's goal of a 25:1 return on cost of LEAP "may have been too easy a target."

6 — Group Facilitator

Facilitation is important to help the group slow down its process in order to allow sufficient time to reflect on learning. A facilitator (also referred to as a learning coach or a set advisor) may be a working group member (possessing familiarity with the problem being discussed) or an external participant (not necessarily understanding the problem content or organizational context, but possessing action learning facilitation skills).

The facilitator is very important in helping participants reflect both on what they are learning and how they are solving problems. He/she helps group members reflect on how they listen, how they may have reframed the problem, how they give each other feedback, how they are planning and working, and what assumptions may be shaping their beliefs and actions. The set advisor also helps participants focus on what they are achieving, what they are finding difficult, what processes they are employing, and the implications of these processes.

Action Learning at National Semiconductor

National Semiconductor prides itself as a company that creates technologies for "moving and shaping information" by manufacturing products that connect people to electronics and electronic networks. Market segments include business communication, personal computing, automotive, and consumer audio and products such as personal computers, cordless phones, computer security, auto instrumentation, multimedia centers, and microwave ovens. Customers include many of the global 1000 — AT&T, Siemens, Intel, Apple, IBM, Boeing, Sony, Toshiba, and Ford, among others.

A pioneer in the semiconductor industry, National Semiconductor was established in 1959. Since that time, the company has been at the vanguard of revolutionary electronics technologies and is today an acknowledged leader in the design and manufacture of the products that provide all of us access to the information highway. Corporate sales in 1999 topped $2.5 billion. Over 12,000 employees work at manufacturing sites in Asia, Europe, and North America.

Working in action learning teams is seen as a key to increasing productivity and creativity at National Semiconductor. When senior management in the South Portland plant saw that delivery performance was holding National Semiconductor back from providing quality service at AT&T, they decided to do something about it. Choosing eight people from different areas throughout the company, they created a Customer Request Improvement Team to deal with delivery performance.

Team members were chosen from sales, marketing, engineering, manufacturing, planning, as well as someone from AT&T. Meeting for a couple days a month for 3 months, the team eventually came up with a list of almost 40 ideas which resulted in four key action initiatives:

1. Analyzing the delivery misses in new ways
2. Increasing frequencies of lead-time updates
3. Creating critical device lists
4. Developing pre-alert reports

Following the implementation of these initiatives, AT&T recognized National Semiconductor as one of its "world-class" suppliers.

Action/Reflection is the Nucleus

The Action/Reflection subsystem functions as the nucleus of the organizational learning system. It enables the organization to assign meaning to new information, and in doing so creates goal reference knowledge. This chapter has expanded on the actions associated with the Action/Reflection subsystem of actions. The relationship to the other subsystems has been demonstrated through the use of the interchange media. We saw examples of this in the patterns established between the dialogue (sensemaking) and goal reference knowledge, and also the relationship between managerial cognition (structuring) and goal reference knowledge. The efforts of organizations such as General Electric, National Semiconductor, Shell, Spring Branch Schools, and AT&T demonstrate the challenges as well as the successes possible in this subsystem. Let us now examine the Dissemination and Diffusion subsystem, the integrating mechanism of the Organizational Learning Systems Model.

References

Andert-Schmidt, D. and Dorsett, M.E., Innovation and Organizational Learning, American Society for Training and Development, Alexandria, VA, 1996.

Andersen, B. and Boutwell, S., 21st Century Organizational Excellence Awards, Clemson, 1998.

Barr, P.S., Stimpert, J.L., and Huff, A.S., Cognitive change, strategic action, and organizational renewal, *Strategic Management Journal*, 13, 15–34, 1992.

Bohm, D., *On Dialogue*, Routledge, New York, 1996.

Brenneman, W., Keys, J. B., and Fulmer, R., Learning across a living company: the shell companies' experience, *Organizational Dynamics*, (27) 2, 61–69, 1998.

Daft, R., *Organizational Theory and Design*, 3rd ed., South-Western Publishing, Cincinnati, 1988.

Dilworth, R.L., Action learning in a nutshell, *Performance Improvement Quarterly*, 11(1), 28, 1998.

Eden, C., Cognitive Mapping and Scenarios in Strategy Making and Risk Management, paper read at 1997 European Managerial and Organizational Cognition Workshop, Netherlands, 1997.

Fiol, C.M., Consensus, diversity and learning organizations, *Organization Science*, 5(3), 404–420, 1994.

Floyd, S.W. and Wooldridge, B., Managing strategic consensus: the foundation of effective implementation, *Academy of Management Executive*, 6(4), 27–39, 1992.

Froiland, P., Action learning, taming real problems in real time, *Training*, 31(1), 27, 1994.

Garud, R. and Rappa, M.A., A socio-cognitive model of technology evolution: the case of cochlear implants, *Organization Science*, 1994.

Hannan, M.T. and Freeman, J., The population ecology of organizations, *American Journal of Sociology*, 82(5), 929–964, 1977.

Inkpen, A.C. and Dinur, D., Knowledge management processes and international joint ventures, *Organization Science*, 9(4) 454–468, 1998.

Laukkanen, M., Comparative cause mapping of organizational cognitions, *Organization Science*, 5(3), 322–343, 1994.

Levitt, B. and March, J.G., Organizational learning, *Annual Review of Sociology*, 14, 319–340, 1988.

Lyles, M.A. and Schwenk, C.R., Top management, strategy and organizational knowledge structures, *Journal of Management Studies*, 29(2), 1992.

Marquardt, M., *Action Learning in Learning*, Davies-Black Press, Palo Alto, 1999.

Marquardt, M., *Building the Learning Organization*, McGraw-Hill, New York, 1996.

Nonaka, I. and Takeuchi, H., *The Knowledge-Creating Company*, Oxford University Press, New York, 1995.

Nystrom, P.C. and Starbuck, W.H., To avoid organizational crises, unlearn, *Organization Dynamics*, Spring, 53–65, 1984.

Polanyi, M., *The Tacit Dimension*, Routledge and Kegan Paul, London, 1996.

Revans, R.W., *Action Learning: New Techniques for Management*, Blond & Briggs, London, 1980.

Rodan, S., The March Model of Mutual Learning: Exploration and Exploitation Revisited, paper read at 1996 Academy of Management Conference, Cincinnati, OH, 1996.

Sackmann, S.A., Culture and subcultures: an analysis of organizational knowledge, *Administrative Science Quarterly*, 37, 140–161, 1992.

Schön, D., Deutero-learning in organizations: learning for increased effectiveness, *Organization Dynamics*, Summer, 2–16, 1975.

Sheffield, A.D., *Joining the Public Discussion*, Doran, 1922.

Spender, J.C., Organizational knowledge, learning and memory: three concepts in search of a theory, *Journal of Organizational Change*, 9, 63–68, 1995.

Starbuck, W.H., Greve, A., and Hedberg, B.L.T., Responding to crisis, *Journal of Business Administration*, 9, 111–137, 1978.

Thompson, S., Rise of the knowledge society, *Straits Times*, July 19, 1993, 1–2.

Tsoukas, H., The firm as a distributed knowledge system: a constructionist approach, *Strategic Management Journal*, 17(winter special), 11, 1996.

Vaill, P., *Managing as a Performing Art*, Jossey-Bass, San Francisco, 1989.

Walsh, J.P., Managerial and organizational cognition: notes from a trip down memory lane, *Organization Science*, 6(3) 280–321, 1995.

Watkins, K.E. and Marsick, V.J., The Case for Learning, paper read at Academy of Human Resource Development, St. Louis, MO, 1995.

Weick, K., *The Social Psychology of Organizing*, McGraw-Hill, New York, 1979.

Winter, S.G., The case for mechanistic decision making, in *Organizational Strategy and Change*, Pennings, H., Ed., Jossey-Bass, San Francisco, 1985.

7 Knowledge and the Organizational Social Fabric: The Dissemination and Diffusion Subsystem

> By the duality of structure, I mean the essential recursiveness of social life, as constituted in social practices: structure is both medium and outcome of the reproduction of practices.
>
> Anthony Giddens

Structuring Organizational Learning

The Dissemination/Diffusion subsystem's purpose is to move, transfer, retrieve, and capture information and knowledge. The actions of this subsystem are characterized by their ability to meet the integrating requirements of the other subsystems. It includes acts of communication, networking, management, coordination, and the implementation roles supporting the norms associated with the movement of information and knowledge. The actions also include technical processes such as electronic data transfer and audio-visual means.

The actions included in this subsystem can be indicative of dissemination and/or diffusion. Dissemination actions are those that are more purposefully directed and governed by formal procedures and policies. Diffusion techniques represent a more informal process such as rumors and informal communications. Of all the organizational learning subsystems, the Dissemination and Diffusion subsystem is the most concrete and observable.

Structuring is the interchange medium produced within the Dissemination-Diffusion subsystem actions (see Figure 7.1). The nomenclature selected for this medium is indicative of its dynamic nature. It is more than a structure of the organization; it is an integration of organizational structures, roles, norms, and objects and processes that provide a dynamic quantity called "structuring." It is through the structuring media that the organizational learning system is able to integrate the other three subsystems. It is the structuring mechanisms that allow for information and knowledge to move within the learning system and the organization itself. The actions associated with the movement of information and knowledge, in and of themselves, become part of the structuring process. Structuring symbolizes connection and order that facilitate the learning of the organization.

Structuring to Disseminate and Diffuse Knowledge at McKinsey & Company

McKinsey & Company is an international management consulting firm that advises the top management of companies around the world on issues of strategy, organization development, and operations. Tom Peters, Bob Weatherman, and Kenichi Ohmae are just a few of McKinsey's long list of past and present associates.

McKinsey recognizes that learning and sharing that learning are critical for its success. A variety of structures and strategies have been implemented to disseminate and diffuse knowledge.

The company has developed 31 practice information centers — 18 centers of competence for functional specialties like marketing and organizational performance, and 13 of industries like banking, insurance, energy, and electronics. At McKinsey there is an emphasis on the systematic development of

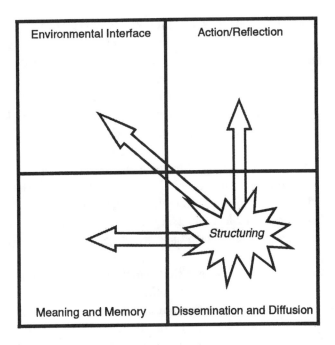

Figure 7.1 Dissemination and Diffusion Output is Structuring

consultant skills so that the firm will have as much "internal knowledge on demand" as possible. The organization has created the ability and structures to tap systematically into what people have learned.

In the past, McKinsey associates had to rely on their personal network of contacts when meeting client requests for information and/or help which fell outside their own individual realm of expertise. The sources for new information were limited by the size of a consultant's personal network. By electronically linking every associate together with LANs and WANs, and at the same time developing knowledge databases containing previous consulting experiences, industry information, and expert contacts, the number of sources for new information available to any single McKinsey associate has been greatly increased. Additionally, discussion databases organized around specific topics have allowed ongoing knowledge sharing between geographically distant employees of the firms. Anyone at anytime in any location could monitor ongoing discussions, take away new insights, or join in and add new knowledge throughout the computer-assisted learning system.

Dissemination and Diffusion Strategies at McKinsey

All too often, valuable learnings, whether from successes or heart-wrenching failures, never leave the minds of the involved individual or group. Learning organizations know how to capture these learnings through a variety of positive and punitive methods. To optimize the capturing of McKinsey knowledge, workers are rewarded for putting their learning into databases within the practice information centers. Consider some of the knowledge management strategies used by McKinsey:

- A Director of Knowledge Management has been appointed to coordinate company efforts in creating and collecting knowledge. (Philip Morris calls the position "Knowledge Champion"; Dow Chemical has a "Director of Intellectual Asset Management.")
- Knowledge transfer is seen as a professional responsibility and part of everyone's job.
- Knowledge development is included in the personnel evaluation process.
- An employee does not get a billing code (and therefore reimbursement) until he or she has prepared a two-page summary of how and what the person has learned from the project.
- Every 3 months, each project manager receives a printout of what he or she has put into the company's Practice Information System.
- An on-line information system called the Practice Development Network (PDNet) is updated weekly and now has over 6000 documents. Documentation also includes the Knowledge Resource Directory (McKinsey's Yellow Pages) that provides a guide to who knows what.
- For any of the 31 Practice Areas of McKinsey, one will be able to find the list of members, experts, and core documents.
- A McKinsey Center *Bulletin* appears at a rate of two to three times per week for each of the practice areas, featuring new ideas and information that a particular practice area wants to "parade" in front of all the company's staff.

McKinsey recognizes the following principles relative to organizational learning and knowledge management:

1. Knowledge-based strategies must begin with strategy, not knowledge or technology.
2. Strategies need to be linked to organizational performance and success.

3. Executing a knowledge-based strategy is not about managing knowledge, but nurturing people with knowledge.
4. Organizations leverage knowledge through networks of people who collaborate, not through networks of technology that interconnect.

Knowledge Sharing at Arthur Andersen

Sharing knowledge and knowledge management, defined as "the process of accelerating individual and organizational learning," are not new at Arthur Andersen; it has always been a major part of the corporate learning culture. Prior to the advent of technology, however, Arthur Andersen relied on individual and team knowledge sharing via a network of strong personal relationships with others in the Firm, enhanced by a unifying corporate culture, a strong focus on training, and documentation of tools and methodologies for global use. With the advent of technology, Arthur Andersen has continued its focus on knowledge creation and sharing through groupware technologies, with the creation of Global Best Practices®, the KnowledgeSpace® Web site, and other knowledge-sharing applications.

In articulating its vision for knowledge sharing, Arthur Andersen addresses knowledge from two perspectives: (1) "personal" knowledge belonging to a single individual and (2) "organizational" knowledge that is contained throughout the Firm. In the past, the Firm's ability to tap into its organizational knowledge was a small component of the overall knowledge that staff brought to bear in serving their clients. Today one's personal knowledge is rarely sufficient to fully satisfy client expectations. As shown in Figure 7.2, associates must provide dramatically more organizational knowledge in order to demonstrate value to Arthur Andersen's clients.

The ramifications of this new corporate manner of sharing knowledge are significant. First, it means that the knowledge that currently exists within Arthur Andersen must be made more accessible to all the individual members. Second, the company recognizes the need to optimize and foster the sharing of personal knowledge. Arthur Andersen has developed a number of implementation strategies to facilitate the organizational and personal transitions required to support these needed changes. The desired goal is a com-

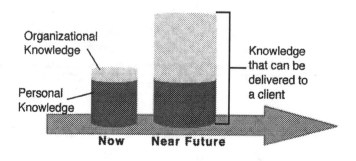

Figure 7.2 Increased Knowledge for Andersen Customers

(Credit: Tomas W. Hoglund, Arthur Andersen KnowledgeSpace®.

prehensive knowledge-sharing system that includes people, process, and technology in an encompassing and systemic relationship.

Arthur Andersen created four interrelated teams to develop the knowledge-sharing system within the Firm:

1. The People Team focused on developing needed competencies, roles, rewards, measures, and learning to support knowledge sharing. People are the origin and destination of all knowledge.
2. The Process Team focused on knowledge-sharing processes, the integration of these processes into our business processes, and the functional requirements and design of KnowledgeSpace Web site. The KnowledgeSpace site is the Firm's intranet "portal" to all its internal knowledge. Processes support Arthur Andersen's people and leadership to effectively create, gather, organize, analyze, and distribute knowledge.
3. The focus of the Technology Team was to define a technical architecture to support the firm's knowledge-sharing needs. Technology was recognized as shaping the context in which knowledge content is presented.
4. The Leadership Team helped put in place the needed structures, processes, and funding to make the system work as well as to serve as role models.

Structuring to Interact with the Environment

Social systems survive because they inherently structure themselves to successfully interact with their environments. These structuring actions are based on the premise that the system must "differentiate" itself to address pressures placed on its boundaries by its environment. For example, McDonald's fast food restaurants respond to the demand of the public for more hamburgers by opening more stores across the country. They have differentiated themselves geographically to insure their survival.

A corollary to the system's ability to differentiate is the corresponding requirement for the system to "integrate" itself. That is, to maintain its integrity as a system, it must coordinate, communicate, control, and couple its elements. Therefore, McDonald restaurants developed highly unique processes of delivery of hamburgers to the public. One can walk into any McDonald's and see the same products, services, and facilities whether one was in New York City or Los Angeles. This uniformity is achieved through policies, regulations, and training that result in McDonald's vision of integrity.

If we examine the phenomena of these two systems — differentiation and integration — we can see a direct relationship. The more an organization differentiates, the more it has to integrate itself; if not it will lose its identity as a system (organization). Thus we see a chain of events that has direct impact on the organization and its structuring. The environment becomes more complex and places more demands on the organization. The organization responds by increasing its differentiation and, of course, increasing the quality and quantity of its integration processes. This in turn results in an increase in the internal system's complexity.

This chain of events exemplifies the law of requisite variety which states "that the variety within a system must be at least as great as the environment's variety against which it is attempting to regulate itself" (Buckley, 1968, p. 495).

Systems integration is the purpose of organizational structuring. It can achieve this integration through highly controlling, tightly coupled actions such as policy manuals and regulations that are reinforced by aggressive management review. Or it can achieve it through loosely coupling mechanisms such as a shared vision and values that allow each element of the system to operate independently within the boundaries of the vision.

Whether an organization is tightly coupled or loosely coupled, the movement of information and knowledge is imperative to its integration processes. This was evident in a small unit of seven people who formed a customer liaison group for a large, highly competitive computer hardware company. The unit's mission was to provide services to the customer and to act as an "online" feedback mechanism for obtaining information concerning customer needs, product performance, and future sales leads. The company, however, felt that it was not gaining enough new information from the unit (thus little goal reference knowledge was being generated). The management of the computer hardware company felt that the reasons could be traced back to the effectiveness of the unit's relationships with its respective customers.

After gathering data from the unit, customers, and other divisions within the company, it was found that there was an abundance of new information within the various parts of the company. However, relations established between the various units and their managers were characterized as "noncollaborative." This was not merely a case of turf wars, but was seen as a pattern driven by values of the highly competitive culture of the company. These values had transcended the organization's external intentions and were being used by the units to make sense of their relationships in an internal context with the rest of the company. When the flow of new information was traced, it was discovered that deliberate structuring mechanisms were employed to retain and use new information for internal competitive reasons rather than for the benefit of the company. Thus, it was not a case of not securing the information from the customers; rather, it was a case of an organizational structure, norms, and reward system that were preventing the movement of information.

This case demonstrates the importance of the dissemination and diffusion actions to the learning system. The computer hardware company had the necessary new information all along; however, the structure of the units and their management were indicative of a noncollaborative, highly competitive environment. Thus the actions of the units emphasized the control of information rather than its dissemination.

The Starting Point for Building Organizational Learning

Since the Dissemination and Diffusion subsystem performs the most tangible functions of the organizational learning system, it is many times the starting point for interventions. The actions of the subsystem involve familiar organizational variables such as roles, leadership, norms, communication processes, and information management systems. This familiarity makes it comfortable for organizations to make changes in these parameters.

Although the parameters are familiar ones, changes in only these will not necessarily result in higher organizational learning capacity. Just as we saw in the above case of the computer hardware company, if change is to occur, all subsystems must be considered because of its nonlinear nature.

Let us now focus on two critical types of actions and their associated structuring patterns to illustrate the importance of the subsystem's actions to learning: (1) the transfer and capture of knowledge within the organization and the importance of organizational norms associated with that process, and (2) the importance of roles within the organization and how they contribute to structuring the movement of information and knowledge. Each of these actions must be concerned with the movement of information and knowledge if the organization's learning system is to achieve its purpose. We will begin a discussion of the first type of action — the transfer and capture of knowledge — by describing how NASA handled knowledge.

NASA — Capturing and Transferring Knowledge

As organizations age, so do the individuals within those organizations. Of course, at some point the individual can retire or leave the organization. This is what happened to the National Aeronautics and Space Administration (NASA). The people who formed and developed the organization began to retire after 30 years of creating the knowledge of the agency. NASA became concerned because its organizational knowledge, which was stored in the individuals, was "retiring out-the-door." Duarte and Schwandt (1996) documented the collective actions taken by the engineering teams to transfer and capture this knowledge.

The agency began a program to transfer the knowledge of its senior engineers to the junior engineers. The engineering directors' workforce is made up of engineers, scientists, and computer scientists. Management structure is lean and most work is accomplished through collaboration of these individuals. The age distribution of the workforce in the engineering directors could be characterized as bi-modal. There were a number of people hired in the late 1960s and again in the late 1980s; there were few employees who were in the middle of the career. Most were either thinking about retirement or just beginning their careers. As a result, the leaders and the engineering directors were concerned that the loss of the more experienced individuals would leave a void that could impact the development of future systems.

The goals of the engineering directors were to: (1) capture and transfer to the younger employees scarce knowledge and skill; (2) develop ways to maintain knowledge and skills apart from experts; (3) create a culture of learning among experts in younger employees; and (4) create a culture where ongoing debate, discussion, and inquiry about technical methods were encouraged.

Specifically, it appeared that most knowledge in organizational memory about technical approaches was stored with specific individuals. Because of a culture that produced minimal interaction between senior experts and younger employees and the nonroutine nature of the information, exposure to this knowledge was limited. There was also an apparent resistance by senior experts to documenting organizational memory in accessible forms such as manuals, training courses, or expert system databases. Finally, the structuring element was also targeted for improvement. In fact, less experienced employees stated that they felt that they lacked an appreciation about the total approach to engineering processes and the directors. This, as well as specific expertise, had never been systematically shared. Communication had been limited due to the small amount of informal interaction with other departments, management, and most importantly senior technical experts.

Because of the diversity in missions, each team developed a plan for the dissemination and diffusion of technical information. They included formal and informal methods designed to transfer information from the senior technical experts to younger employees as well as methods for exchanging information among the younger employees and with other organizational units.

There were a number of formal strategies adopted by the teams. They included electronic bulletin boards that would be updated monthly to focus on new techniques, lessons learned, and other important technical information. Many teams opted for a series of "brown bag" meetings once a month to discuss technical problems and issues among themselves and senior experts. These were advertised across departments to maximize exposure and information exchange. Other teams selected more standard approaches including training and documentation of procedures and processes. Some teams used a combination of methods and instituted a formal lessons-learned program that made technical information available to other teams as it came online through a combination of lunch meetings, electronic bulletin boards, training, and memos. Finally, one team instituted a program for senior experts and younger employees to come together, on an ongoing basis, to hear about current technologies outlined in journal articles or at conferences. In the teams that were the most active, it was the younger employees who took a vigorous role in the process, including scheduling meetings and ensuring that technical experts were available. Teams that focused on less formal activities such as brown bag lunches and development of guidebooks and procedure manuals seemed to make more progress than teams that had planned to develop more formal and complicated processes such as an expert system or databases. After 6 months, many of the younger employees stated that they felt better apprised of nontechnical activities that only a few months ago they considered the domain of senior experts. They also reported a perceived increase in dialogue and team meetings that question established assumptions about doing business. The most common barrier reported was the amount of time that senior experts were willing to devote to the team activities. The second barrier was that senior experts tended to view the problem as training-related and not associated with organizational culture. Many of these barriers were tied to the operating norms held by the senior engineers.

Changing Norms — Increase Absorptive Capacity and Reduce Stickiness

The examples of the computer firm and NASA are not uncommon. Information movement can occur, or not occur, in many ways. The problem is not only knowledge retiring out-the-door as with NASA, but also transferring information or knowledge within the organization, as with the computer company.

Szulanski's research concerning the transfer of capabilities within a firm showed that it is far from easy. Her study of 122 best-practice transfers in eight different organizations found that this process was hampered by what she called "stickiness" — the reluctance of some functions to accept knowledge from the outside.

Intra-firm transfer of best practices was seen as an unfolding process consisting of stages in which characteristic factors usually appear in greater or lesser degree, but also in a certain order. She identified the four stages as initiation, implementation, ramp-up, and integration. The initiation stage involves the decision to transfer knowledge; that is, a need is matched with existing knowledge. The implementation stage reflects the actual flow of knowledge and resources through the actions of the organizational entities. Ramp-up involves the recipient actually starting to use the knowledge. And, finally, integration involves the movement of the knowledge to the routines of the entity (Szulanski, 1996).

Although she warns against broad generalization, Szulanski's findings are quite similar to the NASA case. Movement of knowledge is dependent on:

- The motivation of the participants and their perceptions of need or forming new norms that allow increases in the absorptive capacity of the organization (preexisting knowledge and its impact on valuing of new ideas)
- The creation of flexible organizational structures that bridge unit boundaries to increase movement and retention of knowledge (the ability to institutionalize)
- Providing guides and manuals that reduce causal ambiguity (not clear as to the components and their relationships)
- Creating forums for relationships to form thus preventing arduous relationships (the movement of tacit knowledge requires good communications and intimate interaction) (Duarte and Schwandt, 1996; Szulanski, 1996)

These findings provide some insights into the social dynamics associated with the Dissemination and Diffusion subsystem. One other action that is easy to overlook is adjustments to how we communicate the information or knowledge.

Leveraging Knowledge at Hewlett Packard

Headquartered in Palo Alto, CA, Hewlett Packard (HP) has quickly passed the $50 billion in annual sales, employs over 130,000 people worldwide, and operates in over 120 countries. *Fortune* magazine (March 3, 1998) recognized it as America's Most Admired Computers/Office Equipment Company. Lew Platt, HP's chairman, president, and CEO, recently stated that "Successful companies of the 21st century will be those who do the best jobs of capturing, storing, and leveraging what their employees know."

In keeping with this philosophy, the firm's consulting unit, which offers IT service management, enterprise desktop management, customer relationship management, and enterprise resource planning services, has undertaken a Knowledge Management Initiative to transform the decentralized knowledge of its consultants from a "latent asset into a resource available to everything within the organization."

The sharing of knowledge at HP Consulting was informal and serendipitously based on personal networks or accidental encounters at meetings. However, HP Consulting recognized that success would be "highly dependent on the ability to manage and leverage organizational knowledge — and that this knowledge, appropriately leveraged, was as valuable as financial assets" (Martiny, 1998).

To accomplish greater dissemination and diffusion of knowledge, HP Consulting had to create an environment where everyone was "enthusiastic about sharing knowledge and instituted processes that ensured this occurred." As Martiny observes, "the human side of knowledge management is the hard part — it involves creating a strong foundation where an organization moves from individual knowledge to organization knowledge, where it energizes itself to create knowledge sharing and reuse behaviors to tap its collective wisdom. HP Consulting had come to believe that sharing, leverage, and reuse of knowledge had to become part of its culture."

In 1996 a knowledge management initiative was launched with three key objectives:

1. To deliver more value to customers without increasing hours worked; to bring more intellectual capital to solutions
2. To create an environment where everyone is enthusiastic about sharing knowledge and leveraging the knowledge of others
3. To leverage and reuse knowledge, an initiative that required organizational change, especially on the part of leadership

Jim Sherriff, HP Consulting's general manager, realized that there was a significant opportunity to improve both the value delivered to customers and the profitability of the organization by tapping into the knowledge of the more experienced consultants — or, in his words, "to make the knowledge of the few the knowledge of the many." He strongly believed that all consultants in the organization needed to feel and act as if they had the knowledge of the entire organization at their fingertips when consulting with customers.

HP Consulting launched the knowledge management initiative using pilot programs that focused on the behavioral elements of

- Taking time to reflect and learn from successes and mistakes
- Creating an environment that encouraged sharing of knowledge and experiences between consultants
- Encouraging the sharing of best practices and reusable tools and solutions that could be leveraged by other consultants

Leadership also identified four values for sustaining knowledge sharing, leverage, and reuse in HP Consulting, namely,

1. Leveraging other people's knowledge, experience, and deliverables is a desired behavior.
2. Innovation is highly valued when both successes and failures are shared.
3. Time spent increasing both one's own and others' knowledge and confidence is a highly valued activity.
4. Consultants who actively share their knowledge and draw on the knowledge of others will dramatically increase their worth.

The results have been dramatic and extremely profitable for HP. Along the way knowledge management has progressed from an initiative to becoming a transformation leverage for HP Consulting, a knowledge-based business.

Richness Can Be Found in the Media of Communication

The movement of information can be hampered by very mechanical problems such as misrouting, message summarizing, information delay, and message modification. All of these concepts relate to the ability of a message to accurately arrive at a recipient from a sender. To understand this problem, Daft and Huber introduced the concept of "media richness." A medium is how information is carried from sender to receiver, and may include telephones, computer print-outs, memos, or face-to-face discussions. The richness, or capacity of each medium, is based on a blend of four characteristics: (1) the use of feedback so that errors can be corrected; (2) the ability to convey multiple cues; (3) relating the message to personal circumstances; and (4) language variety. They use this framework to classify several communication media.

Their point for dissemination and diffusion and the organizational learning system is that rich media facilitate interpretive learning. Therefore, if one is interested in the effective transfer of information and knowledge, the process should employ the richest communication media possible. They concluded that the face-to-face medium is much higher than telephone or written communications. It provides immediate feedback, multiple channels for cues, and is highly intimate.

Media richness not only increases the accuracy of transfer, but can also influence the speed of transfer. Zander and Kogut (1995) found that the transfer of manufacturing capabilities is influenced by the degree to which they may be codified and taught. Therefore, it is imperative that the actions of the Dissemination and Diffusion subsystem be deliberate in the selection of the information and how it is coded for transfer within the organization. In addition, the reliability of the transfer is enhanced through the appropriate selection of communication media for the transfer. NASA selected multiple media and provided various avenues for the transfer of information and achieving the knowledge capture that they wanted.

The formulation of the information and knowledge, the selection of the mode of transfer, and enhancing media richness are very important to the dissemination and diffusion processes. However, these can be very mechanical and short-term fixes to the organization's learning problem. Long-term change occurs when the actions in this subsystem reflect a supportive set of norms and role behaviors that will enhance the movement of information and knowledge. This entails structural change.

Diffusing Knowledge at National Semiconductor

Like many organizations, National was overwhelmed with information, retaining data that were not needed and losing valuable data that should have been stored. Employees were uncertain as to what to remember and what to leave behind. In order to cure its "corporate amnesia," the company began developing a corporate database and storage system. Here's how the knowledge management system was described in a recent issue of the company newsletter, the *InterNational News*:

Imagine a city block filled with many different libraries. Stacked on those miles of shelves are millions of books and articles, tons of art and graphics, even videotape, film and audio recordings. Now imagine that you want to seek information, but you have only a single library card, and can enter just one of those libraries. Worse yet, you have heard that other, better libraries exist in other cities around the world, but you have no idea where they are, or what's in them. Frustrating, isn't it? That was the knowledge storage and access situation at National until recently. Now mountains of information stored at different computer systems can be made available to staff throughout the company via a new project called "Knowledge at the Desktop."

Employees at National now have access to all kinds of information such as business plans, materials data, customer support, field sales, public relations, and human resources data. They also have access information from media sources, Sematech, news wires, patent and research records, and bibliographies. Not only text, but graphics, sound, and even video will be available. Fulcrum, a sophisticated new computer program, enables employees to access information on any National system, from whatever type of terminal or work station is at one's desk. A special corporate action team has successfully worked to "create an easy method for people to find their way through the information jungle," according to Mary Holland, Manager of the National Technical Library (Marquardt, 1996).

National Semiconductor cites three key benefits from its knowledge-sharing technology:

1. Increased participation from every part of the organization
2. Automatic knowledge storage and retrieval as well as corporate memory
3. Wider understanding and shared interpretations of knowledge bases

Sharing Learning and Technology

National Semiconductor holds annual in-house International Technology and Innovation Conferences for the purpose of encouraging National's technologists to create and share core technologies to "further National's Aspiration 2000 technology roadmap." Papers were recently presented in the following areas:

Circuit design and simulation
Manufacturing
Device technology and architecture
Process technology
Packaging
Test systems and methodologies
System and software development

Video Compression Technology for Learning

National Semiconductor has invested intensive creativity, time, and research in the development of video technology. Why is video compression so important to National? Because the interactive video capabilities of the new products such as document sharing on real time would not be possible without video compression — the available bandwidth of telephones is too narrow to send real-time motion video, and video data take up too much storage space. Video compression is a critical innovation for video playback, video conferencing, and videophones.

With this technology, National is able to develop a document or share information with co-workers halfway around the world in real time. The data are entered on a PC and it appears instantly on their screens. The team members receive feedback immediately. Together they can finalize specifications for a new run of chips or create a proposal for a new customer more quickly and conveniently than was ever thought possible before.

A Social Phenomenon Called "Structuration"

Do individuals control their behaviors in organizational situations, or does the situation dictate behavior of the individuals? This question is especially important in a free society in which learning is imperative to the survival of the organization. Organizations, by definition, will delimit actions and information through their structures.

In order to enact the social practice of the organization, individuals must draw on a set of rules. The members of the organization socially create these rules. This duality of structure relates to the recursive character of social life and expresses the mutual dependence of social structure on the individual and the individual's impact on the situation. Giddens (1979) makes the point that the implementation of social practices may have both intended and unintended consequences which give rise to unacknowledged conditions of action. These conditions then "structure" new action. In the conception of "structuration," the possibility of change is recognized as inherent in every circumstance of social reproduction.

Giddens feels that every action is a production of something new, a fresh act; but at the same time all action is connected with the past, which supplies the meaning of its initiation. He employs the terms "structure," "system," and "structuration" in ways that differ from traditional social science usage. By "structure," Giddens means rules and resources organized as properties of a social system; "system" is defined as the reproduced relations between individuals or organizations, organized as regular social practices; and "structuration" are those conditions governing the continuity of transformation of structures and, therefore, the reproduction of systems.

Structuration theory may provide a conceptual framework for analyzing the reasons why organizations do not appear to change, despite restructuring and other planned efforts to transform organizational culture. Although possibility of change is recognized as inherent in individual, Giddens suggest that recursive social practices, institutionalized in roles, structured by rules, power relations and locale, and ordered in time and space may prove difficult to modify (Biggs, 1996).

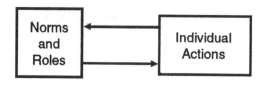

Figure 7.3 Learning as a Loosely Coupled System

Figure 7.3 illustrates this circular relationship between structure (norms etc.) and the actions of the organization and its members. In some sense, Giddens' concept is pessimistic because the organization may not be able to break its pattern of regenerating itself in its old image. However, the learning process can change the norms (and the culture) through inquiry into the basic assumptions. If we employ more flexible structures that provide more freedom we have a higher probability of breaking the cycle.

Loosely Coupled Systems

In a complex environment, the learning system must be open to a large variety of information. This means that the single point-of-entry of new information is not likely. What is more likely is that information enters all organizational subunits at all levels of management and individual interaction. As soon as we try to control, or delimit, these processes, we will defy the law of requisite variety and the organization's survival will be in question.

How do we achieve this variety yet maintain the ability of the organization to transfer information and knowledge to all of its elements? Orton and Weick (1990, p. 204) suggest loosely coupling as an option:

> Loose coupling has proven to be a durable concept precisely because it allows organizational analyses to explain the simultaneous existence of rationality and indeterminacy without specifying these two logics to distinct locations. Loose coupling suggests that any location in an organization (top, middle, or bottom) contains interdependent elements that vary in the number and strength of their interdependencies. The fact that these elements are linked and preserve some degree of determinacy is captured by the word *coupled* in the phrase *Loosely Coupled*. The fact that these elements are also subject to spontaneous changes and preserve some degree of independence and indeterminacy is captured by the modifying word *loosely*. The resulting image is a system that is simultaneously open and closed, indeterminate and rational, spontaneous and deliberate.

This concept has several possible effects on appropriate structuring to increase the learning system's capacity (see Figure 7.4). It is not necessary to counteract the phenomenon of loose coupling to achieve organizational integrity. In fact, in highly complex environments, the learning system must be loosely coupled so that it may anticipate and act as changes occur. As Orton and Weick postulate, the roles of the organization (i.e., leadership) can be used to compensate for loose coupling. We would agree, however, that these roles could also be designed to enhance the loose coupling actions to facilitate the movement of information and knowledge.

Moving and Creating Knowledge through Integrative Roles

Organizations are structured around a set of social roles that are defined by their functions, responsibilities, abilities, and social interactions. As Giddens

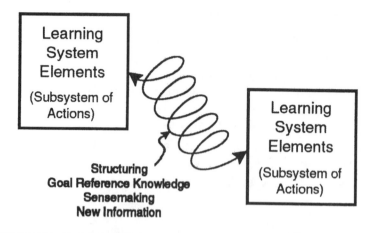

Figure 7.4 New Structuration Because of Information Systems

has pointed out, the implementation of these roles is a complex, cyclic interaction between the role actions and the norms that the organization holds for these actions. We will examine the actions of two roles (not always distinct) that the organization relies on to establish a structure: (1) the leader and (2) the manager.

The Role of a Manager/Leader in Structuring

Just as only changing the media richness level of an information transfer mode will not create a learning organization, neither will just changing the role behavior of managers increase the learning capacity. However, McGill et al. (1992) suggest that, in conjunction with structural changes such as the rewards system, organizational learning capacity is enhanced by managers' behaviors that reflect five dimensions:

> *Openness* requires that managers be willing to suspend their need for control. The second form of openness is cultural functional humility. In order to process multiple levels of experience, managers must be able to see their own values, background, and experiences as not necessarily better or worse than the values, background, and experiences of others. Managerial practices that promote openness:
> - Commitment to cultural functional diversity and selection, development, and promotion

- Use of multifunctional across functional work groups
- Conflict servicing, conflict resolving skills
- Ready availability of all information to all members

Systematic thinking is the ability to see connections between issues, events, and data points — the whole rather than its parts. It means framing structural relationships that resemble dynamic networks as opposed to static pattern interactions that are relationships predicated on one's position in the hierarchy. Management practices that encourage systemic thinking include:

- Sharing of accurate organizational histories that promote a sense of temporal continuity
- Recognizing the importance of relationships based on information, goods and services exchanges, and feelings (example, liking each other), in addition to traditional, line authority-based relationships
- Removing the artificial distinction between line and staff
- Explicit attention to the interrelationships between actions across the organization and between the organization and external forces

Creativity has two aspects that are particularly important for learning: personal flexibility and a willingness to take the risk. Managing in a learning organization requires an orientation that sees failure as feedback leading to further creativity. Managerial practices that promote personal flexibility:

- Long-term policies
- Mobility across divisions and functions
- Growth-oriented personal development
- Supportive "plan" culture

Personal efficacy allows a manager to feel that he/she can and should learn to significantly influence his/her world. Personal efficacy and proactive problem solving are promoted by:

- Clear vision
- Celebrating people that do make a difference
- Linking learning to action

Empathy allows managers to be sensitive to and have concern for human nature, and be interested in (and capable of) repairing strained relationships. Managerial practices that are socially responsible and respectful of individual dignity:

- Strong sense of ethics in dealing with employees and customers and clients
- Active corporate citizenship
- Recognition encouragement of employee contributions outside the workplace
- Willingness to take responsibility for relationships

These behaviors of managers are quite different from those that have been hammered into us by business schools that profess control, conformance, rules, and other mechanisms that were created to support rational organizing. Changes in the manager's role has also forced a rethinking of the role of leadership and organizing.

An example of structuring can be found in the role definition of leader or manager. If the role is defined as one of facilitator and teacher, rather than controller or monitor, the integrating capacity of the learning subsystem will be increased. Arthur Andersen, for example, does this by referring to supervisors as "learning coaches," workers as "learners," and the office as a "learning environment" (Marquardt, 1996). This is an example of positive structuring which is input to the meaning-memory subsystem to aid in creating meaning, and to the action/reflection subsystem to aid in reflection and the movement of goal referenced knowledge.

Leadership and Learning at U.S. Shell

In order to unleash the potential of Shell's people, the company is moving to systems of governance that disperse authority and responsibility throughout the organization and aim to create a greater sense of ownership and enlarged opportunities for personal growth. Shell believes that leadership skills can be broadened and deepened in everyone. Through leadership development workshops, the company is helping managers understand their personal potential and discover new ways of thinking and doing. These transformational activities are taking place under the Learning and Performance (LEAP) program. This corporate initiative provides the framework within which both individual and collective learning take place. Shell believes that the most powerful learning experiences, the ones that produce the fastest and most lasting results, are those in which real people are engaged in finding real solutions to real problems — an action learning process.

Brenneman and colleagues (1998) postulate the following principles based on their experiences at U.S. Shell:

1. Learning is virtually automatic in organizations characterized by workplace attributes created by top management like clarity of goals, roles and expectations, openness, curiosity about alternatives, respect, and attentive listening.
2. Conditions for learning, when they are not already present, must be created by new or transformed powerholders who articulate, model, and reinforce the learning attributes. Training or experiential workshops cannot replace these conditions.
3. Only the truth about cultural current reality can set an organization free of the invisible undiscussables that constrain learning and performance. To find that truth requires the power of managerial accountability modeling and insisting on rigorous fact-based, systemic reasoning to break out of event thinking.

Successful organizational learning competencies for leaders, defined by Shell, include the ability to build a shared vision, an in-depth knowledge of the business, the skill to think systematically, and the ability to communicate through open and honest dialogue. Although these competencies are established at the corporate level, they are not viewed as "edicts from on high." LEAP actually works with the operating units to "sell them" on the expediency of these competencies and on the need for each leader to build his/her own "teachable point of view on leadership."

Roles of Leadership in the Learning System

No other role in organizations has received more interest than that of the leader. The traditional argument of leader or manager has now been replaced with the search for "leadership." This behavior, characteristic, or trait does not have to be manifested in one individual or in a single role.

Leadership has truly become a social phenomenon that is necessary for the integration and transformation of social systems. This is true of both learning and performance actions systems. It is linked with organizational innovation, profitability, and survival. Bouwen and Fry explored the role of the leader during innovation, which is a time that demands a high organizational learning capacity. They defined innovation as (Bouwen and Fry, 1991, p. 37):

> ... the development and implementation of new ideas by people who are over time engaging in transactions with others within an institutional order. The emphasis is on the interactive process among people about new ideas and organizational context. Innovation is not confined to the new technology of products. Turnarounds, mergers, restructuring, total quality, continuous improvement programs, globalization projects, and so on are at the forefront of many transformations. They require the organizational capacity to learn how to translate ideas or intentions into new actions.

Their premise was that the quality of the dialogue during the innovation would define the quality of the organizational learning taking place. They found that the role of the leader can be quite different in the transformation from an existing dominant logic to a more innovative frame of reference.

Their research resulted in defining four possible role models for the leader: (1) the power model, (2) the sales model, (3) an expert model, and finally (4) the confrontational learning model. The power model uses the leader to direct the innovation from the top down. The sales model was indicative of the leader assuming a salesperson's role with a smooth approach to selling the innovation. The expert model relied heavily on the leader as expert and expert knowledge to convince members that the innovation was rational. The learning model relied heavily on coaching; that is, the leader assumed a role of facilitator with process knowledge.

Learning was "facilitated through confrontation processes, that is to say cognitive emotional restructuring. The basis for the decisions in the learning model was through consultation and consensus validation. The sequence of actions in the learning model were experimenting, evaluating, questioning, and then recycling" (Bouwen and Fry, 1991, p. 38).

The leader as learning facilitator resulted in longer-term change. However, it relies on a shared "common sense" and meaning that is supported by open and flexible communications up and down the organization's structure. This becomes a key role — action for the leader.

Leadership can occur not only in the individual role but also in collective roles. Croswell's study of nonprofit organizations and their governing networks found that the network as a collective employed two patterns of leadership —

dialogical leadership and appreciative leadership. Dialogical leadership is the dynamic exchange between the governing network and the members that results in both effective communications and the empowering of the membership. When the third variable of cultural leadership is added, dialogic leadership seems to also become appreciative of relationships and the organization's culture as a system.

> Members of the governing network of the nonprofit organization used new information about the environment to make decisions and determined collective goals for their actions. At the same time, members of the governing network shared new information by communicating with other members in a way that added valence to mutually shared understanding and meanings. In short the governing network was continuously moving information and assigning meaning to it. For instance, members of the governing network used their roles as leaders to disseminate and diffuse information. At the same time they used leadership in the interface with the environment to collect and move new information. (Croswell, 1996, p. 182)

The manifestation of leadership by the collective is intricately linked to the learning process of the organization. The leadership role as a visionary and facilitator is imperative for the movement of knowledge and information, both within and between organizations as can be seen by the following leader, Ricardo Semler.

Ricardo Semler — Semco's Visionary Leader

Semco manufactures a varied roster of products, including pumps that can empty an oil tanker in a night, dishwashers capable of scrubbing 4100 plates per hour, cooling units for air conditioners that keep huge office towers comfortable during the most sweltering of heat waves, mixers that blend everything from rocket fuel to bubble gum, and entire biscuit factories, with 6000 separate components and 16 miles of wiring. Semco is presently one of the fastest growing companies in Brazil; 1997 revenues were over $100 million with profits of $8.2 million (Wheatley and Blount, 1997). It is considered one of the most innovative companies in the world.

Much of Semco's success is attributed to its maverick leader, Ricardo Semler, who has helped Semco not only survive, but thrive in a country that barely blinks at 3000% inflation:

"The threat of competition keeps us all on our toes," says Semler. "Recently, we have encouraged employees to start their own companies, leasing them Semco machinery at favorable rates. We buy from our former employees, of course, but they are also free to sell to others, even to Semco's competitors. This program has made us leaner and more agile, and given them ultimate control of their work lives. It makes entrepreneurs out of employees" (Semler, 1994).

Semler has also developed a new "hierarchy" of leadership. The Semco bureaucracy has been whittled from 12 layers of management to 3 and replaced with a new structure based on concentric circles to replace the traditional, and confining, corporate pyramid. There are still leaders in Semco — but instead of a pyramid hierarchy, there's a more complex geometry: a ring of "counselors" — including Semler — who handle Semco's general policies and strategies; a slightly bigger circle of partners, who head up Semco's seven business units; a large pool of associates, which comprise most of the workers; and all sorts of triangular, coordinating configurations in-between. Circles would free our people from hierarchical tyranny; they could act as leaders when they wanted and command whatever respect their efforts and competence earned them.

Innovations and Learnings Built on Trust

As a result of Semler's numerous innovative changes, Semco has been revolutionized from dark ages-style management practices by innovations which would challenge the thinking of even the most progressive organization. The key thrust of Semler's vision is founded in his faith that when people say they will do something, in general, they do. He has thus sought to create a company which is free from fear and insecurity and is characterized by freedom, trust, learning, and commitment. He has brought new dimensions to the term "empowerment."

Building trust and teams is seen as essential for any organization to be innovative and to learn as an organization according to Semler. Thus, Semco does away with the formalities that discourage team development. "We encourage movement between projects and areas within the organization which help team creation and recreation. Because we work on 6-month operations budgets, there is a tendency to have to rethink things every couple of months. Then there is the transparency — the fact that everyone knows what is going on. Also, we do balance sheet training programs and these include the janitors. That helps trust. There is no classified information whatsoever in the company" (Lloyd, 1994).

Semler presents himself as the questioner, the challenger, the catalyst, as the person who asks basic questions and encourages people to bring things down to the simplest level in making key decisions shaping their work performance. By challenging the status quo at every turn and allowing people to come up with appropriate solutions, the attack on bureaucracy and conventional styles of management became more and more dramatic, leading to many novel innovations such as the spinning off of factories and other business units into separate, self-regulating units; widespread profit-sharing; the hiring and firing of mangers by their employees; and the idea that to keep employed you've got to find a way of adding visible value so that your team will continue to want to include you as part of their 6-month budget. As a result of these innovations on the part of his employees, Semler prides himself on the fact that he is now completely dispensable and spends less and less time working for the company.

Semler realizes that the only real source of power within an organization is information, and the real test of an organization's approach is whether this is really shared and open. By the democratization of information, you can take out layers of management, thus really encouraging teamwork. Sharing power grows responsibility, and that encourages people's growth and trust.

At Semco, there is a true commitment to democracy in the workplace. In addition, Semco has a system where all our strategic or long-range planning is done through a series of meetings in which these decision-making discussions are open to anyone who wants to attend. As one union representative has noted, "Only at Semco are workers treated like responsible people."

Semler notes, "We treat our employees as adults. We trust them. We get out of their way and let them do their jobs. We don't condone symbols of power or exclusivity such as executive cafeterias or reserved parking places. We give people an opportunity to test, question, and disagree. We let them determine their own training and their own futures. We let them come and go as they want, work at home if they wish, set their own salaries, choose their own bosses. We let them change their minds and ours, prove us wrong when we are wrong, and make us humbler" (Semler, 1993).

"It's time to really involve employees," continues Semler. "The era of using people as production tools is coming to an end. Participation is infinitely more complex to practice than conventional corporate unilateralism, just as democracy is much more cumbersome than dictatorship. But there will be few companies that can afford to ignore either of them." As Semler has often stated, "Only the respect of the led creates a leader."

Learning and Sabbaticals

Semler believes that everyone in Semco needs to be constantly learning. Employees can take what Semler calls "hepatitis leave," i.e., a sabbatical to recharge and "do what you would do if you had hepatitis and couldn't come to work for a month or so." This sabbatical allows associates to take a few weeks or even a few months every year or two away from their usual duties to read books or articles, to learn new skills, or to redesign their jobs.

Another way in which Semco people are forced to learn quickly is through regular job rotations. People stay in jobs for a minimum of 2 years and maximum of 5 years. This obliges people to learn new skills, which makes life interesting for them and makes them more valuable to the organization. It also discourages empire building and gives people a much broader perspective of the company. This form of organizational learning also forces the company to prepare more than one person for a job and generates opportunities for those who might otherwise be trapped in the middle of the pyramid. A final value of job rotation is that it encourages the spread of diverse personalities, outlooks, backgrounds, and techniques, thus injecting new blood and fresh vision throughout the company (Semler, 1993). At Semco the offices for the various departments such as purchasing and engineering are scrambled so that everyone sits together. The idea is that "we all can learn from one another."

At Semco, "we encourage everyone to mix with everyone else, regardless of job. Nearly all of our workers have mastered several jobs, which has caused conflict with the unions' need for narrow job classifications, but is critical for our company's survival." Over a period of years, however, Semco has develop a "learning trust" with the labor unions, one that has been helped by the development of a course to teach everyone, even messengers and cleaning people, to read balance sheets and cash flow statements.

Semler attributes the company's success, despite some of the harshest economic conditions imaginable, to its ability to keep on learning, to continuously recognize and adapt to change or, as he puts it, "We have learned to see the need for change and have been smart enough to seek our employees' help in making change happen."

Structuring External Relationships

In Chapter 5 we discussed the use of partnership and joint ventures as organizational actions that would increase the amount and quality of new information that was available to the learning system. This mechanism will provide new information; however, the relationships have to be structured to facilitate the movement of the information into the organization.

Barlow and Fashapara's study of partnering in the U.K.'s construction industry explores the role of the construction industry "partnering" — development of closer collaborative links between firms — and the stimulation of organizational learning. Their research of partnering relationships involving large clients (British Petroleum, NatWestBank, McDonald's, Selfridges, Safeway) and over 40 other contractors and suppliers identified four factors which can either facilitate or hamper the transfer of knowledge between organizations (Barlow and Fashapara, 1998, p. 90):

1. There may be inherent tensions in conflict between clients and suppliers if they are driven in different directions due to the nature of the competitive environment. For example, one partner may have innovation as his intent, while the other partner was expecting cost reduction.

2. The transferability of knowledge between organizations is shaped by two important parameters, the degree which it can be codified — structured according to a set of easily communicated identifiable rules — and its complexity. Information that is readily codified and simple is more easily transferred as opposed to information that is more embedded in the organizing principles by which people work and cooperate within organizations.

3. The mere existence of a partnering relationship is not in itself sufficient — firms need to be able to recognize the value of knowledge and its application. This "absorptive capacity" depends in part on the ways in which knowledge is retained and distributed. This suggests that the internal and external communications structures of the organization will be an important influence on absorptive capacity as well as the turnover of staff.

4. The question of absorptive capacity highlights the role of internal political and cultural environments in aiding or hindering appropriate communications structures and organizational forms. It has been argued that since communication is an exchange of information and

words, ideas, or emotions, true communication is only possible between people who to some extent share a system of meaning.

One of the consistent findings of this structural research is that attempts to improve the retention and distribution of information and develop less hierarchical communications structures were a common feature in all the case studies. These generally involved cutting out a chain of command or allowing key people in each organization to talk directly to one another (Barlow and Fashpara, 1998).

Reengineering and Learning at CIGNA

CIGNA is a leading provider of health care, insurance, and financial services throughout the U.S. and around the world, with assets of approximately $109 billion and over 47,000 people providing services to 12 million people and 21,000 companies.

CIGNA introduced business reengineering into its organization 5 years ago and saved more than $100 million. There are lessons, positive and negative, that can be drawn from CIGNA's experiences. Its success in business reengineering started small — in a pilot project in a vulnerable division of the company. That pilot was a success — a quick hit. The organization then ramped up from this success, transferring the knowledge learned from this "experiment" into larger and more complex parts of the organization. This was not a smooth transition; there were many difficulties along the way. But business reengineering effectively worked and was sustained — from the bottom up, with learning transferred "across" the entire organization.

By the end of 1993 all of CIGNA's nine business divisions had completed business reengineering projects, some with mixed results. Overall, however, a detailed financial analysis of more than 20 projects suggested that each $1 invested in reengineering ultimately returned $2 to $3 in benefits.

Two key lessons were gained about organizational learning and transfer from these reengineering efforts:

1. **Diffuse and leveraged learnings from each project**. Personal transfers from CIGNA's reengineering group back to business areas were an effective way to enable knowledge sharing, as was the creation of a reengineering database on completed projects.

2. **Learn from failure.** Reengineering involves radical change in a number of areas including organization structure, systems, culture, and, increasingly, strategy. Radical change is hard to accomplish. To succeed, one must be willing to accept failure, learn from it, but remain focused on the end goal. Multiple trials were sometimes necessary to enable success with reengineering. The senior corporate management created a culture where failure was tolerated as long as the organization learned from it (Caron et al., 1994).

We have seen from the above discussions that the ability of the Dissemination and Diffusion subsystem to move information and knowledge is dependent on the social integration capacity of the organization. This integration is achieved through the structuring interchange media. Patterns of interchange involve the richness of the communication media, the norms of the organization, the organizational roles, and the coupling of system elements through mechanisms such as partnerships. All of these aspects are important when we look to information systems to solve our integration problems.

Structuring through Information Management Systems

No one today can disagree with the statement that computer technology is involved in all aspects of our organizational lives. With the exception of a few problems (YK2), organizations are benefiting from their investments. If we consider the factors discussed above, we must consider the structuring that is now being supplied (or supplanted) by technology and these systems. However, much of the initial use of information technology was to control the organization's information and to increase efficiencies.

One of the earliest attempts at linking information technology to the structuring concept was the work of Barley (1996). This research described the changes within the social structure of a hospital radiological department when a new information technology was introduced. The author's foundational premise revolves around the notion that organizations are in a constant state of recreating themselves in varying forms, but always within the context of resident social force behaviors, actions, and interpretations. This is very similar to Giddens' concept of structuration. In other words, although constantly shifting, organizations tend to stabilize around the socially constructed norms of the organization members.

The degree of centralization of decision-making within an organization tends to serve as a critical determinant of the number of middle managers when implementing information technology. In other words, "when there is extensive centralization of decision-making, information technology will tend be used by higher level management to reduce the middle management workforce" (Hinds, 1995, p. 81).

Of course in today's organization, information management systems have gone far beyond the simple replacement of levels of management. Shoshana Zuboff, in her classic work, *In the Age of the Smart Machine,* viewed information technology as having both an automating and informating society. Automate refers to the traditional concept of automating routine functions which replaced human work. On the other hand, informate refers to providing new information which is becoming perceptible by virtue of an automating process (Zuboff, 1988).

Edgar Schein used Zuboff's concepts to describe the leader's visions of information technology's possible impact on organizations. He found four visions:

1. An automate vision — the leader views information technology as a means to automate human activities.
2. An informate-up vision — leader envisions the use of information technology to automate human activities and can provide data to achieve greater control of the organizational processes.
3. An informate-down vision — the opposite view of the informate-up, where the leader automates human activities and empowers workers with the additional data.
4. A transform vision — the leader views information technology as an enabler to completely recast the organization (Schein, 1992).

Schein's more recent report of the leader's perception of information systems appears to support Zuboff's concerns about information and its potential when she says, "It must be an unwritten law of social life that hierarchies will utilize any means available as a potential method for reproducing, extending, and heightening those experiences through which elite groups win legitimization" (p. 303).

A more recent study by Hinds (1995) of top leaders in the military information management field found that these concerns of both Schein and Zuboff are somewhat changing to different concerns. His research resulted in the following conclusions:

- Information technology acts as an enormously powerful exploiter of organizational structures. This appears to be especially true when considering information technologies' ability to circumvent or otherwise ignore formal structure. In other words, an organization's information flow does not seem to be confined to any mandated formal design. This results in flattening the organization, whether the leadership wants it or not.
- Information policies are not necessarily the same as the policies that govern information technologies. Many organizations have not completely made sense of the use of information systems and what that means.
- Information technology has introduced new and increasingly complex ethical issues, such as the protection of personally sensitive information.
- Overall, the consistent pattern described by the participants in the study was that both individual and collective roles are in a constant state of flux largely because of information technology. Where information technology enables greater individual and collective work capacities, flexibility, and time management, there is also a potential of opposing costs because of information overload.
- A particularly revealing aspect of the study was that information technology tends to accentuate a leader's basic decision-making skills. The relevant circumstances and background information available to the leader are probably also available to his or her subordinates.

These results reflect Zuboff's idea that technology radically alters the context of what is possible. Information systems and their potential have now forced us to consider another dimension of structuring. The availability of information is outrunning our collective ability to reflect. The past structuring patterns that included norms, roles, and structures are being challenged by information systems.

A different view of Giddens' structuration, as seen in Figure 7.5, portrays this new complex interaction. Here we see almost separate structuring processes in place. The information system is almost in competition with the other structuring variables. This competition will work against the movement of information and knowledge. What is desirable is the integration of the two structuring entities so as to increase the organization's learning capacity. It may rely on a new conceptualization of the organization and its structure (Zuboff, 1988, p. 350):

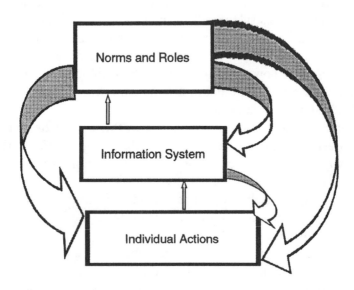

Figure 7.5 Analysis of Interchange Media

It rests on a new collectivism in which "the many" view themselves and each views "the other." Horizontal visibility is created even as vertical visibility is intensified. The model is less one of Big Brother than of a workplace in which each member is explicitly empowered as his or her fellow worker's keeper. Instead of a single omniscient overseer, this panopticon relies upon shared custodianship of data that reflect mutually enacted behavior.

Federal Express — Moving Learning as well as Packages

Federal Express (FedEx) is the world's largest express transportation company, delivering over 2 million items in 200 countries each working day. Headquartered in Memphis, TN, the numbers at FedEx are large and growing — over 110,000 employees, daily flights into more than 325 airports, 1400 staffed facilities, and more than 30,000 drop-off locations. The company prides itself for setting "the standards in the shipping industry for reliability, innovative technology, logistics management, and customer satisfaction." FedEx has received numerous awards, including the Malcolm Baldridge National Quality Award.

Under the guidance of CEO Fred Smith, FedEx has made a conscious and deliberate effort to create a learning organization and to use technology in improving the speed and quality of learning within the organization. FedEx leaders are quick to point out that technology has significantly boosted the company's intellectual capacity, agility, and resourcefulness.

Huge Investments in Learning Technologies

FedEx has made enormous investments in building its learning technology resources — more than $40 million in 1200 systems in 800 field locations. Each location is stocked with 30 interactive videodisk programs, which have been used to train many of FedEx's 30,000 couriers and customer service employees.

Focused employee training using technology has been going on at FedEx for more than 10 years, but in 1995 FedEx launched a new interactive training system using multimedia workstations made by Silicon Graphics. These screens combine TV-quality video with text, graphics, and voice to teach basic interaction skills such as customer-contact methods and features of service categories for its 35,000 couriers and customer service agents. People are trained at a pace that's more personal for them and more customized that the stick-and-pointer classroom. A certain amount of training is required annually, but because it is done using interactive multimedia, there is more flexibility than in the past when classroom time needed to be scheduled. Now training can occur at the beginning or end of a shift, or whenever the individual can best fit in what will be very personalized instruction.

In recent years FedEx replaced some of its classroom training programs with a computer-based training system that uses interactive video on work station screens. This training system can capture and interpret input from learners to determine whether a task is being performed correctly. If a learner makes a mistake, the system recognizes the error, points it out, and shows the proper method.

The interactive video instruction system presents training programs that combine television quality, full-motion video, analog audio, digital audio, text, and graphics using both laser disk and CD-ROM. Learners can interact with the system using a touch screen or keyboard.

The interactive video training closely correlates with job testing. Using the system, employees can study about their job, company policies and procedures, and brush up on customer service issues by reviewing various courses. Currently, there are over 1200 interactive video instruction units placed at more than 700 FedEx locations. All workstations are linked to the FedEx mainframe in Memphis. Each location has 21 videodisks that make up the customer-contact curriculum. There is virtually no subject or job-related topic that the customer contact workers cannot find on the interactive video instruction platform.

Once the CD-ROM courseware is written, FedEx knows that it is imperative to keep it updated. The work force relies on the fact that the system provides accurate and current information. For them, out-of-date information is worse than no information at all. For this reason, a new CD-ROM is sent to each location every 6 weeks. This CD-ROM updates the curriculum through text, PC graphics, and digital audio. Over 1000 updates are made on an annual basis.

Performance Improvement through Interactive Video Instruction

FedEx recently created a mandatory performance-improvement program for all of the company's employees who deal with customers either face-to-face or over the phone. The primary goals of this program were (1) to completely centralize the development of training content while decentralizing delivery and (2) to audit the employees' ability to retain what was learned.

The pay-for-performance program consists of job knowledge tests that are linked to an interactive video instruction (IVI) training curriculum accessed on workstations in more than 700 locations nationwide. More than 35,000 FedEx customer contact employees around the country are required to take the job knowledge tests annually via computer terminals at their work locations. The tests, which measure employees' knowledge in their specific jobs, correspond with employees' annual evaluations. In fact, the results of the tests make up approximately one tenth of the employees' performance ratings.

By testing customer contact employees on product knowledge services, policies, and various aspects of their jobs, FedEx obtains two major benefits, according to William Wilson, manager of training and testing technology, namely:

1. All employees operate from the same book, ensuring that all customers will receive accurate and consistent information during each transaction. This helps the company maintain its high service levels and commitment to quality.

2. Managers have an objective way to measure job knowledge for all customer-contact employees.

FedEx provides many incentives for workers to quickly increase their learning. For example, employees are paid for 2 hours of test preparation prior to each test, 2 hours of test time, and 2 hours of posttest study time. Workers use the interactive video instruction programs for over 132,000 hours/year. Compared to traditional training, this equates to approximately 800 1-day classes for 20 employees per class, yet no trainers are necessary and no travel costs are incurred.

The Integrating Subsystem for Organizational Learning

The Dissemination and Diffusion subsystem moves, transfers, retrieves, and captures information and knowledge, and thus provides the integrating requirements of the other subsystems. In this chapter we looked at the actions associated with the Dissemination and Diffusion subsystem of actions as well as its relationship to the other subsystems through the use of the interchange media. We saw examples of this in the patterns established between the roles of managers (structuring) and knowledge capture (goal referenced knowledge), as well as the relationship between partnerships (structuring) and new information transfer. Nine case studies, including McKinsey, Arthur Andersen, NASA, Hewlett Packard, National Semiconductor, U.S. Shell, Semco, CIGNA, and Federal Express were presented to demonstrate the challenges and experiences of organizational learning in the Dissemination and Diffusion subsystem. Let us now examine the Memory and Meaning subsystem, the most difficult and highly critical subsystem to truly implement organizational learning.

References

Barley, S., Technology as an occasion for structuring, *Administrative Science Quarterly*, 3(1), 78, 1996.

Barlow, J. and Fashapara, A., Organizational learning and inter-firm "partnering" in the UK construction industry, *Learning Organization*, 5(2), 86–98, 1998.

Biggs, M., The Exercise of Authority by Team Managers during the Implementation of Self-Directed Work Teams: A Case Study, Dissertation, Human Resource Development, George Washington University, Washington, D.C., 1996.

Bouwen, R. and Fry, R., Organizational innovation and learning, *International Studies of Management and Organizations*, 21(4), 37–51, 1991.

Brenneman, W., Keys, B., and Fulmer, R., Learning across a living company: the Shell companies experience, *Organizational Dynamics*, 27(2), 61–69, 1998.

Buckley, W., Society as a complex adaptive system, *Modern Systems Research for the Behavioral Scientist*, Buckley, W., Ed., Aldine, Chicago, 1968.

Caron, J., Jarenpaa, S., and Stoddard, D., Business reengineering at CIGNA Corporation, *MIS Quarterly*, 18(2), 233–251, 1994.

Croswell, C.V., Organizational Learning in Nonprofit Organizations: A Description of the Action Patterns of Professional Association's Governing Network and Leadership Role in Turbulent Times, Dissertation, Human Resources Development, George Washington University, Washington, D.C., 1996.

Duarte, D. and Schwandt, D.R., Using Organizational Learning in an Action Research Intervention to Maintain Critical Technical Knowledge and Skills, Paper read at Academy of Human Resource Development, Minneapolis, 1996.

Fierman, J., Winning ideas from maverick managers, *Fortune*, 131(2), 66–80, 1995.

Giddens, A., *Central Problems in Social Theory: Action, Structure and Contradiction in Social Analysis*, University of California Press, Berkeley, 1979.

Hinds, R.C., Information Technology and Organizational Learning: A Case Study of Structuring in a Military Environment, Dissertation, Human Resource Development, George Washington University, Washington, D.C., 1995.

Lloyd, B., Maverick! An alternative approach to leadership, company organization, and management, *Leadership Organization Development Journal*, 15(2), 8–12, 1994.

Marquardt, M., *Building the Learning Organization*, McGraw-Hill, New York, 1996.

Martiny, M., Knowledge management at HP Consulting, *Organizational Dynamics*, 27(2), 71–77, 1998.

McGill, M.E., Slocum, J.W., and Lei, D., Management practices in learning organization, *Organizational Dynamics*, Summer, 5–17, 1992.

McNerney, D., Maverick: the success story behind the world's most unusual workplace, *Organizational Dynamics*, 24(2), 92, 1995.

Orton, J.D. and Weick, K.E., Loosely coupled systems: a reconceptualization, *Academy of Management Review*, 15(2), 203–223, 1990.

Schein, E.H., The role of the CEO in the management of change: the case of information technology, in *Transforming Organizations*, Kochan, T.A. and Useem, M., Eds., Oxford Press, New York, 1992.

Semler, R., *The Maverick*, Warner Books, New York, 1993.

Semler, R., Managing without managers, *Harvard Business Review*, 67(5), 76–84, 1989.

Semler, R., Why my former employees still work for me, *Harvard Business Review*, 72(1), 64–71, 1994.

Szulanski, G., Exploring internal stickiness: impediment to the transfer of best practice within the firm, *Stategic Management Journal*, 17 (Winter Special Issue), 27–43, 1996.

Wheatley, J. and Blount, J., The maverick, *Latin Trade*, May, 59, 1997.

Zander, U. and Kogut, B., Knowledge and the speed of transfer and imitation of organizational capabilites: an empirical test, *Organization Science*, 6(1), 76–92, 1995.

Zuboff, S., Automate/informate: the two faces of intelligent technology, *Organizational Dynamics*, Autumn, 4–18, 1985.

Zuboff, S., *In the Age of the Smart Machine: The Future of Work and Power*, Basic Books, New York, 1988.

8 The Essences of the Learning System: The Meaning and Memory Subsystem

> As we move from that which is rational, through that which is natural, to that which is open, we concurrently move from structures, processes, and environments that are less ambiguous to those that are more so. And with these moves comes a greater premium on sensemaking.
>
> Karl Weick, 1995

Breakdowns and Sensemaking

How many times have we heard people in organizations say, "What are we doing? It just doesn't make sense to me." These words, and this language, are symbols of a breakdown in the capability of the individuals within an organization to understand why the organization thinks and operates the way it does, to be able to use the organization's cultural assumptions and values to place new information in an understandable perspective.

The reasons for this breakdown can be from one of many sources. For example, it could be because the organization's values and assumptions do not permit the matching of the new information; i.e., it does not "fit" with the organization's understanding of the world and its culture. Or, it could be that the new information is not available for reflection because of the inflexible, or tightly controlled, structuring. Or, it could be that the organization does not provide time or the opportunity to reflect on the meaning of the new information, or the meaning of their closely held assumptions.

The ability of an organization to make sense of what is happening to it and remember the knowledge that is critical to its survival is an organizational imperative. The Meaning and Memory subsystem is responsible for these functions. It is the hardest of the four learning subsystems to objectify. Just like Parsons' subsystem of pattern maintenance, its actions are many times "latent." That is, the actions are present and capable of becoming visible, though they may not now be visible or active. The actions of this subsystem are intrinsically linked to the organization's culture — which is also many times not visible, but yet always present.

The Foundation for the Other Subsystems

The Meaning and Memory subsystem provides the foundation from which the other subsystems draw guidance and control. It maintains the mechanisms that create the criteria for the judgment, selection, focus, and control of the organizational learning system. The conceptual base for this subsystem is that learning for the organization is dependent on a certain level of shared understanding, values, and meaning. In addition, it evokes sentiments and behaviors, and plays an essential role in the Action/Reflection subsystem as it creates goal referenced knowledge. An example of this interpretation of symbols and actions is the use of an employee identification badge symbolizing organization membership and/or status.

Although the subsystem is made up of interpretive assumptions, its primary content consists of symbols that include language, social objects, and human actions that are based on, or represent, those assumptions. Also included are those acts directed at sustaining and creating the cultural beliefs, values, assumptions, and artifacts of the organization.

The subsystem is constructed so that knowledge can be stored and retrieved to affect the actions of the organization. The Memory subsystem contains a series of storage mechanisms, each with its own retrieval schema.

These storage mechanisms are the individuals, the culture, the ecology, the transformations, and the structures (Walsh and Ungson, 1991). This subsystem's operation includes both human and technical processes; for example, records, databases, routines, and people. Human processes include collective and individual remembering and the use of consensus to construct history.

Sensemaking as the Interchange Medium

The sensemaking medium is a product of the Meaning and Memory subsystem that carries out the function of pattern maintenance for the organizational learning system. The sensemaking produced and transferred from this subsystem is the product of sets of actions within the organization collective and is symbolically represented by its language and symbols. As depicted in Figure 8.1, it is this medium that the organizational learning system relies on to make sense of its actions in reflection; it is this medium

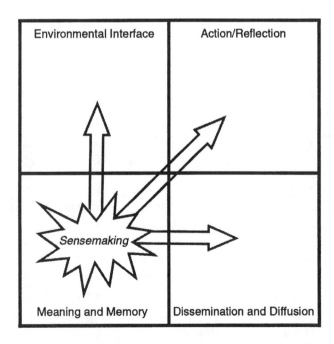

Figure 8.1 Meaning and Memory Output is Sensemaking

that is required to move and classify goal referenced knowledge into stored memory; and it is this sensemaking medium that is required by the Dissemination-Diffusion subsystem to generate appropriate structuring.

Language and symbols provide the means through which the Meaning-Memory subsystem communicates with the other subsystems within the organizational learning system. Language and symbols can be described as the specific words, signals, schemes (interpretive guidelines), and scripts (stored response routines) used by members of the collective in the action-taking process. Language and symbols are the outputs upon which the exchange process is dependent in order to produce useful information, goal reference knowledge, and structure for the organizational learning system.

An example of this medium can be found in the healthcare industry. Many hospitals are implementing a new form of patient-care delivery called "patient-focused care" which is designed to locate all patient ancillary services (pharmacy, radiology, nutritional care, respiratory therapy, etc.) on traditional nursing service floors. This would consolidate and change all patient-care delivery roles. Refocusing the meaning of hospital care to patient-focused care requires the organization to make new sense out of their services, structure, and roles. In turn, the changing of roles, titles, and structures changed the language and symbols associated with patient care (i.e., patient-focused care). This is similar to Giddens' structuration that we encountered in Chapter 7.

Organizational Memory and Sensemaking at Knight-Ridder

Headquartered in Miami, FL, Knight-Ridder owns daily newspapers across the U.S., including such prestigious papers as *The Philadelphia Inquirer*, *The Miami Herald*, and *The San Jose Mercury News*. Together, its newspapers have won an unprecedented 62 Pulitzer Prizes, earning Knight-Ridder the reputation as the best newspaper publishing company in the U.S.

Knight-Ridder's minor role in online information services changed dramatically in 1988 when it acquired Dialog Information Services, Inc. from Lockheed Corporation for approximately $353 million. The purchase of Dialog was the largest acquisition in the history of Knight-Ridder, extending its operations and sales to 87 countries. Thus, Knight-Ridder had vaulted overnight from the periphery of the online information business to its very center.

The late 1980s marked the beginning of another major initiative inside Knight-Ridder that was to have a dramatic effect on how it produced its basic product — the daily newspaper. This project was labeled "25/43" because its goal was to increase readership among persons between the ages of 25 and 43, often called the generation of "baby boomers." The impetus for the 25/43 project was a concern over declines in readership, especially among these young adults. Accordingly, 25/43 was designed to seek changes in newspaper design that would attract readers in the target age group. More than 300 people from four Knight-Ridder newspapers participated in the project.

Most important, 25/43 produced fundamental changes in the way that many Knight-Ridder newspapers were produced. The "25/43 process," as it came to be known, refocused the product on the changing market by drawing input from readers. Fundamental changes in the traditional newsroom culture resulted in shorter articles, products tailored to readers' interests, and more helpful packaging and presentation.

Wishart et al. (1996) describe how Knight-Ridder adjusted to these traumatic changes:

> Discussions with Knight-Ridder's executives revealed a clear change in two shared cognitions about the organization. First, shared concepts of the identity of the company changed following acquisition of Dialog. Members now regarded Knight-Ridder as a "preeminent deliverer of information services" and "an organization with international interests and international reach." ...Thus, Knight-Ridder's change in corporate identity involved a significant move into electronically mediated information services. Because this change was not a radical departure from the core newspaper business, members of the organization were able to incorporate it into existing memory. (p. 11)

The second cognitive component of Knight-Ridder's organizational memory to change was its shared mental model of the causes of corporate success. Knight-Ridder's original formula for success was that high-quality journalism, combined with an increasing population, would generate increasing sales and advertising revenues. As the company looked toward a future in which information technology would play a prominent role, it believed it would need to expand beyond the production of printed media to the delivery of electronic services.

The willingness to question underlying assumptions was also evident in the 25/43 project. At most Knight-Ridder papers, a strong newsroom culture had grown up around the mental model that high-quality journalism was instrumental to corporate success. Thus, the assumption that quality equals success was modified to include an additional assumption that both relevance and quality were prerequisites to success.

The 25/43 project afforded the best opportunity to see revisions in a behavioral component of organization memory. Although Knight-Ridder's initial goal with 25/43 was to learn the effects of newspaper format and content on readership levels, a more fundamental lesson was learned: how to listen to readers. The project began with market research on baby boomers and brainstorming sessions with employees, followed by focus groups with customers to test out some of these ideas. The focus groups proved to be the key ingredient in the new process of obtaining customer input. Bill Baker, Vice President/News, explained how the 25/43 process had become part of a new culture for all of Knight-Ridder's daily newspapers:

> Routinely now, our papers go to focus groups when they are going to try something new. Many of our editors have established a 25/43 goal, which means they conduct research, involve task forces from their news-rooms and other departments, assess the strengths and weaknesses of their papers, propose changes, and test some of these changes in the marketplace. It sounds so simple, but it is not the way the newspaper business tended to operate.

Descriptions of the 25/43 process appeared in corporate newsletters, providing further evidence that it had become part of the routine at Knight-Ridder.

At Knight-Ridder the ability to continue learning was "ensured through the institutionalization of structures and processes designed to promote learning" (Wishart et al., 1996, p. 14).

Organizational Memory

One possible way of beginning a discussion of organizational memory would be to open with the following statement:

> One of the functions of the Memory and Meaning Subsystem is to store knowledge that is important for the organization's survival. This is predicated on storing only the information that has been valued at some level of reflection. If the learning system is not differentiating between information and knowledge, the memory system will become bogged

down. This results in an "overload" situation for the memory and can hamper further retrieval for the reflection process.

However, this statement would fall into an understandable argument concerning the use of metaphor. It would be characterized by questions such as, "Does organizational memory actually exist? Is there a collective brain or mind? If so, where is that located?" These are critical questions that can distract from the organizational learning construct. People say, "If we can't locate the organizational brain, then how can we discuss memory?" This then undermines the "learning" aspect of organizational actions.

To move the memory argument away from the "metaphor only" position, Walsh and Ungson (1991) posit three assumptions concerning collective (organizational) memory. They first assume the organization processes information much like humans do — sensing, coding, processing, storage, and retrieval. And because of the complexity and variability of the organization's environment, and the ability of the collective to form routines, they assume these processes must imply some type of retention or memory.

Early discussions of memory and knowledge structures at the collective level are found in the field of psychology and sociology with the writings of Durkhiem in the late 19th century. He proposed that there are collective ways of acting and thinking that are "realities" outside of the individual. Walsh and Ungson's third assumption gets to the heart of the issue posed by Durkhiem:

> An organization is a network of intersubjectively shared meanings that are sustained through the development and use of a common language and everyday social interactions. Taken in this context, memory is a concept that observers invoke to explain a part of the system, or behavior, that is not easily observed, rather than a variable that is interrelated with other variables to produce particular outcomes. Organizational memories, therefore, are not variables with dispositional properties that have discrete causal effects on, say, structure and technology. (Walsh and Ungston, 1991, p. 60)

Collective Memory about a Merger

On one level, this assumption about organizational memory is dealing with the "latent" nature of the actions associated with the Memory and Meaning subsystem. This aspect of collective memory can be demonstrated in the following example.

While preparing for the data collection at one of our research sites, we conducted a meeting with the project's Steering Group which was made up of a cross section of the total organization. The members were characterized by a mixture of experience, age, and time with the organization (some were with the organization only 1 to 2 years, while one person had been there more than 20 years).

The purpose of our study was to observe this small organization of 300 people and their process of organizational learning as they consolidated three units into one. The "new" organization was a result of the merger of three smaller units (all of which are contained within the parent organization).

During the meeting the question was posed, "What date should we use to separate the past from the present? Or, in other words, when did the merger actually take place?" In their discussions it became obvious that the organization (the collective body) was trying to resurface knowledge.

They could have adjourned and gone to the files to obtain a date of merger. However, they chose not to. Many answers started to rise, none of which the group could agree to. The collective whole was going through a process of "organizational remembrance." This is defined as a process of searching and testing knowledge that may have been stored in the individual. The group exhibited two characteristics: (1) for an answer they were trying to move toward consensus — thus the criterion for the right answer was only consensus, or agreement, not exactness; and (2) the line of questions to aid in the process was referenced by personal experiences. For example, "The date I entered was two days before the merger" or by an event or symbol "Sam took over just about that time" or "It was right after they closed the cafeteria."

After several minutes the group zeroed in on a plausible date that met with approval. This social process of remembrance is a very concrete example of how the memory of the collective can work. "Oh, by the way, we are still not sure that this was the actual date..." After arriving at consensus, nobody checked.

This case illustrates the process of sharing and organizational interpretation transcending the individual level. This is why an organization may preserve knowledge of the past even when the organizational members leave. Taken collectively, these arguments led Walsh and Ungson to a definition of organizational memory. "The construct is composed of a structure of its retention facility, the information contained in it, the processes of information acquisition and retrieval, and its consequential effects. In its most basic sense, organizational memory refers to stored information from the organization's history that can be brought to bear on present decisions" (Walsh and Ungson, 1991, p. 61).

Organizational Brains Are Segmented

If we assume a memory function, as opposed to a "mind," we can picture the actions of the social system as playing the parts of the brain's neurons. This would help explain the dynamic action aspect of the subsystem and the memory processes, but not the storage of knowledge. Walsh and Ungson postulate six potential storage bins, above and beyond information systems and file drawers, as retention facilities.

■ **Individuals** — Individuals in organizations retain information based on their own direct experiences and observations. They store their organization's memory in their own capacity to remember and articulate experience, and in the cognitive orientations they employ to facilitate information processing. This was apparent in the above example and is also the foundation of the discussion of knowledge structure and maps found in Chapter 5. This also explains the motivation behind NASA's knowledge capture process.

■ **Culture** — Organizational culture embodies past experiences that can be useful for dealing with the future. Knowledge is stored in language, shared assumptions, symbols, stories, and values. These are the elements that individuals turn to for guidance and criteria for the interpretation process. Each time the knowledge is successfully employed, the memory is strengthened. However, Walsh and Ungson warn us that, "because this information is transmitted over and over again some of the detail and context of the various decisions are likely to be dropped or even altered to suit the telling."

■ **Transformations** — Information is embedded in many transformations that occur in organizations. That is the logic — the dice transformation of input (whether it is a raw material, a new recruit, or insurance plan) into an output (via the finished product, the company veteran, or an insurance payment) is embodied in these transformations. Much of this knowledge is stored in routines and standard operating procedures. It is in the unreflected actions associated with these routine transformations that the memory functions.

- **Structures** — Individual roles provide a depository in which organizational knowledge can be stored. The organization relies on roles and structure as a social routine. Many times we find roles in organizations that have been perpetuated without an apparent purpose. These are examples of stored memory that have escaped inquiry.

- **Ecology** — The actual physical structure or workplace ecology of an organization reveals a good deal of information about the organization. In particular, the physical setting often reflects the status hierarchy in an organization. It may also reflect the history and culture of the organization.

- **External Archives** —— Organizations are not the sole repositories of their past. Former employees can retain a great deal of information about an organization. Competitors often chronicle an organization's every move, and the government requires all publicly held companies to record reports (Walsh and Ungson, 1991, pp. 63–67).

Although these five "bins" have in some sense made the collective memory visible and mechanical, the most dynamic portion of this framework is the individual and his/her interrelations with other individuals. It is the people in the organizations and their actions that have the capability to store and change the understanding of the information or knowledge. Walsh and Ungson go on to postulate several uses of memory; however, they capsulate its use and potential misuse:

> The consideration of organizational memory reveals it plays three important roles within organizations. First it plays an information role. The information content housed in memory retention facilities can contribute to efficient and effective decision making (particularly in the prechoice decision stages). Second, organizational memory fulfills a function. It can reduce the transaction costs that are often associated with the implementation of a new decision. The "what's" and "how's" can be housed in many of the storage bins and serve to efficiently shape desired behaviors without incurring expensive monitoring costs. Third, organizational memory can play a political role. Control of information creates a source of dependence with which individuals or groups in power are able to influence the actions of others. The filtering of particular information for memory that supports a particular agenda can serve as a means to enhance and to sustain power. (Walsh and Ungson, 1991, p. 74)

Storing Knowledge at PricewaterhouseCoopers

In July 1998 PricewaterhouseCoopers opened its Global Knowledge Center, a unique, state-of-the-art, integrated facility for knowledge sharing, training, and data warehousing project support. The center is based in Rosemont, IL, located just outside Chicago and within a mile of O'Hare International Airport. This is the first in a number of knowledge centers planned around the world with a location in Europe targeted as the next site.

"The Global Knowledge Center reflects PricewaterhouseCoopers' serious, long-term commitment to data warehousing," said Michael J. Schroeck, Global Leader for the PricewaterhouseCoopers Data Warehousing Practice. "This unique environment, where we will work with global companies and technology providers, will help define the landscape of the industry and drive future developments in data warehousing."

Through the Global Knowledge Center, companies will receive hands-on training in many of the leading data warehousing technologies, have access to continuous market information, and view extensive up-to-the-moment product evaluations. The center will also provide a stimulating environment where clients can work with PricewaterhouseCoopers consultants to design and develop strategic knowledge-based solutions. "In today's fiercely competitive global marketplace, knowledge is the key weapon," continued Schroeck. "At PricewaterhouseCoopers, we help companies harness this weapon's power by combining business knowledge with a deep understanding of the tools, technologies, and best practices needed to implement successful data warehousing knowledge-based solutions."

In designing and building the Global Knowledge Center, PricewaterhouseCoopers leveraged the experience of its 1000 data warehousing consultants as well as the firm's global experience and leadership in the successful implementation of data warehousing, data mining, and knowledge management solutions.

To meet the growing demands for acquiring, analyzing, and storing knowledge, PricewaterhouseCoopers has created a variety of resources for collecting, storing, and transferring learnings of the firm. Based on its innovative management of knowledge in five different areas — strategy, approaches and processes, culture, technology, and measurement — PricewaterhouseCoopers was recently selected as an Emerging Best Practices Company in knowledge management by the International Benchmarking Clearinghouse (IBC) (Marquardt and Kearsley, 1999).

Composition of Organizational Memory

Retention facilities are an important dimension of organizational memory; however, what constitutes organizational memory? Casey (1994) formulated an operational definition of organizational memory — shared interpretations of the organization's past as related by the members of the organization. In her research she found evidence of two types of memory:

> *Episodic memory* — the conscious recollection of personally experienced events. Episodic memory is temporal and has temporal–spatial relations among the memories.
>
> *Semantic memory* — knowledge of the world appears to be independent of personally experienced events; for example, stories that are recollected in which the person recalling did not personally experience the event.

The site for Casey's study was a residential substance abuse rehabilitation program. The program had six therapeutic community settings and an administrative office in a metropolitan area. The purpose of the study was to identify organizational memory types and composition.

Casey found that the collective memory in this organization was predominantly episodic with little reliance on semantic memory. Four primary categories of collective memory were found. These categories were funding crisis, changes in the treatment program, expansion, and the birth of the organization. Birth of the organization was classified as semantic memory. Organizational schema of "survival" and "family" emerged within the stories in each of the categories. These schemas and scripts appeared to be influenced by the mission, values, identity, and major concerns of the organization. The mechanisms for transmitting collective memory were from former residents and staff to current residents and staff of this organization. Also, memory was transmitted through documents and artifacts. The process of transmittal including retention and retrieval appeared to be influenced by the organizational schema (Casey, 1994, p. iii).

The basic assumptions and values of the organization and the profession of rehabilitation anchored the episodic memory of this organization. Schema of "family" and "survival" were both found in the knowledge structures used by the counselors to deal with patients, and also in the way members stored memories about the history and fate of the organization. These values and assumptions were part of the organization's culture and constituted its memory.

Matsushita and a Culture of "Sunao"

Matsushita Electric Industrial, the world's largest consumer electronics maker, sells audiovisual and computer products, home appliances, household equipment, electric motors, and air conditioners in more than 180 countries. The Japanese-headquartered company believes organizational learning is most likely to occur within a corporate culture of "Sunao." What exactly does this mean?

The Japanese word Sunao represents a mind of accepting life in a constructive way. "It enables us to see things as they actually are, without any prejudice or preconceived idea."

With Sunao mind, we firmly dedicate ourselves to the gathering of wisdom; to seeking out the intrinsic nature of reality through independent, self-fulfilling study; and to searching anew each day for the path which will lead us to growth and prosperity.

Within the Sunao culture, the company and its workers endeavor to live out the following five vows:

1. To fulfill cherished ambitions — We pledge to do our utmost, always maintaining our resolve. No matter what obstacle we encounter, we will find a way to surmount it. The key to success is to continue to strive after success until it is attained.

2. To have an independent spirit — Things will not proceed successfully if we are dependent on others. Working independently with self-discipline makes others sympathetic to us. This sympathy allows one to benefit from others' wisdom and strength.

3. To study everything — We pledge to learn from all that we see and hear. We regard all experience as an opportunity for study. In diligence, there is genuine development. Observing everything attentively, all objects become our instructions.

4. To take a leading role in pioneering innovation — Untrapped by stereotypes, we will ceaselessly create and pioneer innovations whose form will shape the future of Japan and the world. Only the person who assumes a leading role in an era can open the doors to a new history.

5. To express appreciation and offer cooperation — No matter what talent we assemble, without harmony, success will not be achieved. We will cooperate with others, always maintaining a sense of gratitude. Cultivating trustworthiness creates genuine development. (http://www.matsushita.org)

Organizational Culture and Learning

From the above discussions we have significant indications that organizational learning and memory are closely related to the organization's culture. To understand this connection we must first understand the concept of culture.

The foundational knowledge of organizational culture originates in the work of Edgar Schein. His conception of organizational culture included a descriptive picture that contained three basic components that were at various levels of visibility. At the most visible level were the artifacts of the organization — its buildings, signs, etc. At the least visible level were the basic assumptions of the organization that are seldom articulated. These assumptions were concerned with the organization's relationship to the environment, the nature of human nature, human relations, and other broad guiding assumptions. The values and beliefs of the organization were at the "in-between" level of visibility. They are many times visible in the actions of the organization, however, their link to the basic assumptions are not always evident (Schein, 1992).

This description of Schein's conceptualization runs parallel to Walsh and Ungson's concept of organizational memory and also provides a foundation for the interpretation of the evidence provided by Casey and her study of the rehabilitation facilities. Memory and its composition and retention facilities reflect all three levels of Schein's organizational cultural framework (see Figure 8.2).

Schein uses the following example to delineate the importance of culture and learning:

A company decided to introduce automatic machine tools into their production process. The idea originated with the engineers who saw an opportunity to do some "real" engineering. The engineers and the vendors developed the proposal based on technical elegance but found that middle management would not push the proposal up to executive management unless it was rewritten to show how it would reduce costs

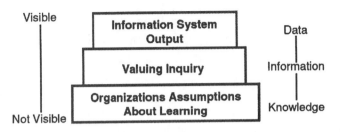

Figure 8.2 Cultural Impact on Memory Actions

by cutting labor. No active figures were available, so the team more or less invented the numbers to justify the purchase of the expensive new machine. As the proposal worked its way up the hierarchy the labor union got wind of the project and insisted that it would not go along unless management guaranteed no job lost and that all the present operators would be retrained. This not only delayed the project, but when machines were finally installed the production process proved to be much less effective and much more costly than had been promised in the proposal. The engineers were highly disappointed that their elegant solution had, from their point of view, been subverted and that all the operators that were to have been replaced had merely been retrained on jobs that the engineers considered superfluous. (Schein, 1996, p. 10)

Schein proposes that in most organizations, there are three different major occupational cultures: (1) the culture of engineering, (2) the culture of CEOs, and (3) the culture of operators. He feels that they do not really understand each other and often work at cross-purposes. "These cultures cut across organizations and are based on what have been described as 'occupational communities.'" He distinquishes the cultures as follows.

- The culture of operators is developed locally in organizations and within operational units. It is based on human interactions that value high levels of communication, trust, and teamwork. This constitutes their basic assumptions and will also drive their memory content and retention processes.
- The engineering culture's assumptions are based on common education, work experience, and job requirements. "In other words, the key theme in the culture of engineering is the preoccupation with designing humans out of the systems rather than into them."

- The executive culture is a set of assumptions that CEOs and their immediate subordinates share. These executive assumptions are built around the necessity to maintain an organization's financial health and are preoccupied with boards, investors, and capital markets (Schein, 1996, p. 15).

The differences in these three cultures mean that the members of these occupations may see the world quite differently. This will have an impact on the values that reference their memories and how they choose to store those memories. For example, the engineer culture is going to be much more dependent on the mechanical systems to store their knowledge, while the operational culture will be dependent more on the individual. This is one of the sources of concern that was generated by the senior engineers at NASA. They felt that the knowledge capture process could be handled by systems engineering.

Schein sees the problem associated with these cultural disconnects as the key barrier to organizational learning.

> Organizations will not learn effectively until they recognize and confront the implications of the three occupational cultures. Until executives, engineers, and operators discover that they use different languages to make different assumptions about what is important, until they learn to treat the other cultures as valid and normal, organizational learning efforts will continue to fail. Powerful innovations at the operator level will be ignored; technologies will be grossly underutilized; angry employees will rally against the impersonal programs of reengineering and downsizing; frustrated executives who know what they want to accomplish will feel impotent in pushing their ideas through complex human systems; and frustrated academics will wonder why certain ideas like employee involvement, social technical systems analysis, high commitment organizations, and concept of social responsibility continue to be ignored, only to be reinvented under some other label the few decades later. (Schein, 1996, p. 19)

Overcoming the Cultural Barriers to Organizational Learning at Canadian Imperial Bank of Commerce

CIBC, a Canadian financial services company, is a global leader in credit card products and PC banking. With over 47,000 employees, it invests more than $40 million in employee development each year, with emphasis on skills enhancement, relationship building, and leadership training.

Michele Darling (1996), executive vice president of human resources, realized that barriers had to be overcome and changes had to be made before CIBC was able to create a culture for organizational learning. As she notes, "the formal decision to become a learning organization can yield some very practical benefits, but it imposes additional demands." For example, a direct focus on knowledge can "unchannel conventional thinking, but it also questions conventional organization." It may also increase responsibility on individuals and changes the responsibilities of management. Inevitably, it focuses attention on recognizing barriers. She adds:

> We all have heard the adage that "knowledge is power." In most organizations, what this really means is that knowledge is saved and put on display at the most opportune moment — likely when the boss is in the room. Rarely is knowledge shared with others at an equivalent level in other parts of the organization. Knowledge hoarding has the added advantage of never having to expose the fact that your knowledge may be partial or stale! People generally use their unique knowledge to reaffirm their position in the organization; if others knew what you knew, then how valuable would you be to your organization? What happens to your indispensability if you dump your knowledge into a pool, where others can take it and make it theirs? There is also the all-too-familiar phenomenon of "not invented here." This is the inevitable urge to disparage the really insightful idea or insight that comes from outside our organization or group simply because we did not think of it ourselves. (Darling, 1996, p. 61)

These reactions, notes Darling, are understandable. The challenge is to break free from these traditional approaches to learning and managing knowledge in the organization. The first step is to create a "knowledge culture." An organization's culture is not decreed by management memo and does not happen by accident. It is that collection of shared values and beliefs that develops over time. It is that unstated consensus of common understandings and conventions — "how things work around here."

So, what is a "knowledge culture?" At CIBC, "we do not yet have a neat, tight definition, but we have developed some insights into its essential characteristics." A knowledge culture should value the following:

1. Values knowledge and puts that knowledge where needed. Knowledge is placed directly at the customer's service and into the hands of the people who deal with the customer.

2. Democratizes knowledge. It is delinked from the individual holder, transferred to others, and valued according to its effectiveness in dealing with problems and meeting customer needs.
3. Values diversity. It recognizes that new ideas and insights are not the preserve of age, experience, race, or gender.
4. Has a subversive effect on traditional management hierarchies. Instead of operating in command-and-control mode, managers must become coaches, advisers, and cheerleaders for their teams, and facilitators, brokers, and networkers to link their teams with others in the organization.
5. Always has its eye on what academics call the "knowledge grid." Succinctly, the knowledge grid examines what we know we know, what we know we don't know, what we don't know we know, and what we don't know we don't know.

Linking Culture and Action

The processes associated with organizational culture and learning are composed of visible and latent actions. Although Schein provides a descriptive framework to help us understand the relationship between culture and memory, we are still interested in "how" does culture work. This would provide us an understanding of the dynamic nature of memory formulation, which in turn can lead to an understanding that the organizational learning system is the path to cultural change.

Mary Jo Hatch extends Schein's model by adding the dynamics that link the elements of culture. Hatch has separated artifacts into artifacts and symbols — the reasoning being that not all organizational artifacts are used by the culture as symbols. She defines these dynamics as:

- **Manifestation processes** — In terms of the cultural dynamics framework, manifestation permits cultural assumptions to reveal themselves in the perceptions, cognitions, and emotions of organizational members. That is, manifestation contributes to the constitution of organizational culture by translating intangible assumptions into recognizable values. The cultural dynamics model suggests that manifestations occur in two ways: through those processes that proactively influence values, and through those processes that influence assumptions via the retroactive effects of value recognition (p. 662).

■ **Realization processes** — In terms of the cultural dynamics model, proactive realization is responsible for the transformation of values into artifacts (for example, rights, rituals, organizational stories, humor, and physical objects) whereas retroactive realization has a potential to transform values and expectations by making them appear differently than they did prior to their proactive realization as artifacts. Proactive realization occurs through activity that gives substance to expectations revealed by the manifestation process. In one case, artifacts realized from values and expectations maintain or reaffirm the values and expectations, whereas artifacts produced by another culture, or by forces not aligned with cultural values, could introduce artifacts that retroactively challenge values and expectations (p. 667).

■ **Symbolization processes** — These processes combine an artifact with meaning that reaches beyond or surrounds it. It is a prospective response that links an artifact's objective form and literal meaning to experiences that lie beyond the literal domain. The retrospective mode enhances awareness of the literal meaning of symbolized artifacts. The important point, from a cultural dynamics perspective, is that not all artifacts are given equal treatment within the symbolic field (p. 671).

■ **Interpretation processes** — Cultural dynamics suggests that interpretation contextualize current symbolization experiences by evoking a broader cultural frame as a reference point for constructing an acceptable meaning. Meanwhile, cultural assumptions, momentarily exposed during the process of interpretation, are opened to the influence of new symbols. In this way, the moment of interpretation makes it possible (but not necessary) for culture to absorb newly symbolized content into its core (Hatch, 1993, p. 675).

Hatch's definitions of the dynamic actions associated with cultural change and maintenance can be used to explain the processes of organizational memory formation, change, and maintenance (see Figure 8.3). The actions of the Meaning and Memory subsystem support the memory functions and the assignment of meaning to the actions of the organization. The product of these actions is the interchange medium, sensemaking.

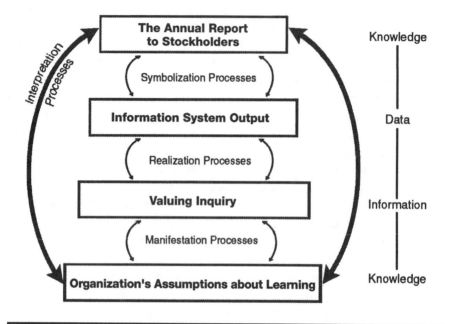

Figure 8.3 Dynamic Cultural Impact on Memory Actions

Linking Learning and Culture at U.S. Shell

Shell Oil Company of the U.S. (SOC), one of 300 Royal Dutch/Shell (RDS) operating companies, employs more than 22,000 employees and generates revenues in excess of $30 billion. Because of the common logo, it is widely assumed that there is one Shell and that its management philosophy and approach are global. To the contrary, RDS, based within Europe, and SOC have quite distinct histories and identities that reveal themselves in their approaches to learning.

It is only recently that U.S. Shell undertook a transformation based on learning, planning, and leadership changes. The focus was internally on the organization's human system, and externally on the immediate customer and business environment.

As Brenneman et al. (1998) note, "the dominant culture in U.S. Shell was difficult to change because Shell, like most organizations, tended to perpetuate its thinking by self-selecting new members in its own image." While RDS had begun to select "systems thinkers," people who see current reality in an organization as only one of many possibilities for the long term, SOC was heavily populated with "event thinkers; i.e., people who interpret current developments as inevitable and view corporate life as a series of unrelated events rather than as connected systems." While the changing environment of the petroleum industry cried out for a reexamination of mental models, little reexamination occurred at SOC. Instead U.S. Shell was characterized by a parochial, short-term orientation, typical of American corporations of the time (Brenneman et al., 1998).

U.S. Shell clung tenaciously to its mental models that included confidence in $30 for a barrel of oil and a success model based on cash generation through financial performance improvement built on short-term cost reduction. SOC in the 1980s was not a model of organizational learning. Little changed at SOC until the early 1990s when a new CEO, Phil Carroll, arrived on the heels of the worst business results in years. Carroll wasted no time in seeking alternate paths for SOC.

Supported by these resources, Phil Carroll has led SOC toward a significant transformation of its corporate culture. It is comprised of a new vision, a new business model, a new system of governance, a new concept of leadership, and the use of learning as both the foundation of Shell's transformation and a permanent part of its culture. The transformation, initially known as the learning and development initiative, began with a process designed to create a mission, with vision and values powerful enough to engage the minds and hearts of SOC's people.

The emerging dialogue from this process also invited people to look within themselves and discover their personal visions. The new business model allows the company's leaders to build winning strategies by recognizing where they can exert the greatest leverage and add the most value. When fully implemented, it will give every employee a better understanding of his or her contribution to the company (Brenneman et al., 1998).

Sensemaking

The field of organizational studies is now taking the "cognition" approach to understanding organizations quite seriously. We are moving past the learning organization and are now confronting issues associated with the dynamics of nonlinear social systems, strategic processes, and even the formulation of knowledge as the basis of a dynamic theory of the firm.

One of the critical facets of the cognition construct is the concept of sensemaking and its relationship to the dynamic nature of the organization. Sensemaking is defined as structuring unknown contexts and/or actions and assigning meaning to the construct.

The term sensemaking conjures up images of the individual and his or her search for personal meaning. Some researchers have pursued this path and have defined the actions associated with the construct as private and have only referenced it to the assumptions and values of the collective (Gioia and Chittipeddi, 1991). Others, such as Weick, have conceptualized the construct as "grounded in both individual and social activity... and possibly not even separable" (Weick, 1995, p. 6). If this is the case, then the chain of relationships of several constructs such as organizational institutionalism, dynamic cultural processes , organizational memory (Walsh and Ungson, 1991), and organizational identity should be explored for their linkages to sensemaking and organizational meaning.

It is an assumption of this book that social action theory can form the basis for the discussion of cognition in such a manner as to better link them to the dynamic nature of both organizational performance and learning. With the advent of complexity theory and chaos in the social sciences we are no longer just interested in change, but we are interested in differentiating change as either characterized by punctuated equilibrium (Gersick 1991), or as continuous change described by the application of complexity theory and time-paced evolution. Whatever the nature of the change, be it continuous or punctuated, the unanswered collective, cognitive question is concerned with the role played in those changes by collective memory, shared meaning, and the associated knowledge structures that are constructed by organizations in terms of mental models, schemas, and scripts.

If indeed the sensemaking construct is considered a dynamic social activity, and even as a social imperative, it is important to understand what form these social actions take and how they are linked to creating meaning for the individual and the collective. This path of investigation has the potential to explain the relationship between constructs such as organizational culture, identity, learning, and possibly autopoietic processes involved in self-generating social systems. However, little empirical work has been accomplished to date that would provide a bridge from a theoretical construct of sensemaking to the practical world of managing an organizational environment that promotes inquiry and dialogue (Bohm, 1996) and that continuously creates useful knowledge for the survival of the system. This lack of empirical results may be due to several reasons, the least of which may be a lack of definition and/or agreement as to the nature of the construct or processes and our inability to observe these constructs in a highly complex social environment. One large step forward has been Weick's description of sensemaking.

Weick's Conceptualization of Sensemaking

How the collective uses its cultural dynamic processes to motivate collective actions may be attributed to its ability to continually provide an interchange medium in which the collective can assign meaning to its learning actions of the Environmental Interface, Action/Reflection, and Dissemination and Diffusion subsystems. Weick (1995) refers to this process of assigning meaning to organizational actions as sensemaking. His examination of sensemaking produces seven properties that distinguish it from other explanatory processes such as understanding, interpretation, and attribution. He defines these sensemaking characteristics as a process that is

1. Grounded in identity construction — an intricate combination of self-identity of the actor and the identity of the organization that forms and sustains the socially constructed meanings assigned to events.
2. Retrospective — sensemaking is characterized by meaningfully lived experience. The key is the past tense nature of assignment of meaning after one sees what he has experienced.
3. Enactive of sensible environment — action is a precondition for sensemaking. People often produce part of the environment they face.
4. Social — sensemaking is never solitary because what a person does internally is contingent on others. Shared meaning is not what is crucial for collective action, but rather it is the experience of the collective action that is shared (Czarniawska-Joerges, 1992).
5. Ongoing — sensemaking is ongoing and neither starts fresh nor stops cleanly.
6. Focused on and by extracted cues — context affects the extraction of cues and small, subtle features can have surprisingly large effects on sensemaking.
7. Driven by plausibility rather than accuracy — sensemaking is about plausibility, pragmatics, coherence, reasonableness, creation, invention, and instrumentality.

Weick makes a strong case for the extension of his observations concerning sensemaking in highly critical situations, such as forest fire fighting, to more routine organizational settings. These so-called normal settings can also be characterized by high noise levels (poor communications), no clear reasons to change, lack of trust, high reliance on cause–effect relationships, lack of skills, fear of admitting to failure, social dynamics such as pluralistic ignorance, and individual commitments to strong professional cultures (identity) (Weick, 1995).

Sensemaking at Drug Rehabilitation Centers

Casey performed a post hoc analysis of her study of drug rehabilitation centers using Weick's sensemaking characteristics to ascertain their applicability to these normal situations. Her analysis provided excellent, visible examples of sensemaking in action.

Identity Construction

Using Weick's sensemaking criteria, the organizational schema of family and survival was continually renewed in the collective stories of significant events in the organization's history and through the dominance of the scheme in the industry as a whole.

Enactive of Sensible Environments

Actions reflected in newer scripts, that of experimentation with time frame for treatment and approaches to treatment, ultimately began to reshape their image of themselves and what it meant to be the therapeutic community.

Social

Although the collective memory was primarily episodic memory, or memory of personally experienced emotional events, the collective stories emerged and were continually shaped by the telling and retelling of stories by people who experienced them together. One of the few semantic memories recounted was a story of the birth of the organization. This event was only experienced by three of the current staff, yet all staff knew the story because it had been told and retold over a period of 25 years by the staff who were there during that era, and who had passed the story along through orientations, manuals, and brochures.

Retrospective

Weick also proposes that there are usually too many meanings that may be attributed to events and that "values, priorities and clarity about preferences" help people in organizations to be clear about which events or projects are important. In this organization, values were clear and reinforced through the work of the organization and the value base of the therapeutic community industry as a whole.

Ongoing/Focused on and by Extracted Cues

In essence, these organizational stories were the "moments out of continuous flows" of events. This process appeared to be ongoing and mutually reinforcing in that the cues were extracted from the collective stories of "moments"; and the cues also seem to prompt why these events were selected and why and how the stories developed. These cues also influence organizational meaning and actions in current crises and framed how the collective stories emerged as these events transpired.

Plausibility

Although the organizational schema appeared to be the key to which events were considered significant to the interpretation of current events, they did not appear to dictate which scripts were to be used. Different scripts emerged in the stories, yet the scripts were all framed within the schema of how to survive as an organization when threatened and how to stay as a family (Schwandt et al., 1997).

Sensemaking and Collective Learning

Weick has gone one step further in relating the human aspect of sensemaking to the contextual nature of organizational environments. His characteristics provide a finer level of distinction for describing the dynamic nature of social sensemaking in the context of generating knowledge and meaning as collective learning.

Geigle (1997) found in her studies of an organization going through reengineering that experiences from individuals passed in the form of memories. They were connected to each other and made accessible for ongoing sensemaking through schemas. Current experiences are the stimuli that elicit schemas deemed relevant by the individuals and provide new information inputs that can reinforce or disconfirm existing schemas. The most powerful influence on the reengineering work group during the project was not observing sessions; it was not reading a bulletin board; it was not attending briefings with unit representatives on the reengineering team. It was the organization's past experiences of reorganizing. These experiences were stored in and made accessible through cognitive structures known as "scripts" (Geigle, 1997, p. 246).

The sensemaking medium is critical to the organization because of the role it places in creating knowledge. Not all knowledge created by the organization contributes to its survival; organizations learn and store knowledge that can also lead to less-than-desirable outcomes. The consequences of these actions of memory and assignment of meaning are extremely important to the organization. There is no better place to see these consequences than in the strategic thinking processes, especially those involved in sensemaking around human resources and their place in the organization. For it is here that critical decisions are made about the linking of the learning system to the performance system.

Is It Strategy or Is It Learning?

Inherent in the construct of human resource strategy is the search for knowledge and ways of knowing that will raise the likelihood of survival of the organization through more effective and efficient utilization of human capacities. More often than not, the search is focused primarily on issues of performance. Human performance, either perceived as contributing to rational planned change or as a means of continuous improvement and survival, has almost become synonymous with change itself. Today's environmental complexity demands that we consider change to be more than performance; it requires us to examine the organization's ability to increase its collective capacity to perform while also increasing its collective potential to learn.

A society's movement into the "knowledge era" places a different emphasis on the concepts of strategic human resource development and management. Until now these concepts have been seen as means to an end. The end has traditionally been defined as production, return on investment, or other indices that measure organizational performance. However, in the transformation from an industrial to a knowledge society these human resources are no longer just means; they have now become the ends in themselves. Human resource strategy is no longer just the concern of the human resource department; it has become a focus for all organizational functions and all levels of management.

Albeit the importance of human resources has increased, executives and managers continue to apply strategic thinking that pertains to production measures supported by their present organizational performance paradigms. Prahalad and Bettis pose an explanation of this behavior as "dominant logic" which involves, "…mental maps developed through experience in the core business and sometimes applied inappropriately in other businesses" (Prahalad and Bettis, 1986, p. 485). Although their propositions were directed at the concept of corporate diversification, the basic argument also applies to the manager's use of strategic thinking logic that has been used in performance situations being misapplied to learning situations.

The complexity of the environment in which organizations operate today requires the application of systems thinking to the role of strategic planning and managing of complex human performance and learning. This makes it mandatory for the organization's human resource functions to align their strategic planning with the business objectives. In doing this, traditional human resource activities — selection, staffing, compensation, training, etc. — become the focus of the strategic alignment. Of course, the dominant logic of past practices is embedded in these activities and may not be the appropriate framework for formulating human resource strategy for a learning organization. What is required is a logic that allows the organizational learning dynamics to influence the present dominant performance logic (Schwandt et al., 1995).

Organizational learning has not been seen as a primary goal of organizations, only as a supportive activity in the adaptation to its environment through imitative or entrepreneurial strategies. It is not simply the adaptation of the organization to its present environment that should be of concern; rather it is the understanding of the internal and external processes used to establish relationships with its environment that is of importance — this necessitates understanding organizational learning as dynamic collective actions.

Andersen Worldwide — Focusing the Learning on Organizational Strategies

Andersen has recently introduced Goal-Based Scenario (GBS) training. The core of GBS is a simulated task that makes clear to participants what skills they need and why, what problems they are likely to encounter and when; what is the most effective means of dealing with those problems; and why they are effective. Teaching and learning always take place within the context of a clearly perceived need, as part of the larger goals of the organization. GBS provides a motivational framework that serves not only to facilitate the acquisition of individual skills and facts, but also to enable staff to understand how these skills and facts can solve client business problems.

Originated by Roger Schank, director of the Institute for Learning Sciences at Northwestern University, GBS is not simply a realistic simulation of some problem situation. Rather, as Andersen Associate Partner Alan Nowakowski states, GBS is "an artifice, carefully constructed to teach specific skills, lessons, knowledge, and abilities. And it must be executed in a manner that will in fact ensure that these things are learned by participants. For instance, this means that the unfolding of the scenario must be controlled so that learners see all of the important consequences of their actions, good and bad."

GBS contains the following components:

1. Learners are presented with an end goal that is motivating and challenging.
2. This goal is structured such that, in order to successfully meet it, learners are required to build a predetermined core set of skills and knowledge.
3. The environment is holistic. Skills and knowledge are taught as part of an integrated whole.
4. The learning environment is designed to take advantage of the different sets of experiences, cultural backgrounds, interests, and motivations of the learners.
5. Learners are able to explore and develop other than the predetermined set of skills.
6. Learners have the freedom to select their own strategies for meeting the end goal.

7. The stress level is appropriately managed by including a reflection, a genuine focus on the learning, and the availability of easy-to-use resources that support the learner's pursuit of the end goal.
8. Learners use the resources on as-needed, just-in-time basis.
9. The environment often includes real-world tasks, learners working in teams, and human coaches who are experts in both content and process.

Self-Study, Point-of-Need Learning

To promote and enable continuous self-development, Andersen is also focusing more and more on delivering self-study, point-of-need learning that provides staff with opportunities to learn by doing as well as to develop individual skills. Since an individual's learning needs typically derive from his or her current job assignments, accessible-upon-demand skill training has become increasingly important.

Andersen's learning programs feature built-in flexibility for building critical job skills at the individual level. Focus is on the increasing need and benefits of individualized self-paced instruction as determined by the learner. Instruction must increasingly be provided on a just-in-time basis, since most learning will need to occur just prior to the time such knowledge and skills must be applied.

At Andersen, a key pathway to personal mastery is the development of metacognitive skills where the individual learners are learning how to learn, and this will be a key component in the future. The firm recognizes that the more metacognitive skills that the individual can gain, the stronger his or her chances of keeping current with change.

Ready for the Steps and Strategies of Organizational Learning

This chapter has developed and exemplified the actions associated with the Meaning and Memory subsystem. The relationship to the other subsystems has been demonstrated through the use of the interchange media. We saw examples of this in the patterns established between the human resources strategy (structuring) and the resistance to dominant logic (sensemaking), and also the relationship between values (sensemaking) and new information transfer. Case studies of Knight-Ridder, Canadian Imperial Bank of Commerce, PricewaterhouseCoopers, Matsushita, Shell, and Andersen demonstrated the challenges and experiences of organizational learning in the Meaning and Memory subsystem. Having now examined in depth each of the four subsystems, we are ready to discuss steps and strategies for building organizational learning in your company, the focus of Chapter 9.

References

Bohm, D., *On Dialogue*, Routledge, New York, 1996.

Brenneman, W., Keys, B., and Fulmer, R., Learning across a living company: the Shell Companies' experiences, *Organizational Dynamics*, 27(2), 61–69, 1998.

Casey, A., Collective Memory in an Organization: Content, Structure, and Process, Dissertation, Human Resource Development, George Washington University, Washington, D.C., 1994.

Czarniawska-Joerges, B., *Exploring Complex Organizations: A Cultural Perspective*, Sage, Newbury Park, CA, 1992.

Darling, M., Building the knowledge organization, *Business Quarterly*, 61(2) 61–71, 1969.

Geigle, S.L., Schemas and Sensemaking during Radical Organizational Change: A Case Study of Reengineering in a Federal Agency, Dissertation, Human Resource Development, George Washington University, Washington, D.C., 1997.

Gersick, C.J.G., Revolutionary change theories: a multilevel explortaion of the punctuated equilibrium paradigm, *Academy of Management Review*, 16(1) 10–36, 1991.

Gioia, D.A. and Chittipeddi, K., Sensemaking and sensegiving in strategic change initiation, *Strategic Management Journal*, 12(6) 433–448, 1991.

Hatch, M.J., Dynamics of organizational culture, *Academy of Management Review*, 18(4), 1993.

Marquardt, M. and Kearsley, G., *Technology-Based Learning*, St. Lucie Press, Boca Raton, 1999.

Prahalad, C.K. and Bettis, R.A., The dominant logic: a new linkage between diversity and performance, *Strategic Management Journal*, 7, 485–501, 1986.

Schein, E.H., *Organizational Culture and Leadership*, 2nd ed., Jossey-Bass, San Francisco, 1992.

Schein, E.H., Three cultures of management: the key to organizational learning, *Sloan Management Review*, Fall, 9–20, 1996.

Schwandt, D.R., Learning as an organization: a journey into chaos, in *Learning Organizations*, Chawla, S. and Renesch, J., Eds., Productivity Press, Portland, 1995.

Schwandt, D.R., Casey, A., and Gorman, M.D., In Search of Organizational Sensemaking, paper read at European Conference on Managerial and Organizational Learning, Namur, Belgium, 1997.

Schwandt, D.R., Johnson, C.G., and Gorman, M.D., Changing the Dominant Logic of Strategic Human Resources Planning through the Development of Deep Structures Social Systems Thinking: A Three Year Case Study, paper read at Strategic Management Conference, Mexico City, 1995.

Spender, J.C., Making knowledge the basis of a dynamic theory of the firm, *Strategic Management Journal*, 24, 289–305, 1996.

Tulving, E., *Elements of Episodic Memory*, Oxford University Press, New York, 1983.

Walsh, J.P. and Ungson, G.R., Organizational memory, *Academy of Management Review*, 16(1), 57–91, 1991.

Weick, K.E., *Sensemaking in Organizations. Foundations for Organizational Science*, Whetlen, D., Ed., Sage Publications, Thousand Oaks, 1995.

Wishart, N., Elam, J., and Robey, D., Redrawing the portrait of a learning organization: inside Knight-Ridder, Inc., *Academy of Management Executive*, 10(1), 7–20, 1996.

9

Steps and Strategies for Bringing Organizational Learning to Your Organization

To raise new questions and new possibilities, to regard old problems from a new angle, requires creative imagination and marks real advance in science.

Albert Einstein

This book has thus far presented a comprehensive framework that allows managers and OD/HR practitioners to weave an organizational learning quilt that is comprised of the fabrics of world-class theory, research, and practice. The case studies that exemplify these fabrics of the quilt are not meant to be mimicked; they are presented so that the reader could see the "weave" or underlying connections between social actions and the cognitive capacity of an organization. Let us now examine how to turn these world-class theories and the Organizational Learning Systems Model into reality and success for your organization.

Seven Steps for Starting the Organizational Learning

The process of increasing an organization's learning capabilities does not start by selecting your favorite consultant (and his or her model) or by merely having a vision or wish as to what you want your organization to become. It must start with an understanding of what represents the organization's present capabilities in both the performance and learning systems. It is this "wrestling" with your own learning capacity that begins the steps toward increasing organizational learning. Figure 9.1 depicts the steps that provide the starting point for a continuous process of organizational learning.

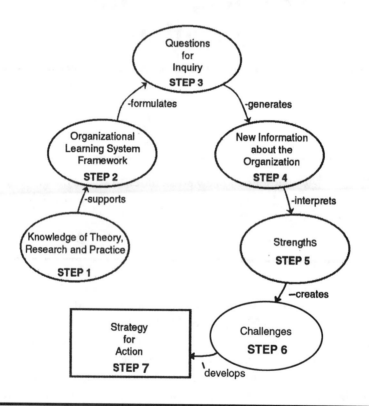

Figure 9.1 Steps for Starting the Organizational Learning Process

Step 1: Knowledge of Theory, Research, and Practice

By reading this book you have already taken the first step. Understanding that there are multiple theories (and associated research) that address, in some cases, only parts of an organizational learning system builds a foundation for valuing information about your organization's actions. Remember that theories are not natural laws, they are simply explanations of social phenomena that have to be continuously tested within the context of your organization.

Step 2: Understanding of Organizational Learning Systems Model

If you accept our arguments as presented in this text, you also have a framework that allows you to integrate the many theories, research results, and stories of practice into a quilt or map. The organizational learning system provides a dynamic social basis for judging organizational actions of both learning and performing.

Step 3: Asking Questions for Inquiry

Using the Organizational Learning Systems Model as a framework offers four sets of introspective questions, one set for each of the subsystems of learning actions. By asking these questions, the organization begins the process of generating new information concerning its learning system. This analysis is facilitated through the use of the following analytical questions for each of the subsystems and their interchange medium.

New Information and the Environmental Interface Subsystem

- How does the organization define its organizational environment?
- What are the processes used to scan the environment?
- What segments of the environment are scanned?
- What criteria are used to determine the nature of the environmental scan?
- What kind of information does the organization create?
- Is scanning environmentally intrusive or passive?
- What role does experimentation play in developing new information?

Goal Referenced Knowledge and Action/Reflection Subsystem

- What criteria does the organization employ to distinguish routine issues from exceptional issues?

- At what organizational level are our problems defined?
- To what extent are employees involved in the decision-making processes?
- How open is the organization to critical inquiry and dialogue?
- Does the organization support experimentation?
- Are there mechanisms in place for reflection of the collective and specifically the executive/managerial levels?
- Does the organization critically question established technical methods? If so, how?
- How does the organization evaluate the success of technical methods and approaches?

Structuring and Dissemination and Diffusion Subsystem

- To what extent are performance data available: individual and strategic?
- How is the role of leadership defined in the organization?
- How are knowledge and information shared: vertically and horizontally?
- How are success and failure documented?
- How is the organization structured to facilitate the integration of information and knowledge at the necessary levels?
- How are well-established technical methods communicated throughout the organization? How are new methods?
- Are there formal mechanisms to distribute technical knowledge (e.g., expert systems, newsletters, training sessions)? If so, describe them.
- What is the accuracy and relevance of the information that is communicated formally and informally?

Sensemaking and Memory and Meaning Subsystem

- How is information about technical expertise stored?
- How do you access this information when you need it?
- How does the organizational culture facilitate or inhibit information sharing?
- How does the collective create meaning?
- What value is placed on learning? Performance?
- What are the basic assumptions of the organization concerning learning?
- What are the basic assumptions of the organization concerning performance?

- Where is organizational memory stored and how is it accessed?
- What is the relationship between stored knowledge and the meaning of that knowledge?

(Note: These questions have been incorporated into a survey that measures the learning and performing tendencies of the organization. The survey is available through the Center for the Study of Learning, George Washington University, Washington, D.C., e-mail: csl@gwu.edu Phone: 703-729-8203.)

Step 4: Convert the New Information into Meaningful Knowledge

These questions will generate new information about the organization that can be valued as to its meaning. Information is not knowledge. If it is converted directly into actions associated with performance, then the organization is not learning; it is simply moving information. This type of action will not lead to learning; rather, it will lead to more confusion and lack of sense-making. The process of learning begins with understanding and assigning meaning to the information through reflection. This process will identify the strength and the challenges that the organization may face in increasing its learning capacity.

Step 5: Analyze the Inputs and Outputs of Each Subsystem

The system's nature of organizational learning requires us to examine the inputs of each of the subsystems to ascertain the nature of the outputs. This was discussed in Chapter 4 as the "black box" analysis. The analysis of the new information, using the context of the organizational learning system, allows the organization to develop knowledge of its strength and challenges. Using the black box analysis approach, we have selected three typical challenges that organizations may find as a result of their reflections.

Step 6: Respond to the Challenges of Each Subsystem

Challenges of the Environmental Interface Subsystem

The Environmental Interface subsystem of actions requires the input of sensemaking, structuring, and goal reference knowledge to understand the influence of these actions on the production of new information. Figure 9.2 graphically portrays this analysis.

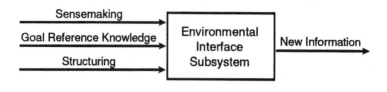

Figure 9.2 Analysis of Interchange Media

The analysis provides us three patterns that the learning organization must be aware of to maintain quality new information and its learning capacity:

> *Challenge I — Inappropriate Screening.* Perceptions concerning the environment and/or the boundary-penetrating actions of the organization either ignore or dilute the development of a sufficient variety of new information.
> *Challenge II — Lack of Variety of Environmental Interface Actions (Modes).* Insufficient number, variety, and levels of interactions for scanning environmental sectors reduce the quality of new information.
> *Challenge III — Lack of Understanding of the Role of Management Cognition and the Environmental Interface Subsystem.* Managers' actions and their cognitive schema can influence scanning outcomes.

Challenges of the Action/Reflection Subsystem

The Action/Reflection subsystem of actions requires the input of sensemaking, structuring, and new information to understand the influence of these actions on the production of goal reference knowledge as shown in Figure 9.3.

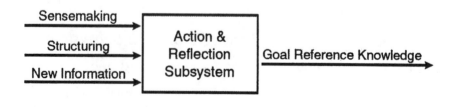

Figure 9.3 Analysis of Interchange Media

The analysis provides us three additional patterns that the learning organization must understand and appreciate:

> *Challenge IV — Lack of Organizational Reflection.* If organizations do not reflect on their actions, new information automatically becomes the goal referenced knowledge. A "pass-through" of information without any valuing characterizes this situation. This results in organizational confusion and frustration because every piece of new information becomes "the word."
>
> *Challenge V — Resistance to the Dual Nature of Knowledge.* Organizations will reject the social construction of knowledge, or the need to transform tacit knowledge to explicit knowledge. This situation is characterized by devaluing dialogue and diversity in their deliberations.
>
> *Challenge VI — Lack of Readiness.* Organizations do not prepare themselves for inquiry into their assumptions. Cultural assumptions are not even identified, let alone queried. The organization must develop new information about itself before it begins the reflection process.

Challenges of the Dissemination and Diffusion Subsystem

The Dissemination and Diffusion subsystem of actions requires the input of sensemaking, goal reference knowledge, and new information to understand the influence of these actions on the production of structuring (see Figure 9.4)

The following three challenges encounter organizations as they attempt to maintain effective structuring and to support its learning capacity:

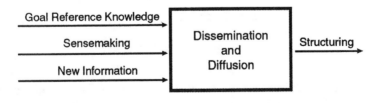

Figure 9.4 Analysis of Interchange Media

Challenge VII – Lack of Information Movement. The norms of the organization and its members do not reflect the sharing of information. The reward systems are reinforcing the noncollaboration within the organization and the lack of openness to external information.

Challenge VIII – Inappropriate Alignment of Roles. The roles of the members of the organization may be defined more as controlling and directing than as facilitating and enabling. This is especially true with respect to managerial and leadership roles.

Challenge IX - Lack of Understandable Policy Regarding Information. Organizations must formulate the meaning of information and its use so as to avoid the competition between Information Management Systems and the social dynamics of the organization. This meaning has to be articulated to all members of the organization.

Challenges of the Meaning and Memory Subsystem

The Meaning and Memory subsystem of actions requires the input of structuring, goal reference knowledge, and new information to understand the influence of these actions on the production of sensemaking. Figure 9.5 graphically portrays this analysis.

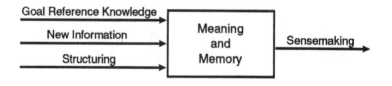

Figure 9.5 Analysis of Interchange Media

The analysis provides us three patterns that the learning organization must be aware of to maintain effective sensemaking and to support its learning capacity:

Challenge X — Lack of Alignment in Multiple Organizational Memory. The organization can have multiple memories that are influenced by very different subcultures. This difference is not bad in and of itself; however, if the organization is not aware of the difference, then the creation of knowledge can be frustrating.

Challenge XI — Lack of Cultural Profile. The organization must surface its basic assumptions so that it may understand the impact it is having on its sensemaking processes.

Challenge XII — Thinking You Can Fix Only One Subsystem at a Time. The organizational learning system is a nonlinear social system framework. This means that everything is connected to everything else. Thus, organizations have to implement multiple changes simultaneously to effect change.

Step 7: Take Action

One of the questions that occurs in this reflection process is "Once we have the information and have identified the challenges, where should we start?" Not all of the learning subsystems are equal in their influence on the organizational learning system. They all have necessary functions; however, the guiding function of the Meaning and Memory subsystem is the most influential and is also the most remote and impenetrable to change. It contains the critical links to the organization's culture and is therefore the hardest to see or manipulate. Its power lies in its cybernetic relation to the other subsystems.

The concept of cybernetics refers to two phenomena associated with systems theory — the relative source of energy and information for the subsystems, and the relative control of the subsystems in their consumption of energy and information. In his work with social systems, the concept of cybernetic hierarchy and control provided Parsons with a schema that explained the importance of the relationship between and among the subsystems of action. Figure 9.6 illustrates the cybernetic relationship between the four organizational learning subsystems. Each subsystem of actions is subject to control or influence by the higher-order subsystem. That is, the Environmental Interface subsystem is the point of articulation with the learning system's environments. Through its acts of adaptation it secures the means (resources, information) that are required by the total organizational learning system. The Action/Reflection subsystem controls the resources by orienting them to the goals of the learning system. In a similar manner the Dissemination and Diffusion subsystem has control over the Action/Reflection and Environmental Interface subsystems because it must integrate all subsystems into one learning system. And finally, the Meaning and Memory subsystem controls all other subsystems by providing the basic assumptions

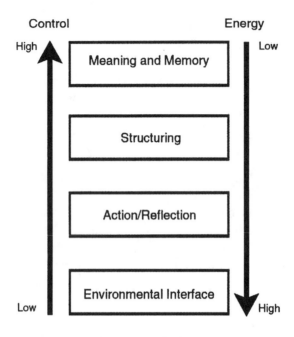

Figure 9.6 Cybernetic Hierarchy of Learning Subsystems

(From Schwandt, D. R., Organization learning, in *Advances in Strategic Management,* Vol. 14, Walsh, J. P. and Huff, A., Eds., JAI Press, Stamford, CT, 1997. With permission.)

and meaning upon which the other subsystems of actions determine their relative meanings and functional purposes. It is apparent, through this cybernetic relationship, that the pattern maintenance function, as enacted through the Meaning and Memory subsystem, is a critical factor in understanding and possibly adjusting the organization's learning capacity.

Whirlpool — Applying the Model in Product Development

Whirlpool Corporation is the world's leading manufacturer and marketer of major home appliances. Its home is in Benton Harbor, MI. There are over 45,000 people in the Whirlpool family who manufacture appliances in 13 countries and market them under 11 major brand names in approximately 140 countries around the world.

Under the guidance of Nancy Snyder, Corporate Director for Organization Development and Leadership, and Debbie Duarte, an organizational learning consultant, Whirlpool recently incorporated all the four subsystems of the Organizational Learning Systems Model in the process of developing new worldwide products. The product development effort was a multidimensional strategy that coupled work in advanced products and product development with organizational learning. Let us examine how principles of the model were applied.

Environmental Interface Subsystem

An important early step in the development of new products was the information gathering from existing product development teams who described factors relating to success and failure, real exchanges with teams both internal and external to Whirlpool, and environmental scanning of academic and practical literature related to product development.

Best Practices conferences were used for gathering data, interpreting data, sharing lessons learned, and identifying ways of storing critical knowledge. The conferences brought together people who were Whirlpool participants who were held in different regions around the world as well as participants from other global companies.

Action/Reflection Subsystem

Throughout the product development efforts, various methods were employed to analyze the information as well as learnings. This included contacting other team members who had experience dealing with specific problem areas, training and team development activities, developing a structure to analyze lessons learned at the end of projects, as well as benchmarking other companies.

A template was developed for teams to analyze their key learnings at the end of the product life cycle that included the following:

- Document what went well and what needs improvement — in every step of the process.
- Discuss openly what happened and why.
- Focus on the content, process, and premise of team activities.
- Obtain as many different perspectives as possible.

- Be open to multiple interpretations and a systems perspective.
- Suggest a range of options for improvement that target a system's perspective.

Duarte and Snyder (1997) noted that what attracted participants was "the potential for interacting with people like themselves who have faced similar challenges and really digging into issues. The dialogue that occurred ranged from how to deal with obtaining management support on a project, to handling multicultural team membership, to the issues involved in building a truly global platform in emerging markets."

Dissemination and Diffusion Subsystem

Special efforts were made to identify numerous ways to distribute the information on a just-in-time basis to people and product development teams. Methods included team mentors, training, interventions, documentation, and handbooks. Duarte and Snyder designed a number of courses, activities, and events to perpetuate the exchange of key learnings and best practices.

One of the most popular was a series of panel discussions that focused on key learnings. In an open forum, individuals with experience shared their best practices with the class and entertained questions. They also taught sections of the course that pertained to their areas of expertise. This provided a real-time way to share information as well as a way for course participants to network.

The courses were designed to require global representation among the learners so as to facilitate global integration as well as the sharing of best practices and lessons learned. This created a worldwide network of individuals with expertise in product development, with the expectation that these participants would call on one another to assist with problems in the future

Memory and Meaning Subsystem

High values were placed on the learnings and they were distributed throughout Whirlpool and had a significant impact and leverage on other company efforts. These were fed into the existing product development process to improve and streamline it. The learnings from the sessions were documented and stored using text and video so that others who could not attend could access the results. Teams were matched with a mentor who could help with sharing learnings from their product development team experiences.

Rover's Successful Journey into Organizational Learning

Let's now look at what one organization — Rover — has done over the past 10 years in building a culture of organizational learning. It has been a long and arduous journey, one that the company realizes is never completed, but one in which all four subsystems of the Organizational Learning Systems Model are continuously being enacted through the actions of people in all parts of the organization.

Rover's Incredible Turnabout

In the late 1980s, Rover, the largest car manufacturer in Great Britain, was in trouble. Losses were exceeding $100 million per year. Quality performance was low and going lower, union-management relations were wretched, leadership was seen as ineffective, future opportunities appeared bleak, and employee morale was sinking.

Today Rover is the darling automobile maker in the world. It cannot produce enough cars to meet the demands of buyers in North America and Asia. International sales have nearly doubled in the past few years. Rover has won nearly every award for quality that exists, including Design UK Quality Award, Engineer of the Year Award, Engine Management Systems Award, and the Queen's Award for Technology. The luxury Range Rover is the new "King of the Road." The Rover 600 has powered itself into a worldwide bestseller.

Rover now produces over half a million vehicles a year with annual sales of $10 billion to over 100 markets worldwide. In 1997 sales worldwide increased dramatically at a time of only partial recovery in the world's car markets. In the past 10 years, Rover has gained in shareholder value and seen huge losses turn into large profits, with average revenue per car sold increasing by 50%. Revenue per employee has jumped by an incredible 400%! Rover Group is a major employer with 39,000 people working for the company in the U.K. and internationally. A further 110,000 people work within companies supplying Rover Group with production materials and services. Rover Group is both the largest automobile manufacturer in Great Britain and the country's largest automobile exporter.

Not only is the company and its workers more productive, but satisfaction of employees is at an all-time high and rising. In the most recent employee survey, over 85% of Rover's 39,000 "associates" stated that they enjoy their jobs, are well-trained, and are committed to improving team performance.

Managers are now seen as supportive partners who are making Rover a better company. And, yes, employees want, more than ever, to learn!

As noted in the company's Web pages: "The Rover Group culture is different to anything you are likely to have encountered previously. Terms such as demarcation and blue or white collar are not only meaningless, they are totally alien to everything we believe in. Rover Group believes in flexibility between jobs and a single status for all associates, plus learning and career development opportunities for all."

Deciding to Create a Culture of Organizational Learning and Become a Learning Organization

What caused these dramatic changes in productivity and results, profits, and worker satisfaction? Top management and employees are unanimous and quick to attribute the new prosperity to Rover's long, arduous, and ongoing "journey" (one that is never finished) in creating a culture of organizational learning.

When Sir Graham Day became chairman of Rover Group in the late 1980s, he quickly recognized the rapidly changing environment of the automotive world — global competition, new technological advances, inadequately prepared employees, and customer demand for quality. Aware that "as a minnow among whales, Rover would be swallowed up if it stood still," Day and other senior managers decided that Rover had no choice but to find ways to increase organizational learning at Rover. At the initial Rover Organizational Learning Conference (the theme was "Learning to Win"), Day stated: "Neither the corporate learning process nor the individual one is optional. If the company seeks to survive and prosper, it must learn. If the organization and individual seek to make progress, learning is essential."

Creation of Rover Learning Business

The first step chosen was to create the Rover Learning Business (RLB) as a distinct entity within the company itself. At the launch of RLB in May 1990, Sir Graham Day noted, "As a company we desperately need to learn." And on that day, Rover served notice to its employees and to the worldwide public that corporatewide learning would become the cornerstone for Rover's survival and return to success.

The role of the RLB was to provide the processes, the resources, and the motivation to the entire company to ensure that learning is part of every individual's and unit's job, that the learning process be a "mainstream activity with Rover — recognized as it should be, as one of the most significant contributors to the Company's prosperity." Through RLB's nurturing and encouraging of companywide learning processes, Rover would benefit from the constantly growing pool of learning and knowledge gained by individuals, teams, and departments (Marquardt, 1996).

The Rover Learning Business had five main thrusts:

1. **Associate encouragement and contribution.** To stimulate, encourage, and provide ease of access for all associates to "climb the learning ladder" in order to develop themselves and enhance their willing contribution to team objectives.
2. **Learning process.** To provide leading-edge learning processes, supported by innovative tools, techniques, and materials for achieving major business changes.
3. **Corporate learning.** To lead and facilitate the design, development, sharing, and deployment of best-practice corporate learning based on internal and external benchmarking.
4. **Extended enterprise.** To support the business objectives of dealers and suppliers with learning support and collaboration to facilitate world-class activities.
5. **World-class image.** To achieve world best-in-class learning.

The inauguration of the RLB marked the beginning of what Rover people now call "a true revolution" within the company. The company began changing from a slow-moving, slow-learning, lumbering organization into an agile, fast-learning, dynamic "success through people" company. The organizational learning culture began to take root.

Establishing Corporate Vision and Beliefs about Learning in Rover

Rover leadership believed that organizational learning would power the company to "world-class levels of performance" and enable it to be "internationally renowned for extraordinary customer satisfaction." To show its commitment toward organizationwide learning, Rover established a culture built on seven fundamental beliefs about organizational learning:

- Learning is the most natural human instinct.
- Creativity, involvement, and contribution are fueled by learning and development.
- Everyone has two jobs — the present job and improving that job.
- People own what they have created.
- People need to be valued.
- Creativity and ingenuity are widely distributed and grossly underused.
- Management does not have all the answers.

Rover also developed several definitions for determining what organizational learning and being a learning organization would mean for Rover:

"A place where inventing new knowledge is not a specialized activity ... it is a way of behaving, indeed a way of being, in which everyone is a knowledge worker."

"A company in which learning and working are synonymous; it is peopled by colleagues and companions rather than bosses, subordinates and workers; and both the inside and outside of the company are being continuously searched and examined for newness."

"A company that monitors and reflects upon the assumptions by which it operates. It is in touch with itself and its environment and thereby adapts and changes as a matter of course, rather than traumatically, as in a crisis."

Aligning Corporate Learning to Quality and Continuous Improvement

Rover realized that quality products, processes, and services were vital to its short-term and long-term success. The principles of corporate learning were clearly aligned with the principles of total quality improvement. Every learning process was to be tested against the following principles:

- **Continuous improvement.** To achieve ever more demanding objectives, there must be a creative application of the learning process within a shorter time frame.
- **Management led.** Management will plan for learning and development opportunities for employees in their own areas.

- **Everyone responsible for quality.** Involve employees in the design and delivery of learning and development programs by integrating the best mentoring, shared experience, and self-development.
- **Companywide.** Each plant is to plan, invest, and report on its learning and development so that corporatewide progress can be formulated.
- **Cost of quality.** Financial and nonfinancial benefits to the organization accruing from the learning programs would be evaluated and reported.

Leaders Demonstrate Commitment to Corporatewide Learning

Rover's leaders realized that it was important for them to demonstrate their commitment to the concept of a learning organization both through role modeling and clear support. The first action illustrating this commitment was for each member of the Rover Group Board of Directors to also serve and actively participate as a member of the Board of Governors of the Rover Learning Business.

The Board and top managers have indeed undertaken a number of learning leadership roles, such as:

- Sponsoring corporate learning events.
- Promoting line managers who demonstrate a commitment to learning.
- Funding all employees who want to learn something outside their normal job responsibilities.
- Leading learning processes and programs from the front of the classroom, thereby acting as role model.
- Championing leadership learning programs.
- Giving recognition for learning achievements at all levels is part of the motivation process.

Streamlined into a Learning Structure

The old management hierarchy was soon transformed into a structure that featured a "lean organization" where greater responsibility and accountability were given to individual workers. Greater emphasis on teamworking was encouraged so that learning barriers would be removed and an environment where there were better working relationships and mutual trust would be created. Each individual was expected to develop and demonstrate a broader range of knowledge, skills, and leadership.

A Corporate Learning Model for Enhancing Business Results

To maximize its learning and make it available throughout the organization (Action/Reflection and Dissemination and Diffusion subsystems), Rover has developed a 13-step Corporate Learning Process Model (see Figure 9.7):

1. Business opportunity — All learning undertaken should contribute directly to bottom-line performance. Without this there is not justi-fication for doing it. Business opportunities can emerge from two main areas: (1) changes that require considerable financial investment and affect a wide range of people and (2) continuation of existing practices where performance requires significant improvement.
2. Champion — The person who identifies with the project's goals and opens doors, motivates, set standards, maintains, and coordinates the key players/expert group. The champion for a major strategic issue will normally be a Rover board director.

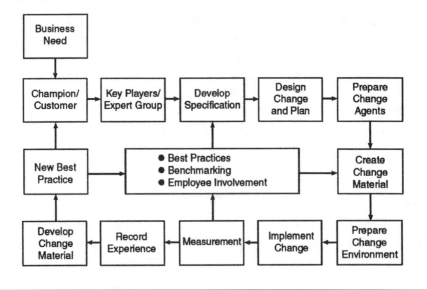

Figure 9.7 Rover Group Corporate Learning Process Model

3. Key players/expert group — Includes the subject experts, experienced operators, motivators, networkers, learning experts, and outside experts.
4. Develop specification — Includes business opportunity, aims, objectives, learning process and methods, venues, timing, and methods for measuring for success.
5. Design process and plan — Lists all the major steps that will absorb time, the leader of each step, any milestones, and the resource for delivering the end objective.
6. Prepare coaches/learners — Describe the project to pertinent employees and subject specialists so they are prepared and motivated to carry out the corporate learning process.
7. Create the learning material — Develop high-quality materials produced to agreed timing that contribute to complete success of the project; can range from a new model to audiotapes, videos, handouts, etc.
8. Prepare learning environment — The learning should be as close to workplace as possible, but, in any case, a high-quality learning environment should be prepared.
9. Implement learning — A combination of off- and on-the-job activity of learners/coaches to capture the learning.
10. Measurement — Measuring the effect of the learning and change process against the original objectives. The bottom line benefits achieved by a well-specified process will strengthen the value of systematic learning to the organization.
11. Record experience — The learning is recorded in a computer system for the organization and in the individual's personal development files.
12. Develop learning material — Develop any learning lessons for future organizational use.
13. New best practice — Revise the best practice standard to share this new experience throughout the organization.

Throughout the corporate learning process, the key players/learners can draw on already established best practice and benchmarking, and engage the involvement of company employees. These are the three internal boxes in Figure 9.7; they provide the foundation for Rover's targeted efforts on building corporate knowledge, called the Group Learning Exchange Network.

Group Learning Exchange Network

Launched in 1993, Group Learning Exchange Network (GLEN) is the definitive corporate database (updated quarterly by inputs from people in all of Rover Group areas) and accessible via IBM-compatible PC discs or directly on company computer networks. It guides inquirers to the appropriate sources of best practice or benchmarking information within the company. Also included on GLEN is a summary of personal learning materials for Rover associates.

Communications of Organizational Learning Activities and Programs

In order to transfer its new ideas as well as demonstrate its commitment to sharing learnings, Rover implemented a variety of programs:

- Regular learning product launches focus on satisfying individual needs to become more effective learners.
- At least one page of every company newsletter is devoted to Rover learning business and learning activities of employees.
- A very main plant has news bulletins which, without exception, feature group and individual learning as a main feature.
- The electronic notice bulletin board at each main plant location features existing and new programs available at employee development centers.
- Company road shows feature learning as a key employee activity.
- Existing best practices are role modeled by groups or individuals through presentations and exhibitions.

New Role for Managers

Ten years ago, managers "pushed" for improvements that would meet set standards (which, in effect, became the ceilings for upper levels of performance). This resulted in a diluted execution of ideas and insufficient upward flow of ideas. Today managers serve primarily as facilitators, coaches, mentors, and motivators empowering the real "experts" (associates). Managers and employees all work together as a potent resource for continuous improvement in both quality and productivity. Since 90% of learning takes place on the job, managers have significantly increased the cost-effectiveness of training through their new capabilities and commitment of facilitating learning on the job.

Managers are encouraged both to build on existing good practice and actively transfer their own experience to other colleagues. This philosophy and practice is called "Copy Plus." Total quality leadership within Rover means that the line managers take full responsibility for creating learning environments in their areas, and for coaching employees in all aspects of their learning.

Extending the Learning Enterprise to Customers, Dealers, and Suppliers

Rover realized that the intensifying industrial competition that existed throughout the world was putting an increasing premium on the company's ability not merely to satisfy suppliers and customers, but to delight them. This was particularly true in the fiercely competitive international motor industry.

The company decided not only to learn about its suppliers, dealers, and customers, but also to have them learn together with Rover. Accordingly, the company offers courses at various Rover facilities as well as at colleges and hotels in an effort to help suppliers meet the auto industry's demanding standards of quality and efficiency.

Significant resources are devoted to learning programs for Rover dealers. Popular distance-learning programs have been initiated that include a library of sales and after-sales skill-improvement videos as well as industry-leading literature/video packages covering sales, product knowledge, and servicing techniques. In addition, service correspondence courses have attracted over 500 participants per year. Rover also offers tutored courses at its various facilities for dealer staff who are willing and able to attend.

Recently, a Rover professionals program was launched in quality management and customer service initiatives. The program provides a structured career path via a "learning and competence accreditation ladder." In its first year, over 2000 dealer staff from over 500 dealerships enrolled in what has been described as a "remarkable confirmation of the continuous learning ethos" at Rover.

Principles for Learning Application

Learning activities in Rover seek to accomplish three purposes: (1) enhance job skills, (2) acquire knowledge of new technologies, and (3) expand both personal and corporate vision, thus creating the environment as well as the opportunities for innovation. Development activities are expected to be consistent with the following principles of learning:

1. Active participation. Learners should be involved in the design of their own training and its future application. Prebriefing of learners is essential.
2. Knowledge of results. Learners should know how they are doing during and after training. Feedback mechanisms must be in place to ensure that this happens.
3. Learning transfer. Where learning is off job, opportunities need to be created to transfer to job application.
4. Reinforcement of appropriate behavior. Where learners demonstrate changes in behaviors, this should be actively recognized and feedback as well as encouragement given.
5. Motivation of learners. Individuals must recognize the need to learn something; and managers need to utilize the learner's own drive and purposes.
6. Willingness to change. Visible support from the manager is most likely to encourage the learner to change.
7. Practice and repetition. It is necessary to provide opportunities to practice on real work situations without "fear of failure."
8. Time for reflection. All learners need time and space to assimilate learning by talking to others and having questions answered — thinking and planning are real work.

Success through Organizational Learning

As John Towers, former CEO at Rover, notes, "Rover has achieved and will continue to achieve dramatic progress through people who are perpetual learners, people who are skilled in the application of that learning, people who are committed to the application of those skills in the improvement of their company."

Begin the Weaving and the Organizational Learning!

As these pages have shown, organizational learning is not a simple concept or process. But only through an appreciative comprehension of its complexity can one truly hope to convert the ideal of a learning organization to a reality. To successfully weave an organizational learning quilt that is comprised of the fabrics of world-class theory, research, and practice requires an understanding of the "weave" or underlying connections between social actions and the cognitive capacity of an organization. A number of organizations have seen the benefits of applying the Organizational Learning Systems Model. They are creating organizations which "continually expand their capacity to create results they truly desire, where new and expansive patterns of thinking are nurtured, where collective aspiration is set free, and where people are continually learning how to learn together" (Senge, 1990, p. 3). We hope that you now have the knowledge, the resources, and the courage to weave a culture of organizational learning in your company, to convert the world-class theories into best practices for your organization.

References

Duarte, D. and Snyder, N., Facilitating global organizational learning in product development at Whirlpool Corporation, *Productivity Innovation Management*, 14, 48–55, 1997.

Marquardt, M., *Insights into World Class Learning*, WILL Publishing, Brussels, 1996.

Senge, P., *The Fifth Discipline*, Doubleday, New York, 1990.

Vaill, P. B., *Managing as a Performing Art*, Jossey-Bass, San Fransisco, 1989.

Appendix A: George Washington University's Center for the Study of Learning and the Organizational Action Survey

The Center for the Study of Learning (CSL) at George Washington University focuses on those issues of organizational effectiveness that involve complex organizational systems that enhance and/or prevent organizations, teams, and individuals from performing and learning. Its goal is to bring together practitioners and academicians an effort to improve both theory and practice. This partnership between CSL, the University's Executive Leadership Doctoral Program, and organizations is the pivotal point of the Center's approach to knowledge creation and dissemination.

CSL's objective is to bridge this gap between theory and practice by developing and sharing knowledge about important practical issues facing organizations today. To accomplish these objectives, CSL focuses its efforts on applied research with its partners, conducts developmental seminars, and publishes books, articles, and working papers.

The Center for the Study of Learning is an international research and development organization devoted to issues of learning in the field of Human and Organizational Studies. CSL provides high quality services to

251

all types of organizations through specific projects in Organizational Strategy, Organizational Learning, Cultural Assessment, Human Resource Systems, Reorganizing, and Transformational Leadership.

The Center for the Study of Learning has been studying organizations to develop an applied theory of Organizational Learning. From these studies, CSL has worked with organizations from all sectors — public, private, and nonprofit. This work has allowed the Center to develop a diagnostic tool for assessing an organization's performance and learning capabilities. The Organizational Action Survey is an instrument developed to measure dynamic social actions as they relate to organizational performance and learning. Developed in the mid 1990s, the survey was developed to identify (1) an organization's learning and performance orientation; (2) functional emphasis of organizational actions as they pertain to the learning and performance systems; (3) measures of organizational learning and performance actions; and (4) organizational sensemaking patterns.

To contact the Center for the Study of Learning:

Chris G. Johnson, Associate Director
Center for the Study of Learning
The George Washington University
20101 Academic Way, Suite 228
Ashburn, VA 20147
Phone: (703) 729-8203
Fax: (703) 729-2538
E-mail: csl@gwu.edu
Web site: http://www.chaos.va.gwu.edu/cslprog/csl.html

Appendix B:
Internet Resources for
Organizational Learning

- The Society for Organizational Learning
  http://www.sol-ne.org/
- European Network for Organizational Learning
  http://www.orglearn.nl/
- Knowledge Management & Organizational Learning
  http://www.brint.com/OrgLrng.htm
- Learning Organization Archive (Sponsored by Innovation Associates)
  gopher://ftp.std.com:7011/archives/Learning-org
- Stanford Learning Organization WEB
  http://www.stanford.edu/group/SLOW/
- Learning, Change, and Organizations
  http://www.euro.net/innova-
  tion/management_base/man_guide_rel_1.0B1/LCOrg.html
- Organizational Learning and Cognition
  http://choo.fix.utoronto.ca/FIS/OrgCog/Orgcog.html
- The Learning Organization
  http://world.std.com/~lo/LOinfo.html
- The Learning Organization Home Page
  http://www.albany.edu/~kl7686/learnorg.html
- Knowledge Management and Learning
  http://www.sveiby.com.au

Index

DATE DUE

OCT 2 0 2002	
NOV 1 0 2002	
FEB 1 4 2003	
DEC 1 2 2006	
FEB 2 4 2007	
APR 2 0 2007	